A Question of Commitment

A Question of Commitment

Australian Literature
in the Twenty Years after the War

Susan McKernan

Routledge
Taylor & Francis Group

LONDON AND NEW YORK

First published 1989 by Allen & Unwin

Published 2020 by Routledge
2 Park Square, Milton Park, Abingdon, Oxon OX14 4RN
605 Third Avenue, New York, NY 10017

Routledge is an imprint of the Taylor & Francis Group, an informa business

National Library of Australia
Cataloguing-in-Publication entry:

McKernan, Susan.
    A question of commitment: Australian literature in the
    twenty years after the war.

    Includes index.
    ISBN 0 04 355032 0.

    1. Australian literature—20th century—History and
    criticism. 2. Literature and society—Australia.
    I. Title.

A820'.9'003

Set in 10.5/11.5 pt. Caledonia by Setrite Typesetters
Ltd, Hong Kong

ISBN-13: 9780043550328 (pbk)

Contents

Acknowledgements

I would like to thank the many people who helped me both directly and indirectly in the writing of this book. In particular, I thank Judith Brett, Alec Hope, Michael McKernan, Margaret McNally, Adrian Mitchell, Bruce Moore, Venetia Nelson and Richard White.

Introduction

In the years since the Second World War there has been a period of literary creativity in Australia which completely overshadows the nation's earlier period of literary activity at the turn of the century. The postwar years have seen both a growth in the number of poets, novelists and dramatists in Australia and the creation of literary work of exceptional quality and range. Furthermore, the literary impetus which was evident after the war in the work of writers such as Patrick White, A.D. Hope, Judith Wright and others has not dwindled but has led to continued literary activity through the sixties, seventies and eighties.

Today Australia has at least a dozen novelists of recognised distinction—such as David Malouf, Elizabeth Jolley, Helen Garner, Frank Moorhouse, Thomas Keneally—as well as many less well-known but exciting fiction writers, and it can claim many established and emerging poets as well as a handful of impressive playwrights. But this widely acknowledged achievement in literature is not sudden or unprepared—it has come in the wake of the earlier achievements of the fifties and sixties.

In the eighties it is easy to overlook the fact that in the fifties the older generation of Australian writers did not have this assured achievement to build on. In particular, younger writers and critics such as John Tranter or John Docker have labelled poets such as

1

A.D. Hope, James McAuley and Judith Wright as an 'establishment' of Australian poetry as if these poets did not have to win recognition for themselves in a society unwilling to listen to poets. Yet before the Second World War Australia did not have a group of poets of the status to be taught regularly on university courses or to be included in major international anthologies. Before the war, Australia did not have university courses in Australian literature. The growth of all aspects of Australian literature and its support—tertiary and secondary teaching, literary journals, government grants for writing and publishing—has occurred in the forty years since the war. In the comfort of the late eighties this growth may now be accepted as inevitable but it was by no means an assured outcome in the immediate postwar years. The tendency to view the now elderly writers of the fifties as an establishment should not obscure the facts that in the mid-fifties they were not established and that they faced considerable argument about their achievement and their role in Australian society.[1]

One of the principal charges which a younger generation levels at the writers who emerged in the late forties and fifties is the charge that, in retrospect, they were conservative. This use of the word 'conservative' tends to categorise the poets, in particular, as a group with common aims, common techniques and common politics. During the fifties, poets such as Wright, Stewart, Campbell, Hope and McAuley did use formal, traditional techniques. All of them wrote poems which dealt with declared subjects in a clear and logical manner and they rarely abandoned rhyme or accepted stanza form. However, this general agreement about the appropriate form for a poem did not imply shared beliefs about the purposes and nature of poetry and, most especially, it did not indicate a shared commitment to political conservatism.

Many writers in Australia in the early fifties were committed to communism or a less doctrinaire socialism. These writers, too, employed traditional techniques. Communist poets such as John Manifold and David Martin were no less willing to write imitations of Pope or tightly structured sonnets than A.D. Hope or James McAuley. In fiction, the communist writers of the early fifties espoused the official party technique of socialist realism. Though this technique was associated with a radical political program it was based on the traditions of the nineteenth century realist novel and socialist realist writers were inclined to see literary experiment of any kind as linked with the degenerate nature of capitalism or the extremes of fascism.

Introduction

The apparent literary conservatism of Australian writers in the postwar years cannot be linked simply with conservative political attitudes. Nor should Australian writing of this period be seen as adopting static attitudes to art and society. Over the period individual writers adapted and responded to the changes in their society and to their own changing perceptions of their art. A closer examination of individual writers reveals both the individual nature of each writer's response to the social world and some broad similarities in those responses.

This book examines the changing responses of Australian writers to their society and their art in the twenty years from 1945 to 1965. It is a literary history but it is not a history which records and describes every major literary achievement of those years. Instead, it examines some of the broad groupings of writers in the period and it places the work of some individual writers in the context of these groupings. The book begins with a consideration of the socialist realism practised by communist writers and its links with a nationalist tradition. Then it discusses the reaction against communism by Cultural Freedom and, in particular, the way in which anti-communism influenced the poetry of James McAuley. The different responses to current debates about politics and literature will be considered in the work of A.D. Hope, Douglas Stewart, Judith Wright, David Campbell and Patrick White. Finally, the book considers the significance of the drama of the late fifties in establishing new directions in literature and it ends with some consideration of the breakdown of the old political/literary groupings in the early sixties.

In reading and researching I found that it was difficult to ignore the political and social changes occurring in Australia and the world at the time because the writers themselves were so aware of such changes. Frank Hardy, for example, proclaims his belief in a communist future in his fifties novels, while Judith Wright's poetry and criticism anxiously watch the triumph of technology and James McAuley warns of the dangers of totalitarianism. It would seem absurd to classify Australian writers of the eighties according to their political commitments because these are so various and ill-defined, and because the idea of literature as an instrument of social change has been largely abandoned. Of course, even in the fifties there were writers such as A.D. Hope and Douglas Stewart who maintained that the literature of commitment was successful only by accident and that art had no place in political movements. But the prevailing climate in the early fifties was one of extreme political positions and the question of commitment needed to be considered even by the uncommitted.

This thread of argument about commitment runs through the literary work and essays of most Australian writers of the fifties. Indeed, a writer's choice of genre, form, subject matter and style during this period might be seen as a declaration of commitment. A novelist, for example, who wrote a clearly told narrative about the hardships of a small selector and his wife might be classed as a nationalist with left-wing sympathies. Patrick White's *The Tree of Man*, however, which is a narrative about the life of a small selector and his wife, confused the categories of commitment because its nationalist subject was framed in a style which suggested a greater concern with form than with subject—an attitude associated with 'formalism' and right-wing politics. Similarly, a poet who wrote on subjects which were 'universal' rather than national might be seen as anti-nationalist and Anglocentric, and hence imperialist in politics.

Because these simple political categorisations of fifties writers have lingered in some recent critical discussions, particularly those stimulated by John Docker's books *Australian Cultural Elites* and *In a Critical Condition*, it is important that some understanding of the complexity of these writers' social and artistic views should be reached.[2] The fifties offered very different social, political and artistic conditions for writers from those of the eighties, and writers did not take an unchanging attitude to art and commitment. In teasing out the complexities and changes in the writers' art and attitudes I hope to show that the question of commitment was not a simple matter of a writer endorsing one political ideology but a matter of expressing an ideology through art which might or might not align itself with broad political categories. In seeking out the ideological commitments and attitudes of these Australian writers through their art I hope to show not only the individual nature of their responses but also how these responses relate to each other and to an understanding of the wider social and cultural changes taking place in Australia at the time.

The years from 1945 to 1965 were a period of vast social, political and cultural change in Australia. They encompass a period of recovery from war and argument about the future of postwar Australia and possible world peace. They include, in the first half of the fifties, the period of the Cold War and an Australian military commitment to Korea. In the last years of the fifties and the early sixties the extreme positions of the Cold War dissolved as communism receded as a threat both to Australia's international safety and its internal politics. By the late sixties, however, political lines were redrawn for a new generation as Australia entered the Vietnam war and a conservative government introduced conscription for military service.

These changes are not only apparent in the broad view of Australian history; they are evident in the changing attitudes and interests of Australian writers. When reading Australian fiction and poetry of the fifties and the comments of writers about their art, it is difficult to deny that social questions were important to writers. In particular, the question of a writer's political and social commitment arises again and again. In the immediate postwar period there was intense worldwide debate about the role which art may have played in the rise of European fascism. Equally, Stalin's interest in art as part of his political plan for the Soviet Union—with writers as the 'engineers of souls'—forced artists throughout the world to consider their relationship to the state. In Australia, these questions were complicated by a revival of nationalist feeling among writers during the war years and many writers felt a responsibility to assist in the development of a new nation free from the shadow of Britain or its successor in Western power, the United States of America.

In the early postwar years many writers were committed to Australian nationalism and to the hope that the future Australia would put into practice the longstanding nationalist claim for a true egalitarianism. But the alliance between nationalism and socialism aroused the suspicions of other writers who wanted a nationalism without a left political program. Still others saw nationalism as a stifling and provincial tenet for art and some deliberately avoided any kind of nationalist reference.

In the late fifties and early sixties a number of important works specifically criticising nationalism—such as Ray Lawler's *Summer of the Seventeenth Doll* and George Johnston's *My Brother Jack*—were written and, during the sixties, nationalism could be debunked without risk of the charge of political reaction. By the late sixties nationalism was often associated with the militarism which endorsed commitment to the Vietnam war or it was caricatured as a national joke. It no longer implied a set of egalitarian, humane values.

In the forties, however, when white Australians had faced the first real (as opposed to imagined) threat to their nation and when the whole nation, both at the war front and at home, became aware of the possibility of loss, nationalism was a serious and deeply felt belief. In the world of writing, arguments about the role of literature in a nation at war and then recovering from war can be seen clearly in the two major literary journals which came into being at the beginning of the war years, *Southerly* (1939) and *Meanjin Papers* (1940).

The Australian English Association, a sub-branch of the English Association (London), produced *Southerly* as part of its aim to promote and teach the English language and to maintain its purity. Four Queensland poets produced the first issue of *Meanjin Papers* as a small brochure of their own writing but the response to a second issue was such that it expanded into a fully fledged literary journal and later became *Meanjin* quarterly.

Both journals saw that Australian literature had been neglected by critics and, for different reasons, set about remedying this state. In the early issues of *Southerly*, for example, critics began to establish a canon of Australian work which contributed to the wider canon of literature in English. They sought out neglected Australian writers and, occasionally, whole issues were devoted to individual writers. *Meanjin* saw a more urgent and more clearly nationalist task: its editor Clem Christesen saw literature as essential to the building of a better Australian society.

The criticism in these two journals during the forties and fifties gives some idea of contemporary attitudes to literature and the demands which critics placed on writers. In *Southerly* critics considered the possibility of an Australian tradition with a 'distinctive' national flavour. But if the tradition was to follow the bush tradition of Henry Lawson and Joseph Furphy there were difficulties in translating this tradition to the city life which most Australians lived in the forties.

Marjorie Barnard defined the tradition in a *Southerly* review of 1948 as demanding bush rather than city themes, democratic sympathies, and an often picaresque plot spiked with sardonic humour. This was conveyed in a colloquial, unpolished style because any experimentation or variation in approach might appear artificial—and realism was the guiding star of the tradition. But Barnard criticised the tradition because it led young writers to the nostalgic subjects of country life and away from the increasing problems of the city.[3]

In the postwar years various *Southerly* reviewers lamented the sparseness of city themes in Australian writing and the writers' lack of interest in the internal life of individual characters. Kathleen Barnes, for example, commented in a review of Colin Roderick's collection of short stories, *Australian Roundup*, that there was a 'pervading gloom, a rarely interrupted adherence to the stark, sunburnt and terrible school of Australian literature, and its comrade in the urban scene of squalor, hopelessness and want'. But some of these critics also felt that writers should show a national loyalty of a kind, that Australian writers had a duty to write great novels of which the nation could be proud. In 1948 Cecil Hadgraft, for example, thought that the time had come for Australian writers to face the urban reality of Australia: 'One might expect the next stage to be here now—the urban. The general tendency in a literature is from the outer to the inner life...But the great Australian novel of the great Australian cities has not been written.'[4]

In poetry Max Dunn found the peculiarly Australian features to be poetry of statement rather than suggestion, with little profundity except for the work of Christopher Brennan and little lyrical invention except for the work of John Shaw Neilson. Dunn thought that Australians were conformists in 'both life and literature'.[5] In reviews of both fiction and poetry *Southerly* critics often commented on an 'immaturity' in Australian writing or referred to the need to achieve 'manhood and nationhood'. It was as if one of the tasks for literature after the war was to express a coming of age of the nation.

Unlike *Southerly*, *Meanjin* discussed literature as a social force rather than limiting its comments on society to aspects emerging unavoidably from literature. *Meanjin*'s editor, Clem Christesen, was the inspiration and driving force behind the journal and he had clear ideas about Australian society and its literature. Lynne Strahan's study of *Meanjin* to the mid-sixties confirms the impression that Clem Christesen was responsible for much of the journal's peculiarity and enthusiasm.[6] Without the support of an association or official group Christesen produced *Meanjin* because he believed passionately in the cultural contribution it made to Australia.

Meanjin Papers began in Brisbane in 1940 as a brochure of contemporary Queensland verse; the first issue contained two poems each by James Picot, Paul Grano, Brian Vrepont and Christesen. The second issue expanded to include a critical article by James Picot which aroused interest, antagonism and new contributors and correspondents. By 1945 *Meanjin* was significant enough to gain the support of the University of Melbourne and Clem Christesen moved to Melbourne.

Christesen found inspiration in the crisis of war. In his view, now was the time for the national culture to be revitalised. As Australian civilisation became endangered its literary and artistic heritage grew more precious and *Meanjin* aimed to strengthen the threatened culture. Christesen responded to most political events by considering their effects on Australian culture. He saw political and social changes to Australian life as directly influencing the writer. If there was war then this made the creative writer's achievements more valuable as a bulwark against despair; it also threatened the physical conditions of writers and, furthermore, it provided them with new material as Australians fought an enemy overseas and suffered deprivation at home. Looking back on *Meanjin*'s beginnings from the security of 1951 Christesen wrote:

> When *Meanjin* was initiated the nation was being mobilized for a momentous struggle for survival; and as the war grew nearer to our shores the issues became clearer. The physical energy generated had its counterpart on the cultural front. There was a quickened mental alertness, a heightened consciousness, a fresh hope for the nation's future. The promise of a cultural renaissance surpassing that of the 80s and 90s was tremendously exciting to some of us.[7]

In Christesen's view the war had a beneficial effect on creative literature, and in 1943 he had been anxious that writers should take advantage of what he saw as an inspirational environment; at that time, he wrote: 'The continent today is teeming with material for the poet, story writer and documentary reporter.'[8] He was an editor with definite ideas and hopes for the literature he published.

From the beginning *Meanjin* also entered the 'distinctively Australian' argument. The editor made literary excellence his criterion for publication but he made it clear that he hoped that the best work would also be distinctly Australian. But there were two sides to the argument. In one issue *Meanjin* quoted on its inside page Norman Bartlett asking for Australian writers to write about Australia because 'It is the only way we can become an adult, spiritually mature people' and, later in the same issue, published A.R. Chisholm regretting that:

> In literature: to be a good Australian you must assume that letters began in 1788, that the scene of all novels has to be laid in Australia, that only gums and wattles grow in heaven, that people like reading

about sun-drenched plains. . . There is, of course, another school: those
who indulge in pale imitations of would-be European revolutionaries
and iconoclasts in order to be 'different'. [9]

Chisholm's article suggests that there can be an Australianness
other than that of the sun-drenched plain and *Meanjin*'s contributors came time and again to the question of where that Australianness might lie. Manning Clark's 'Letter to Tom Collins' in *Meanjin*
in 1943 expressed dissatisfaction with prevailing attitudes to Australianness by changing the term 'mateship' to the derogatory
'mateyness'. In a *Meanjin* article in 1949 Clark developed this
idea, arguing that Australian literature must be considered in
the light of historical development. In Clark's view, Lawson
and Furphy succeeded in expressing the creed of a pastoral,
anti-British and pro-labour society—'social equality, mateship,
independence'—but the way of life presented in their writings
quickly disappeared and by the end of the 1930s Australian life
centred on the cities. Clark saw writers as coping with this change
by using the pastoral era as an escape, recommending suffering and
hardship as a form of nobility or following the old tradition as an
inspiration for the working class. Clark thought that the speed of
material development in Australian society prevented writers from
developing stylistic skills and dealing with the inner life. [10]

Like *Southerly*, *Meanjin* performed the duty of informing writers
of the tradition and it also began to reexamine that tradition. In
Meanjin, Arthur Phillips tackled this task by applying the American
frontier thesis to Australian literature. He agreed with Clark that
the tasks of settlement had kept Australians too busy to develop a
sophisticated literature and he thought that urbanisation might
bring literary maturity but at the cost of the hard-won national
tradition. To Phillips and to Christesen the tradition was important;
it was something for Australians to hold onto at a time when
enemies and then allies, in the form of Britain and the USA,
threatened to dominate Australian cultural life at all levels.

In the fifties the arguments about the Australian tradition were
compounded by the Cold War. Writers and critics with radical
political sympathies came increasingly to see the bush tradition as
an expression of republicanism, democracy, even socialism. In
their views, writers had a direct responsibility to Australian society;
they must not be sidetracked by the self-indulgence of art for its
own sake. The political polarities of the time meant that the
Australian tradition was annexed by the left and writers who did

not share left political sympathies resented this. The new definitions of the Australian tradition, formulated during the forties and early fifties, declared that only writers with socialist sympathies could be truly nationalist. It could be no surprise that non-socialists began to find serious failings in the tradition.

At the same time, Christesen had pressing reasons to fear the loss of liberty in Australia of the early fifties. He, with his Russian-born wife Nina, was one of the innocents called before the Royal Commission on Espionage (the Petrov Commission) in 1955 to answer questions about their contacts with Soviet officials and communists. No reader of *Meanjin* issues of the fifties can doubt that this experience influenced Christesen's interpretation of Australian society. In his view, the conservative political forces in Australia were threatening the freedom to criticise Australian society. They threatened intellectual life and the very existence of the creative writer.

In his *Australian Cultural Elites* John Docker has argued that *Southerly* and *Meanjin* represent the different intellectual traditions of Sydney and Melbourne. He claims that the libertarian tradition of Sydney produced *Southerly*, a journal devoted to literary discussion without politics, as well as a range of writers who decried social purpose such as Norman Lindsay, A.D. Hope and Patrick White. Melbourne, in Docker's argument, creates an environment of commitment exemplified by *Meanjin* with its insistence on the social role of literature. The theory places too much emphasis on the 'intellectual environments' of Australia's two largest cities and it does not take into account the movement between the cities or the fact that *Meanjin* began its life in Brisbane. However, it does identify two positions (not necessarily Sydney and Melbourne) in the argument about commitment in literature, an argument which was particularly important in the years after the Second World War. The question of commitment was much more important before 1960 than it has been since then, and the changes in writers' attitudes to commitment need to be considered in detail over time. The two categories of a Sydney libertarian tradition and a Melbourne tradition of commitment are too simple to explain the variety of changing attitudes in the twenty years after the war.

Southerly's interest in Australian literature was part of the English Association's aims of promoting the English language and its literature as a civilising force. When *Southerly* critics examined the Australian literary achievements of the past it was in an attempt to evaluate them and establish a canon of literature which Australia could offer the world. *Meanjin* critics had much more immediate concerns and literature took its place alongside political and social issues. For *Meanjin* critics, literature was important in promoting political freedom and social morality. However, these two views of literature were not mutually exclusive and many writers and critics contributed to both journals during the forties and fifties. The important difference for the purposes of this book is the way in which *Southerly*, for the most part, discussed literature apart from contemporary social and political concerns while *Meanjin* insisted on the social and political role of literature. The attitudes of the journals were related to the question of the political and social commitment of writers and, as we shall see, by the late fifties some writers, such as A.D. Hope, had strong views that the writer should not be committed to causes while others, such as James McAuley, were committed to causes in opposition to those of Clem Christesen and *Meanjin*. The two significant literary journals to emerge from the Cold War period, *Overland* (1954) and *Quadrant* (1956–57), began as journals of commitment but unlike *Meanjin* they were journals of commitment to specific political positions and their associated political parties—*Overland* to the Communist Party, *Quadrant* to anti-communism and thereby to the Democratic Labor Party, the Liberal Party and the right wing of the Australian Labor Party.

The kind of left-wing nationalism promoted by *Meanjin* in the forties and early fifties also informed three books published in the fifties: Vance Palmer's *The Legend of the Nineties* (1954), A.A. Phillips' *The Australian Tradition* (1958) and Russel Ward's *The Australian Legend* (1958). All three books looked to the Australian past, particularly the 1890s, to define an Australian national tradition. These books suggested that the Australian character was naturally egalitarian, unconcerned by social form and appearances, and a likely basis for a truly democratic society. Phillips and Palmer traced this national character in Australian literature and suggested that there were appropriate ways for the true Australian to write. Palmer claimed that Australian fiction

is never, or very rarely, written from the eyrie of a detached observer, well above the crowd, but from some point in the working community. The idiom, too, is often that of the man on the job, with his slang and colloquial rhythms... In our novels there is not much emphasis on the interior life of the individual; there is more on his activities as a social being or on his experiences at work.[11]

Phillips argued that the writers of the tradition shared

> the same belief in the importance of the Common Man, the same ability to present him without condescension or awkwardness, the same square-jawed 'dinkum' determination to do without the fripperies, the modes—and sometimes the graces—of aesthetic practice, the same unembarrassed preference for revealing the simple verities rather than the sophistications of human nature. It is by such qualities that an Australian writer usually reveals to the knowledgeable reader his national ethos, and his inheritance—reaching back through Lawson to the 'isocratic irreverence' of the Pastoral Era.[12]

Russel Ward's history concluded with the view that the Australian legend should be adapted to postwar Australian life. The publication of all three books at this particular time suggests that their authors hoped to influence the direction of Australia's future, but some reviewers of the books commented that, in the latter part of the fifties, they were already out of date and society had moved on to more sophisticated ideals.[13]

Certainly, in the early part of the fifties, there appeared a spate of books on Australia which offered more critical views of the Australian character. Some of these were published in honour of the royal visit in 1954, others appear to have been information books for British immigrants. Ian Bevan's *The Sunburnt Country* (1953), V. J. Aughterson's *Taking Stock; aspects of mid-century life in Australia* (1953), George Caiger's *The Australian Way of Life* (1953), and Stanton Hope's *Digger's Paradise* (1956) all found Australians to be easygoing, friendly and unwilling to stand on form. They also found Australians to be anti-authoritarian, complacent, and suspicious of foreigners.

Most of the contributors to these books believed that Australia was a classless society but they thought the pleasures of material prosperity were marred by a lack of respect for the non-material. Australia was a society without religion and without the respect for culture which might modify consumerism. In Bevan's book George Johnston attacked the xenophobia of his countrymen. In Caiger's book F.W. Eggleston complained about a lack of respect for education and artistic achievement and, in Aughterson's book, P.H. Partridge lamented the lack in Australia of even a 'cultured minority' which could appreciate or respect learning.[14]

So, in the eyes of some contemporary observers the cult of the
Common Man meant mediocrity rather than cultural achievement.
To them, equality meant conformity, and material well-being for
all denied the value of the mind and the soul. Nationalism, which
had been at its strongest during the war years, by the early fifties
had to contend with charges that it was anti-intellectual, xeno-
phobic, racist and philistine. Nationalist critics such as Palmer and
Phillips promoted nationalism because they endorsed the humane
values and political liberty which they saw enshrined in it. However,
the criticisms of nationalism apparent in commentaries of the early
fifties grew stronger as the fifties progressed so that, by the early
sixties, even writers with left political views had joined the chorus.
This was made possible partly by the breakdown of the Cold War
polarities which had allied nationalism to the left.

One of the features of international art which nationalism kept
at bay was the modernism which influenced European literature
and art in the years between the wars. Australian literature has
almost completely resisted modernism, with a widespread acceptance of modernist techniques coming only in the period after 1960
which many critics now call the 'post-modernist' period. This
resistance to modernism came not only from nationalist writers
but also from those who found nationalism an inhibiting literary
ideal. Modernism challenged Australian writers in a number of
ways and it is important to recognise that most of them rejected
modernist techniques for considered reasons, not simply because
the writers were old-fashioned and isolated from the centres of
European culture.

Modernism is a broad term for a method apparent in a range of
twentieth century arts—painting, sculpture, music, drama and
writing. Clear evidence of modernist attitudes can be found in
some literature and painting of the late nineteenth century, but
widespread recognition of a new kind of art occurred after the
First World War and modernism was most evident in the art of
the twenties and thirties. In English literature, the publication of
T.S. Eliot's *The Wasteland*, Virginia Woolf's *Jacob's Room* and
James Joyce's *Ulysses* in 1922 offer a convenient marking of the
arrival of modernism as a major force in English literary art.

It is difficult to define modernism in simple terms and this is
partly because one of the features of modernism is its defiance of
definition and convention. However, in all the arts modernism
expressed a dissatisfaction with the limits of traditional form. In

fiction, the restriction of narratives to a chronological time-sequence of events and to an account of the external activities of characters was cast aside. By using modernist techniques the novelist could move from one time scale to another and probe the flow of associations within the mind of characters. Modernism meant that the novelist need not adhere to an orderly and logical development of story and character, but could jump from time scale to time scale and from thought to thought so that readers must actively make links for themselves.

In poetry, modernism made it possible for writers to abandon traditional formal restrictions such as rhyme, traditional metre or stanza form, and it allowed them to play with disjunctive syntax, new symbols, and with illogical word associations. In reading a modernist poem the reader must seek the associations and allusions of the poem in order to discover its meaning; meaning is no longer given to the reader but emerges from the reader's response to the text of the poem.

These techniques meant that literature moved away from the clear depiction of a subject and away from the notion that literature was in any sense a mirror of life. Modernist writing forced readers to actively seek meaning from its often obscure and illogical patterns.

Allied to modernism in the twenties and thirties were a number of attitudes which suggested ideological allegiance. The figure of the victim (often the artist) alienated from an uncaring society often appears in modernist work and the presentation of this figure throws out a challenge to the orderly nineteenth century humanist social values. Modernist art suggests that this humanist order has failed to accommodate the full range of human desire and that humanist notions of progress brutally deny full expression to the individual, particularly the artist. Modernist art offered disorder as a challenge to the self-satisfied orderliness of Western society and in some ways it seemed to reflect the actual breakdown of that society in the first half of the twentieth century with the European War, the Great Depression and a second major war.

When most Australian artists and writers encountered modernist art in the twenties and thirties they did not dismiss it simply because they found it meaningless. Certainly, there have always been Australians willing to dismiss modernist art on these grounds, but most writers rejected modernism for more considered reasons. Norman Lindsay may not be regarded highly as an artist today but

14

he was influential in the twenties and thirties and he regarded modernist art as an expression of the breakdown of European civilisation. For Lindsay, modernism demonstrated the corrupt nature of European art and it confirmed his belief that Australians must preserve the best of European traditions in their own art. In 1948 the poet R.D. FitzGerald argued that 'Old-world disintegration which commenced with the smashing of sane and beautiful form in art and literature, and has gone on now to total violent physical destruction is surely out of place in a young soil.'[15]

After the trauma of the Second World War and the revelations about Nazism, modernism was often seen as the artistic expression of fascism. Some writers noted the anti-humanist elements in modernism, others saw that several of the great modernist practitioners such as Eliot and Ezra Pound had been associated with reactionary political views, and many connected the rise of fascism in Europe with the contemporaneous rise of modernism. Obviously, nationalists who espoused liberal humanist beliefs could not accept an artistic approach which challenged the traditions of liberal humanism. A.R. Chisholm's remark that the alternative to the 'wattle and gum' nationalism appeared to be 'pale imitations of would-be European revolutionaries and iconoclasts in order to be "different"', rejected the relevance of modernism for Australia.

As well, the Soviet Union, which in the thirties was seen by many radicals throughout the world as the triumph of Marxism, had declared that formalism—the concern with literature as structure rather than with literature as meaning—could not be accommodated in socialist goals for writing. Most modernist writing could be identified as more interested in form, even when it meant the destruction of traditional form, than in subject and so it was unacceptable to Marxists. In Australia, some writers' commitment to communism endured well into the fifties so that these arguments against modernism continued to be raised by the left.

The condemnations of modernism as allied to right-wing political ideologies were not without foundation. Liberal humanist views during the nineteenth and twentieth centuries have upheld the human power to change society and to order it in a rational way so that the benefits might flow to all. Beliefs in human equality, democracy and the goal of physical well-being for all people have been founded on the possibility of a logical organisation of society and of improvements to the general human condition. Modernist art challenged the ordered, rational, logical beliefs of liberal humanism and undermined the possibility of human ability to improve social conditions. As Richard Quinones comments in *Mapping Literary Modernism*, 'Modernism has been denounced by Marxist critics and others of the left as reactionary, and attacked by reactionaries for being part of the liberal froth of modern time.'[16] As we shall see, both responses were strong in Australia.

Many proponents of literary modernism might argue that modernist techniques were not only radical in artistic terms but also radical politically. Certainly, where literary conventions are entrenched the decision to experiment can imply a radical ideological position. Many of the poets emerging in the late sixties in Australia saw their experiments in this way, so that a poet such as Michael Dransfield could attack A.D. Hope alongside mining companies and industrialists as a 'poet of the state'.[17] However, the linking of technique and ideology is not a simple equation and Australian writers emerging in the period after 1960 appear to be remarkably innocent of the earlier association of modernism and fascism. They can experiment without the ideological implications which impinged on the work of their predecessors.

The Ern Malley hoax of 1944 where an Australian modernist literary group was fooled by an invented modernist poet may now seem to reflect Australians' literary ignorance, but it also came from serious concerns about the nature of modernism. This hoax, together with the court case in the same year against William Dobell's 'modernist' portrait of Joshua Smith winning the Archibald prize, led to a public debate about art and encouraged Australians to dismiss modernist art as meaningless. These two events led Kenneth Slessor to warn Australian writers that they wrote in a fairly hostile environment.[18] Ignorance has always been a factor in public resistance to modernist art, which appears obscure and difficult to untrained people, but this difficulty can also be seen as elitist. Modernist art seems directed towards the select few who are trained to understand it. This feature of modernist art also had implications for writers in postwar Australia because if art had a social role to play then it needed to be accessible to all intelligent, literate people. One of the remarkable aspects of Australian literature, even in the years since 1960, is the continuing concern with the social world which has led most novelists, poets and dramatists to seek clarity rather than experiment in art.

Though the modernist question, like the question of political commitment, was complicated in postwar Australia by literary nationalism, the phenomenon of a return to traditional literary forms in the years after the Second World War occurred in other English literatures of the time, and for similar reasons. In Britain and the USA there was a similar reaction against modernism in the postwar years. Rubin Rabinovitz argues in his *The Reaction Against Experiment in the English Novel 1950–1960* that English novelists turned to the models of the nineteenth century for a variety of reasons. Like the Australian left nationalists, British novelists such as Kingsley Amis, Angus Wilson and C.P. Snow saw experimental writing as elitist and celebrating the interests of the individual over society. They shared a distrust of the personalism apparent in much modernist writing and they also associated modernism with fascism.[19]

American novelists also favoured traditional models in the years after the Second World War. Though the reaction against experiment was not so universal nor so longstanding as in Britain, writers such as John Cheever, Mary McCarthy, Saul Bellow and J.D. Salinger developed their own kind of realism. Despite some similarities with the socialist realism promoted by communists in the thirties and forties, the traditions embraced by British and American novelists in the fifties were realist without being Marxist. Anti-communism was as much a part of British and American life in the early fifties as it was of Australian life, and writers sought techniques which asserted humane values without offering associations with fascism or communism. In Britain, the return to tradition also had nationalist elements as critics and writers recognised that the 'great tradition' of English writing was a realist, socially concerned tradition. Patrick White's famous comments about the dullness of Australian postwar fiction have always been taken as directed at a peculiarly national form of writing and so have offended national pride, but they might have been applied to most fiction written in English in the immediate postwar years.

During the fifties, critics in the English-speaking world also sought a tradition of humanism and moral value which might inform the wider society. The massive crisis in Western civilisation during the thirties and forties forced them to consider what role literature may have played in the crisis. In particular, the 'great tradition' claimed by F.R. Leavis and his followers offered a social and political role for literature which was humane without being Marxist. After the war, the New Criticism, which emerged in the

USA in the wake of Leavis, sought qualities in literature which transcended historical contexts and offered moral, humane, and even spiritual values, in resistance to the machinelike demands of modern industrialism. New Criticism's interest in the metaphysical and its ahistoricism must be placed in historical context. It was a phenomenon of the postwar concern to free literature from its associations with the political commitments which had devastated the world.

New Criticism did not influence the teaching of English in Australia until the sixties, and even F.R. Leavis was not popular among most academic English teachers in Australia in the fifties. This stemmed from the simple fact that most university teachers of English in Australia in the fifties had been trained in the historical traditions of Oxford rather than the Leavisite traditions of Cambridge. In the early sixties, New Criticism caused some controversies in Australian universities but, although its influence spread in the late sixties, in its early years it was confined mainly to the English Department of the University of Melbourne. John Docker has argued that Australian university English departments have favoured writers with 'metaphysical interests' over those with social and political interests as a result of the influence of New Criticism and Leavis. This may be true of Australian literature teaching since the late sixties, but Leavisites and New Critics in Australian English departments have often scorned Australian literature because, as Professor Sam Goldberg put it in 1966, they considered the literature 'generally too mediocre to withstand much scrutiny however sympathetic, much less provide the centre of a liberal education'. When the teaching of Australian literature in universities was being pioneered it was usually through the efforts of academics pursuing the Oxford tradition of historical approaches to literature. The important point for this discussion of Australian literature is that the writers themselves—even academics like A.D. Hope and James McAuley—were not influenced by the Leavisite or New Critical theories and that Docker is referring to the attitudes of critics writing after the mid-sixties.[20]

Docker's 'metaphysical' writers include James McAuley, A.D. Hope and Patrick White, all writers who emerged in the postwar years when questions of commitment were being hotly debated. It may be true that academics trained in New Criticism during the late sixties and early seventies have emphasised the universal or 'metaphysical' concerns of these writers at the expense of their

18

social and political interests, but it is wrong to suggest that these writers had no social or political interests at all. In fact, social, political and historical factors influenced these writers greatly even when it led them, like A.D. Hope, to reject political and social commitment in their art.

Australian writing of the late forties, the fifties and early sixties should not be seen, then, as a monolithic stand against literary experiment or a simple literary reflection of the prevailing socially and politically conservative values of postwar Australia. The writers of that period cannot be dismissed as 'metaphysical' in their interests and so divorced from important political and social issues. The situation of the Australian writer in the years after the war was complex, and the responses of writers to their situation were also complex.

Because the historical situation of the early postwar years—with the aftermath of war, the rapid growth of technology and the development of the Cold War—demanded some response from writers and because various groups in Australia at the time demanded social and political commitment from writers, the problem of commitment was widely debated. It is this question of commitment which emerged as a unifying concern for writers in the immediate postwar years and dissolved in the early sixties. Since the most obviously committed writers in Australia in the fifties were the socialist realist writers in the Communist Party I will begin with them and their links with the radical nationalists, before considering the attitudes of anti-communists in Cultural Freedom.

1

Pursuing the National Tradition

An interest in nationalism of all kinds is likely to grow at a time of national threat. In Australia during the forties, the interest in a national literary tradition was not merely part of the patriotic sentiment of a people resisting invasion but it also offered a link between literature and politics. Critics such as Phillips, Palmer and Christesen linked the tradition of Lawson with a left-wing democratic socialist political view.

A renewed determination to establish a national culture was evident in many areas of Australian life after the war. Many historians, critics and writers were tired of the shadow of Britain and Europe and they saw a new threat to Australian independence in the growing cultural influence of the USA. In 1950 Phillips coined the phrase 'the cultural cringe' to describe the lingering unwillingness of many Australians to accept the achievements of their own culture in comparison with that of Britain. It is a phrase still in use but it belongs essentially to that period after the war when there was a strong reaction against the denigration of things Australian.[1]

Arthur Phillips and Vance Palmer indicated the directions which postwar writers might take in pursuing a national literary tradition. As Phillips put it, the national tradition was concerned more with 'simple verities' than 'the sophistications of human nature', with straightforward storytelling rather than with the 'fripperies of aesthetic practice'. Sophisticated literary ideals were no more relevant after the war than they had been to Lawson when he warned critics to keep out of 'the tracks we travel'.[2]

On this rising tide of nationalism a large number of novels were written in Australia in the period between 1945 and 1956. Though all of this fiction was in keeping with the national tradition's call for realism, for concern with the social world, for praise of the Australian character, and in keeping with the tradition's refusal to experiment technically, it may be placed into several distinct groups. The first group includes the novels of Vance Palmer and Katharine Susannah Prichard who formed a link between the writers of the turn of the century and those of the postwar period. Both novelists had established themselves in the years between the war and both wrote novels which reflected their political commitments—Prichard to communism and Palmer to left nationalism. In the postwar years each of these writers published trilogies—Palmer's *Golconda* trilogy and Prichard's *Golden Miles* trilogy—which seem to be their authors' final attempts to write Australian novels of grand proportions.

In the forties, younger writers who shared Palmer's kind of left nationalism began to emerge. Alan Marshall published a novel of factory life, *How Beautiful Are Thy Feet*, in 1949 and his well-known partly autobiographical *I Can Jump Puddles* in 1955. Kylie Tennant, too, accepted the bush tradition in her early novels but seemed less interested in politics with each novel after *The Battlers* (1941). Dymphna Cusack, on the other hand, developed a nationalist novel which retained the realism and social concerns of the tradition but directed its attention to contemporary problems. In the immediate postwar years, she wrote *Come In Spinner* (1951) with Florence James, then *Say No to Death* (1951) and *Southern Steel* (1953) and she went on to write novels which addressed racial prejudice and fascism. Marshall, Tennant and Cusack wrote novels which used the techniques of the national tradition to portray the lives of people in the Australian cities. Their novels had political sympathies with the left but did not form part of a political program.

In 1948 Ruth Park published her first novel about life in the slums of Sydney, *The Harp in the South*. Although this novel also adopted the clear narrative techniques of the national tradition and identified the true Australian as the Irish-Australian, it was distinguished from the work of Cusack because there were no obvious political or social goals behind it. *The Harp in the South* was one of several novels written in the early postwar years which exploited the nationalist tradition for its 'exotic' subjects and strong narratives. Other novels of this kind returned to the bush to find true Australians: Jon Cleary's *The Sundowners* (1952), D'arcy Niland's *The Shiralee* (1955) and Nevil Shute's *A Town Like Alice* (1956).

In each of these novels the national character which had been identified and promoted by left nationalists for political motives became a romantic or exotic figure. There was no political program behind Cleary's itinerant Irish-Australian shearer or Niland's Irish-Australian fighting swagman or Shute's returned soldier; they were simply hard-drinking, hard-fighting larrikins with generous hearts. In 1957 John O'Grady turned the cult of the national character into a comedy by creating an Italian immigrant, Nino Culotta, who studied the national character, language and customs in *They're a Weird Mob*.

Apart from novels which made open reference to the national tradition, either by a bush setting or by a deliberate adapting of the bush style to city subjects, there were novels which continued the traditions of the realist narrative and the concern for external event but applied them to new aspects of Australian life. For example, Brian James' *The Advancement of Spencer Button* (1950) offered a comic account of promotion in the New South Wales teaching service, Tom Ronan's *Moleskin Midas* (1956) satirised the respectability of squatters like Kidman, and Dal Stivens' *Jimmy Brockett* (1951) experimented a little with the autobiography of a gangster.

Many of these realist novels remain rewarding to read and we should beware of dismissing them as dull simply because they do not conform to more recent notions of novelistic technique. Often they were 'journalistic' in the sense that writers like Tennant and Cusack wrote about aspects of Australian life which they researched and then cast into stories. Most of these novels were more concerned with plot than with character and there was little psychological insight or complexity of social discussion. The novelists did not see themselves as technical innovators and the main value of their novels lies in the attention they gave to aspects of Australian life and history, and the cheerful extroversion with which they treated these subjects.

However, more ambitious programs for the national tradition emerged from the political commitments of the forties and fifties. As these political commitments dominated Australian literature for some time it is important that the more consciously political applications of the national tradition be considered in detail.

During the war years, the Communist Party of Australia had attracted some Australians' interest in the possibility of a new society after the war, one which put into practice those ideals associated, correctly or not, with the egalitarianism of the 1890s. Though in Britain, Europe and the USA the Communist Party reached a peak of influence in the thirties, in Australia membership of the Party peaked in 1945. It seems that where in other parts of the English-speaking world the experience of the Spanish Civil War and Stalin's alliance with Hitler had disillusioned many communists, in Australia the Party offered a program for the future which attracted nationalists anxious to throw off the influence of Britain and the USA.

The Communist Party also had a program for writers which was part of its political program and this fitted very well with current notions of a national literary tradition. In the years since the breakdown of Stalinism among Western communist parties, Marxist critics have developed sophisticated and complex theories of literature. These theories combine an understanding of literature as a dynamic part of society with an awareness of the subtlety of literary communication. Since the seventies Marxist literary theory has challenged the division between political writing and writing with 'universal' interests above politics.

However, in the forties and fifties communists who adhered to their Party's doctrines were offered the theory called socialist realism as official party guidance for art. At the time, the work of Marxist critics such as George Lukács or Bertolt Brecht, who continue to be respected as literary theorists, was either unavailable to Australians or was banned by official Party decree. In pursuing a simple form of socialist realism Australian communists were not alone or particularly backward by comparison with communists in Europe or America. Socialist realism was the theory adopted by communists throughout the world, in particular in the Soviet Union, which was regarded as the source of communist truth by most communists until 1956.

The Marxist literary theory available to Australian writers in the forties and fifties provided a simple statement of the relationship

—
23

between art and reality. It was based on readings of the accepted English Marxist critics—Christopher Caudwell's *Illusion and Reality* and *Studies in a Dying Culture* or Ralph Fox's *The Novel and the People*—supplemented by material which came from Soviet sources through the Party publications and more accessible works such as *Literature and Reality* by the American novelist Howard Fast. This version of socialist realism had its roots in a 'reflection' or 'mimetic' theory of art—in which the role of art was to mirror reality. But Marxism meant that reality was seen from the perspective of a Marxist political understanding. Writers with a Marxist commitment were obliged to examine the economic forces at work in society, and the reality which they reflected emphasised the relationships between those economic forces. This kind of realism sought not merely the external, obvious features of social interaction but a truth which exposed the bases of this interaction. Socialist realist art is not simply a 'mirror of life' but a mirror which selects and emphasises the conflicts in economic and political power within society in order to teach the true nature of these conflicts.

The obvious criticism which such a theory invites from non-Marxists is that socialist realism distorts the mirror of life for propaganda purposes and that socialist realist artists surrender their independence to a preconceived political theory. Many of the critical pronouncements reaching Australian writers did offer crude notions of the writer's task. They knew, for example, the explanation which Zhdanov (now infamous for his part in Stalin's purges) offered in 1934 for Stalin's description of writers as the 'engineers of human souls':

> It means, in the first place, to know life, in order to depict it truthfully in works of art, to depict it not scholastically, not lifelessly, not simply as 'objective reality', but to depict actuality in its revolutionary development. Moreover, the truthfulness and historical concreteness of artistic description must be combined with the task of the ideological transformation and education of the working people in the spirit of socialism. This method of literature and of literary criticism is what we call the method of socialist realism.[3]

The theory in the hands of such spokesmen was principally didactic and writers were part of a team putting into practice the political ideas formulated at another Party level. In the Marxism of the period, literature was not part of the base of political, social and economic activity where revolution occurred but part of the superstructure which could only reproduce and communicate these activities. Literature was apart from the revolutionary developments of the political, social and economic world, and its main role was to educate revolutionaries about these developments. This positioning of literature meant that writers were not significant in the formulating of political theory nor even in developing literary theory. Their art could be revolutionary only in the sense of assisting revolution at a political level.

In their insistence on the descriptive or representative role of literature and in their emphasis on literature as part of a superstructure determined by the base of political struggle, these versions of Marxist literary theory were artistically conservative and deterministic. Socialist realism attached radical politics to non-innovative art; it linked a belief in the ability of the working people to change the conditions of their lives with a refusal of the writer's ability to change the conditions of art. Literature was the tool of the revolution rather than an expression of it and communist artists were obliged to accept the formulations of their political theorist comrades rather than explore new possibilities through literature.

On the other hand, Marxist sources also warned against the writing of propaganda. Frederick Engels' letters to Minna Kautsky in 1885 and to Margaret Harkness in 1888 argued that a socialist novel need not offer social solutions nor even display the writer's own political views: 'The more the author's views are concealed the better for the work of art. The realism I allude to may creep out in spite of the author's views.'[4]

Despite the arguments about Marxist literary theory which can be traced through the writing of Engels, Lukács, Brecht and others, there is little evidence that Australian communist writers were very interested in literary theory. Most Australian discussions of socialist realism at the time centred on the links between the national literary tradition and the Marxist literary tradition. The writings of Lawson and Furphy were taken as instinctive, pre-revolutionary attempts at socialist realism. Australian writers felt that a national tradition lay waiting for them to renew in a revolutionary and communist way.

In 1944 groups of Australian communist writers began to meet to discuss their work and the nature of the writer's role. Members of these groups included Frank Hardy, Eric Lambert, David Martin, Jean Devanney, Walter Kaufmann, Ralph de Boissiere,

25

Laurence Collinson, Mona Brand, John Morrison, Bill Wannan, Ian Turner and later John Manifold, Judah Waten and Dorothy Hewett. The Melbourne Realist Writers Group began publishing a journal, *The Realist Writer*, in 1952 and produced nine numbers before incorporating it into *Overland* in the spring of 1954. The first issue of *The Realist Writer* proclaimed that: 'The old order is dying and the old literature, the old criticism, the old journalism with it. We aim to assist in the birth of a new order and its new literature.' *The Realist Writer*'s philosophy was set out in an unsigned article entitled 'The Writer and the People'. The author (probably the original editor, Bill Wannan) named Graham Greene, T.S. Eliot, Jean-Paul Sartre and Ezra Pound as writers who reflected the breakdown of capitalism by defeatist or elitist writing. He explained the place of socialist realism in Australia in terms of a history of workers' struggles. The songs of Eureka and the ballads demonstrated the creative spirit of ordinary people 'standing together against the exploitation of tyrants'. Realism, simply defined as 'word pictures of life as it was lived', had always been the method of the people's art, but under capitalism it had been corrupted into modernism whose only purpose was the display of 'indecision, futility, boredom'.[5]

'The Writer and the People' called for writing which understood the processes of history and saw that the future was with the people. Modernism was associated with reaction and despair; socialist realism alone could show the way forward. The article was not so much an explanation of the methods and ideals of socialist realism as an emotional call for the defence of the people against the forces of reaction. Its rhetoric is typical of that found in Australian Communist Party publications in the fifties.

But the article also promoted socialist realism as a demand that the writer observe and write about the real conditions of life rather than sound the possibilities of technique or proclaim the mysteries of the self. Furthermore, the socialist realist writer was committed to the portrayal of 'ordinary people' in active response to the limiting conditions of their lives. Many contemporary popular novels, for example Ruth Park's novels of city misery, could not belong to a socialist realist canon since they depicted a degraded and passive minority suffering poverty; the socialist realist theory called for a realistic grasp of the whole society, with the working class as protagonists rather than victims.

'The Writer and the People' also indicated the nationalist thread in Australian socialist realism of the fifties: it claimed the songs and stories of Eureka as the foundations of a literature for the people. Later articles in *The Realist Writer* and elsewhere show that Lawson, Furphy, Miles Franklin, Mary Gilmore and other nationalist writers were adopted by the socialist realists as their forerunners. That these writers often had philosophies quite remote from communism was of little account; a working-class subject and a reasonably straightforward approach to storytelling was taken as sufficient evidence of a shared socialist sympathy. With little concern for critical niceties, the socialist realists claimed the national tradition as their own and assumed their place as the contemporary exponents of the national literature.

The few existing statements of Australian socialist realism include Frank Hardy's notes for *The Realist Writer* where he gave a simple and practical account of the method based on his own novel, *Power Without Glory*:

> Socialist Realism: The theory of Socialist Realism was fathered by the great Russian writer Gorki who straddled like colossus the two great epochs of literature, bourgeois realism and socialist realism. This theory was characterised by Fadeyev as 'a combination of historical veracity and artistic generalisation'. Typicalness is basic to Socialist Realism . . . the creation of the type is the basis of character building for the socialist realist writer. Take qualities from several grocers to create one, for instance, taking well into account the social behavior of the small shopkeeper.[6]

Hardy continued by quoting Malenkov on the typical as the essence of a particular social force. It was not a simple matter of writing about bad capitalists and good workers but a matter of capturing the essence of each group and following its role in society. But Hardy's interpretation of the 'typical' seems to suggest a stereotype, for example of the grocer, rather than a recognition of individuality. In the writing of some socialist realist critics, such as Georg Lukacs, the idea of the typical character is a means of linking the portrayal of individuals with their place in a wider society; it is not simply the creation of characters according to their type but an exploration of the place of the individual in society. Hardy's definition seemed to reverse the process by seeking out characters according to social group rather than by examining an individual in terms of his or her social group.

Jack Beasley was the manager of the Australasian Book Society which was set up in 1952 by a group of communists and their friends to publish socialist realist writing. In 1957 Beasley published his own pamphlet, *Socialism and the Novel: a study of Australian Literature*, in which he applied socialist realist theory to Australian literature. This is the only other extended statement by an Australian communist on Australian socialist realism in the fifties. The determining feature of socialist realism as Beasley saw it 'is the truthful, artistic depiction of our living society, in which the decisive, moving force is the struggle of the working class for Socialism. Further, if literature is to serve the interests of the working people and the future of Australia, it must be written from the standpoint of, in support of, the movement for Socialism'.[7] Beasley conceded it was possible to write good realistic literature without being a socialist but maintained that socialist belief made a good writer better. On the question of 'typicality' Beasley took the line that characters should represent the main social forces, that is the working class and its allies, as well as their enemies, the capitalists. This viewpoint

> would help to create many important types, some of them new to Australian literature. Such examples as the small farmer, heavily in debt to the banks and watching the decline of the world wheat market; the manufacturer, worried by the approach of overproduction in his industry, who sees trade with China as his salvation; the right wing union official obedient to the wishes of his monopolist masters; the far-seeing union official or worker who believes that socialism can be achieved by nationalising the big monopolies; the Catholic worker, torn between loyalty to his church and his class; the working class wife and mother, battling to rear her family while the pay slips through her fingers; the brutally arrogant big capitalist, driving for profits and political reaction, prepared to make war, to do anything except something of benefit to the people.[8]

Beasley seemed to be on the point of writing a novel himself with this range of suggested subjects for the writers. In fact, many of these stories were told by socialist realist writers in the fifties and some of them, especially 'the working class wife and mother, battling to rear her family while the pay slips through her fingers', were told many times. The difficulty with such literary criticism is that it amounted to a prescription for writing and the emphasis was on a prejudged categorisation of individuals such as 'the brutally arrogant big capitalist' rather than on an examination of the complex tensions between individuals and their class. A charming and seemingly generous big capitalist, for example, might have presented more promising material for writers than one who fulfilled the role of his class in every aspect of his personal life.

Despite warnings from many Marxist theorists, beginning with Engels, that the typical did not mean casting characters into simple stereotypes, both Hardy and Beasley seemed to be suggesting such an approach. However, they were writing criticism before the event—a kind of recipe for writing—rather than criticism based on texts. In his more recent *Red Letter Days* Beasley has commented that Frank Hardy was never important in the official echelons of the Communist Party and that his views on art should not be taken as representative of those of his comrades. Yet Beasley's own views were similar to Hardy's and, in the fifties, they were friends. Beasley's subsequent attack on Hardy is but one example of the continuing bitterness between communists and ex-communists which confuses the facts of commitment in the fifties.[9]

It is difficult now to assess how seriously communist writers treated such prescriptions for writing. Much of the critical discussion in the Party's journals and newspapers was written by those who, like Beasley, were not writers themselves. Correspondence between John Morrison and Frank Hardy during the fifties suggests that Morrison gave due respect to Hardy's earnestness but stood his ground on questions of political interference with the writer. Dorothy Hewett, in her youth, was inclined to listen to the man who wrote *Power Without Glory*, and Ralph de Boissiere's novel *No Saddles for Kangaroos* seems to follow Beasley's ideas very closely.[10]

From time to time, writers argued about literature in the Party publications. For example, in 1953 when the Australasian Book Society published S.F. Bannister's *Tossed and Blown* and *God's Own Country* several communists were critical of the choice of novels which described such anti-Marxist activities as bootlegging and door-to-door salesmanship. David Martin defended the novels as humane and nationalist:

> Here is a writer who is not a Marxist. To confuse her evident
> ideological weakness with an overall moral weakness, to criticise an
> almost too frank documentary life record of an elderly progressive

Australian, a non-communist, in the same manner as a new novel by Fadeyev, is naive; it betrays political backwardness on the critic's part.[11]

But Victor Williams and Len Fox disagreed. E.M.M. (Enid Morton?) and John Morrison disagreed with them in turn. Morrison made the following statement of his views:

> Here, in the baldest possible terms, is set out an attitude to writing which I have seen growing up over a number of years, and which I believe now more than ever leads straight to literary damnation. An attitude which maintains that literature should be regarded as an instrument in the social struggle and nothing else. As a matter of fact, Williams goes even further, arguing as he so clearly does that writing is good only in the degree in which it serves the needs of a given moment. . . . Am I committing a heresy when I suggest that the function of an artist, no matter through what medium he works, is to move his audience emotionally?[12]

Martin and Morrison were writers rather than critics and they did not develop their disagreements with the Party critics into a challenge to the conventional socialist realism which the Communist Party offered. Instead they continued to write their short stories, novels and poems, presumably with scant regard for the opinions of their more dogmatic comrades. Both writers were sufficiently sure of their own approaches to writing not to be unduly pressured by Party attitudes.

In other disputes, communist writers broke into two groups: those who insisted on the strictest interpretation of socialist realism and those who argued for greater freedom for the individual writer. Frank Hardy, Eric Lambert, Victor Williams and Ralph de Boissiere might be found in the first group; John Manifold, David Martin, John Morrison and Mona Brand appeared in the second. Sometimes, these disputes were simply between writers and the Party critics such as Paul Mortier or Len Fox. They disagreed on issues such as the worth of Ilya Ehrenburg's *The Thaw* or the management of *Overland* or the Australasian Book Society. These were questions of allegiance to the Party, rather than literary issues as such.

Thus the writers in the Realist Writers' Groups in the fifties included those such as Morrison who had reservations about the official socialist realist theory as well as those such as Hardy,

Lambert and Judah Waten, who were prepared to defend it staunchly. One of the differences between the two groups seemed to lie in the age and experience of the writers. The new worker-writers such as Hardy, Lambert, Hewett and de Boissiere apparently found support in the theory for their early efforts as writers, while Morrison and Martin, who had published before 1946, were more confident about their own ideas.

The most positive effect of the socialist realist theory and the groups which promoted it may have been the direction and confidence it gave to new writers. In some ways the goals which the theory offered writers were quite impossible to attain but they were worthy goals which inspired writers. First, socialist realism aimed to be popular both in the sense of representing the lives and aspirations of working people and in the sense of being accessible to and entertaining for them. Second, it linked nationalism to a universal concern with the struggles of humanity. Third, it presented the actual conditions of contemporary society rather than the trials of the past as the material for literature. Most important, socialist realism offered a reconciliation of the two strands of literature, the concern for the life of the individual and the concern for society, by means of the theory of the typical.

In practice, however, the demands of socialist realism were difficult to meet. Literary theories function best after the event of writing, as in the criticism of Lukács, not as formulas for the creation of art. As I have suggested, some communist writers largely ignored the theory in the sure knowledge that their political commitment would emerge in their art willy-nilly. Others professed a version of the theory as their guide. The practice of socialist realism in Australia presented many interesting difficulties as individual communist writers interpreted the theory or ignored it completely.

Stephen Murray-Smith's anthology of short stories, *The Tracks We Travel* (1953), emphasised the nationalist claims of socialist realist writers. The book included stories by non-communist socialists such as Alan Marshall, Frank Dalby Davison, Vance Palmer and Gavin Casey among those by communist writers. In his introduction, Murray-Smith claimed that 'the stories in this collection are a contemporary expression of the mainstream of the Australian tradition', and outlined that tradition through the anti-authoritarianism of the convicts, Eureka, the struggle for land and the

---

development of the trade unions. Lawson, Daley, Brady and Furphy were the writers who expressed the great democratic impulse of the nineties:

> What these writers primarily did was to emphasise the worth of the common man, to realistically depict his life and struggles, and to expose the inequalities that held him down. They reflected the democratic temper of their environment, but they developed that temper, gave new meaning to it and passed on their sword, as Pilgrim did, 'to him that can use it'.[13]

Murray-Smith found evidence that the Australian democratic spirit had survived into the fifties in 'the support by Australian workers for the anti-colonial struggle of the Indonesian people, and the rejection by the whole Australian nation of the 1951 Referendum' (the referendum to ban the Communist Party) though this referendum was only narrowly defeated. So too the writers in his collection continued the work of Lawson, Furphy, O'Dowd, Francis Adams and Miles Franklin:

> Thus, in distinct and happy contrast to recent Australian anthologies, we have rejected 'high writing', psychological preoccupation for its own sake, the 'atmospheric', the grotesque and the introverted story. We are convinced that this sort of story, however well done, cannot constitute literature in the sense that we as pupils of Lawson understand it.[14]

Murray-Smith's version of socialist realism, at least, had no place for the close examination of the individual as part of an expression of social and political forces.

Setting aside the stories by non-communists such as Davison and Palmer, the contributions to *The Tracks We Travel* had certain features in common. Most of them are set in the thirties depression or periods of drought or of particular crisis for working people. Many of them, for example, those by Lyndall Hadow, John Manifold, Flexmore Hudson and Judah Waten, deliver their views of experience through the eyes of a child character. Several support the cause of Aborigines, of Jewish immigrants or factory or mine workers. The device of remembered childhood served to simplify moral issues for the writers, for the deprivation suffered by innocent children provides a greater pathos than the suffering of adults. Similarly, a setting where the evils of capitalism are obvious, such as the depression or the state of Aborigines in the outback, relieved the writer from character exploration. In stories such as Allyn Vaisey's 'Fire in the Pit' or Gavin Casey's 'It Finds its Level' the servants of capitalism are not only evil but also foolish. In some stories, such as Max Bollinger's 'Southland: farewell!' or David Martin's 'Cybalski and the Nightcart Man', the right-thinking workers triumph in simple acts against authority. If this was a new version of Henry Lawson then it was Lawson of the sentimental story and the simple tale, of 'Send Round the Hat' and 'The Loaded Dog' rather than 'The Bush Undertaker' or 'Water Them Geraniums'.

John Morrison's story 'The Judge and the Shipowner' alone demonstrated that the socialist realist story need not conform to the pattern of railing against oppression or manipulated triumph over it. This story declared itself as a worker's fantasy in which those in power learnt about working life. The story was playful and comic, and it did not pretend to reflect actual life. However, its socialist sympathies were absolutely clear.

The Realist Writers' Groups nurtured several socialist poets including David Martin, Laurence Collinson, and John Manifold. These poets found difficulty in expressing their loyalty to communist ideals and their commitment to the people without falling into clichés of public rhetoric or domestic sentimentality. Though their non-political poetry appears in Australian anthologies, all of these poets wrote about appropriate communist subjects such as the death of the Rosenbergs or the glories of Stalinist Russia. John Manifold's 'The Tomb of Lt John Learmonth, A.I.F.' expresses a sense of Australian tradition and a faith in future freedom in recollection of the death of a friend. In other poems, such as 'The Bunyip and the Whistling Kettle', Manifold adapted the Australian traditional ballad form to general socialist ideals. But the most explicit examples of his commitment are the Red Rosary sonnets which include his 'Death of Stalin', which pictures Stalin as a fighter-plane:

Such is his vast memorial's extent!
Here—like a fighter-plane, his petrol spent,
But straining dauntless towards a friendly drome

Whilst all his victories yet blaze in air—
Here at the dawn-lit first perimeter
Of Communism Uncle Joe reached home.[15]

33

Reading these sonnets in the eighties, the most striking element is not Manifold's commitment to communism but the choice of a rigid, traditional sonnet form in which to express his revolutionary sympathies. Manifold celebrated what he saw as various socialist battles—the Eureka stockade, Tito's victories, the Chinese revolution, allied victory in Europe—in a verse form which demands strict discipline and suggests the most refined traditions of European culture.

Manifold is most often cited in critical discussion as the author of 'The Tomb of Lt John Learmonth, A.I.F.' or 'L'embarquement pour Cythère', but the poems in which he openly expressed his political commitment were hymns of praise to communist ideals. Such a commitment may also be recognised in the patriotism of 'The Tomb of Lt John Learmonth' and in the cheerful anti-authoritarianism of his ballads. Yet these qualities are equally apparent in the poetry of a poet such as Douglas Stewart, who had no sympathy for communism.

Similarly, David Martin wrote domestic and social poetry because this expressed his commitment to the people which was part of his communism. But he also addressed the public issues which concerned communists in the fifties, such as the imminent execution of the Rosenbergs in 'A Letter to President Eisenhower':

> In the name of America: open the doors of the death house!
> In the name of the children of slavery: open the door of freedom!
> In the name of the cornfields, in the name of the laughing smoke
>   stacks,
> In the name of the dead that are not dead in America:
> Let the Rosenbergs live, destroy the death house,
> Or the curse of the living will wither and blight and destroy you.[16]

Socialist realism was founded on the novel and could offer poets little help in approaching their task. Laurence Collinson found it difficult to combine his socialist commitment and his taste for love poetry; the very basis of Collinson's view of romantic love would seem to demand a disregard for wider social causes. Communism may have appealed to romantic poets, but it was difficult to see how romantic poetry, with its interest in personal emotion and a world beyond immediate reality, could serve the political goals of communism.

David Martin insisted that poetry could encompass both private emotion and public commitment. In his Preface to *Poems of David*

Martin 1938—1958 he explained that 'true poetry' relied on traditional responses which are bound up with 'man's creativeness in love, work and struggle', so that political and domestic emotions came from the one source:

> Poetry, I believe, will again take its just place in the affections of the living when it is lyrical as well as heroic, public as well as domestic, traditional but of its own time and unafraid of experiment. At all cost, poets must be true to themselves. But to be loved by the people, poetry must be close to its life and must embody its hopes and aspirations.[17]

This was an admirable ambition which offered a poetic equivalent to the socialist realist novel's aim to reconcile the personal and the social. The socialist realist poets were attempting to retrieve poetry for the people while retaining the intensity of individual emotion. Their poetry is always easily understood—there is no obscurity in Collinson's early love poetry or even Manifold's more allusive imitations of Pope. These poets were trying to hold back the tide which has taken serious poetry beyond any significant audience other than poets and academics. And it should be noted that Martin believed that experiment had a place in poetry of the people—tradition and experiment belonged together.

Martin and Manifold approached from a communist point of view the same problems which absorbed non-communist poets and even anti-communist Australian poets in the postwar years. To all of them the modernist experimental poetry seemed inward-looking and meaningless. Douglas Stewart was as concerned by the loss of an audience for poetry as Manifold or Martin. As well, the forms favoured by the communists—the short lyric, the sonnet, the bush ballad, the Augustan satire—were used by writers as various as Stewart, Judith Wright, David Campbell, James McAuley and A.D. Hope. Indeed, Stewart, Campbell and Wright met John Manifold on common ground in the use of the bush ballad as a basis for their writing. Nationalism, even without communism, could lead a writer to the ballad as the 'song of the people'.

The communists, and John Manifold in particular, collected Australian bush ballads, the folk songs of a new country. In performing this task they served the new nationalism in Australia and earned the gratitude of many patriotic Australians. In 1953, Dick Diamond put together *Reedy River* for the communist little theatres, the New Theatre League. The show used a combined storyline from chapter one of Furphy's *Such is Life*, Lawson's *Joe Wilson* stories and the nineties shearers' strikes. Along this line were pegged Australian folk songs. Some were traditional, such as 'Click Go the Shears' or 'The Banks of the Condamine', but others, like Helen Palmer's 'The Ballad of 91' were new creations in the old style. Helen was the daughter of Vance and Nettie Palmer and her ballad reflected Vance's view of the nineties. The shearers of the nineties did not create this song but the postwar nationalists were happy to remedy the omissions of the past.

More than 130,000 Australians had attended *Reedy River* by the end of its first six years of production. The players encouraged the audience to join in the songs and word sheets were handed round. In this way, Australians who may never have heard 'The Ryebuck Shearer' came to claim it as their heritage. They left the theatre perhaps ignorant of the communist nature of the entertainment but rejoicing that they did have a folk culture after all.

The communists served nationalism even if nationalism did not serve communism. Influenced by communism, Ian Turner, Russel Ward and Robin Gollan wrote important histories of Australia. As a communist Stephen Murray-Smith edited *Overland* as a vehicle for Australian stories, criticism and poetry. As communists, Jack Beasley and Joe Waters kept the Australasian Book Society afloat to publish Australian writing.

Then, in 1956, the Soviet leader Kruschev made a speech denouncing Stalin and confirming the nature of the purges instigated by him. When Soviet troops moved into Hungary to quell what appeared to be a nationalist movement, Australian communists were forced into a period of reassessment and conflict. Within the Party the existing differences between members became exacerbated. Some members were expelled; others, disillusioned, left willingly. In 1958 Stephen Murray-Smith left the Party, taking the journal *Overland* with him. Others in the socialist realist groups, including Frank Hardy and Dorothy Hewett, stayed on, to turn bitterly away in the sixties. Judah Waten, who had not been an official member since the thirties, returned to the Party as an act of solidarity; John Manifold and John Morrison retained political commitments which allowed them to pursue their own literary lights.

The 1956 crisis for the Communist Party in Australia was a matter of political allegiance rather than attitudes to literature, but

———
36

writers had gained a deal of emotional support from their political comrades and from the belief in a Soviet society which was committed to the freedom they sought. The failures of the political party which promoted socialist realism did not mean that writers must abandon its literary method, but there are several interesting patterns in the decisions of communist writers after 1956. For example, two writers who did not espouse a strict allegiance to the Party guidelines for literature and who had established themselves as writers before 1945—John Morrison and John Manifold—did not find it necessary to leave the Party in the crisis of the late fifties. These writers seemed able to maintain a political commitment without relying on the Party critics for advice on writing. In John Manifold's case, residence in Brisbane may have kept him from much of the argument within the Melbourne or Sydney realist writers' groups.

The decisions of other writers suggest that personal disagreements and disppointments may have been as influential as political or literary ideas at this time. Eric Lambert, for example, had quarrelled with Frank Hardy and other Party members and left Australia in the early fifties. By 1956 he was denouncing the Party critics and realist writers' groups to his friend Zöe O'Leary and claiming that they had hindered rather than helped his work. Hardy had moved to Sydney by 1956 and began to gather a new group of realist writers around him; his papers suggest that this move widened the differences between him and Melbourne communists such as Murray-Smith. By the sixties Dorothy Hewett had moved back to Perth where she was no longer in the thick of socialist realist discussion; in letters to Hardy, she criticised the vulgar distortion of Marxist theory which, in her opinion, was leading socialist realists to formula writing.[18]

However, neither the political crisis for Australian communists in 1956 nor individual personal circumstances can account for the demise of socialist realist writing in Australia by the early sixties. In 1954 socialist realist writers had a journal to discuss their work, *Overland*, they had a book society to publish and distribute it, the Australasian Book Society, they had a network of supporters and sympathisers, and they had a number of popular and critical successes to their credit such as Lambert's *The Twenty Thousand Thieves*, John Morrison's *Port of Call* and Hardy's *Power Without Glory*. By 1960 *Overland* had become a nationalist journal with sentimental rather than political connections with the left, the

Australasian Book Society could not find enough manuscripts worthy of publication, and many of its writers had either left the Party or removed themselves from Party debate.

One of the main difficulties was the close identification of socialist realism with Stalinism, so that Kruschev's denunciation of Stalin on the other side of the world could undermine the efforts of writers in Australia. If the theory had been understood and developed in Australia writers might not have felt cheated and misled by a Party which had invested its hopes in a dream of Soviet paradise. But the end of the fifties saw a distrust of political commitments of any kind and an increasing criticism of political motivation for writing.

The practice of socialist realism in Australia in the fifties also provides some indications of the difficulties for communist writers. Though Australian socialist realists wrote poems and plays with varying success, the theory was based on the novel, and it is to the novel that most of the writers turned. Socialist realist novels by Australian communists in the period include Frank Hardy's *Power Without Glory* (1950), Eric Lambert's *The Twenty Thousand Thieves* (1951), Walter Kaufmann's *Voices in the Storm* (1953), Judah Waten's *The Unbending* (1954) and *Time of Conflict* (1961), David 'Forrest's' (Denholm) *The Last Blue Sea* (1959), Dorothy Hewett's *Bobbin Up* (1959), John Morrison's *Port of Call* (1950) and *The Creeping City* (1949), and Ralph de Boissiere's *No Saddles for Kangaroos* (1964). Jack Beasley gives a list of the Australasian Book Society's publications to 1978 in his *Red Letter Days*; although only a proportion of its authors were communists, the Society's list gives a fair indication of socialist realist interests.

Of these novels, Frank Hardy's *Power Without Glory* is the best known. It was a bestseller, partly as a result of the publicity of legal action against Hardy, partly because of the qualities of the novel itself. Hardy described the novel as 'critical realism' rather than socialist realism, on the grounds that it was concerned with the past as a necessary step towards a socialist future and it did not examine the contemporary world advocated by socialist realist theory.

The novel diverged from the theory in other ways, too. Its realism was an exaggerated, blown-up version of the 'actual conditions of social life', best described as melodrama. This kind of writing had no interest in the internal life of the individual or in personal psychology, but its characters played obvious roles in the acting out of good and evil. The 'actual conditions of life' were represented in the novel by casting actual people and retelling actual events in terms of a melodrama. Readers could easily identify John Wren in John West, as well as the boxing hero Les Darcy, 'Red' Ted Theodore, Frank Anstey, Archbishop Mannix, Squizzy Taylor and many other public figures in Hardy's lightly disguised characters. This and the verifiable nature of much of its plot gave the novel an authenticity which came from outside the novel rather than through the power of a created realism.

Power Without Glory demonstrated one of the great ironies of literature: verifiable fact is often less believable than created incident. Actual people, their words and actions, may be less convincing than those of the imagination. Hardy interpreted his facts to show that John Wren and the Labor Party were morally bankrupt and that the Communist Party was the only political party likely to serve the interests of the people. His novel amounted to an open attack on the Labor Party, the Catholic Church and the corruption of Australian public life.

The obvious contradiction that real people are accused of crimes in the novel and, at the same time, deprived of their capacity to think and behave like real people must have baffled the Wren family and the court which tried Hardy on a charge of libel. The Wrens used the incident of Mrs West's affair with a bricklayer as the basis of its suit, partly because it is in his portrayal of personal life that Hardy was most obviously untruthful. But the Wrens lost their case because this was where Hardy was most clearly writing fiction.

Jack Lindsay has praised Hardy's novel as the rough and heartfelt creation of an Australian working man. By reading the novel as a kind of document of Hardy's own passionate political beliefs it can be accommodated to both the social novel (dealing with Australian politics since the turn of the century) and the novel of the individual (where the individual is Hardy himself). This distorts socialist realism, but Hardy was quite happy to see the novel as belonging to the pre-revolutionary phase of critical realism. The point is that the theory really has little relevance to Hardy's novel; what he achieved was something apart from Marxist theory and closer to the nationalist writing of Dymphna Cusack.[19]

The fictional elements of *Power Without Glory*—the stereotyped characters and the clichéd speeches—pushed the novel onto a plane beyond realism, and Cusack and Tennant were better skilled at translating researched events into believable human terms. In *Power Without Glory*, for example, each of the characters is sketched with physical attributes to suggest their moral states. John West is described thus:

> From a distance, the first noticeable characteristic was his bandiness, but, at close range, his eyes were the striking feature. They were unfathomable, as if cast in metal; steely grey and rather too close together; deepset yet sharp and penetrating. The pear-shaped head and the large-lobed ears, set too low and too far back, gave him an aggressive look, which was heightened by a round chin and a lick of hair combed back from his high sloping forehead like the crest of a bird. His nose was sharp and straight; under it a thin, hard line was etched for a mouth.[20]

This is the portrait of a villain, and similar portraits are drawn briefly for most of the characters in the book. The novel offered black-and-white moral values, but Hardy had so much material of public interest that he seemed unable to spare the time to move beyond simple character delineation and conventional speeches.

The novel's boldness in exposing the immediate past and portraying Australian public figures marked a new development in Australian writing. No longer were the intrigues of criminals and politicians part of the tales of other lands and other times; Hardy forced Australians to recognise corruption in their own society. The promotion of communism in the novel, which Hardy emphasised to his comrades as evidence of his commitment, paled beside its display of social evil.

Judah Waten's *The Unbending* came much closer to fulfilling socialist realism's ideal of a study of believable individuals at the centre of social change. The novel, like Waten's book of short stories *Alien Son*, tapped the novelist's memories of his own parents, Russian Jews who migrated to Australia in 1905. In describing their struggles in a new land, their naive dreams and unwillingness to face a new reality, Waten wrote with a deep affection and sympathy. His study of a marriage between a clever woman and an extroverted, dreaming man is one of the finest portrayals of marriage in Australian writing, of a kind to be compared with Henry Handel Richardson's *The Fortunes of Richard Mahony*.

At the same time that it is a study of a marriage, *The Unbending* also pursues the struggles of the workers in the small West Australian town where the Jewish migrants come to live. The battles of the Industrial Workers of the World during the anti-conscription campaign of the First World War form a second plot of class struggle and racial intolerance which touches its central concern with the changing relationship in the marriage. However, Waten has some difficulty integrating the two elements in the novel because his main characters see themselves as outsiders and cannot recognise their own place in the class struggle. Solomon Kochansky resists the political arguments of his neighbours because he wishes to become wealthy in Australia:

> Kochansky could not deny there was a lot in what Feathers had said but he would not admit it. Somehow he did not want to come too close to his neighbour; bad as things were at the moment, he did have prospects, a future. And he felt nearer to men of weatlh than to men like Feathers who had nothing to look forward to. That of course should not be.
>
> 'In this country every man should have work and plenty everything,' he said. 'Always great surprise to me men be out of work with Labour Government here and in Melbourne.'
>
> Feathers shrugged his shoulders. 'It doesn't seem to matter what Government's in office,' he said. 'The politicians look after themselves and nobody else. Only strong fighting unions will get us anywhere.'
>
> It was Kochansky's turn to shrug his shoulders. Strong fighting unions! What good would they do him? He clicked to his horse which began to canter.[21]

Judah Waten was aware of this conflict between the central interests of the novel and its overt political interests, and several friends and publisher's editors advised him that this was its major weakness. However, he found that he could not conceive of the novel in any other way because it was important for him to place his family's experiences within a framework of socialist struggle, and, though the novel does not explore the full implications of Solomon's resistance to politics, it certainly raises questions for the reader. It is tempting to speculate whether Waten would have needed to give political speeches to his worker-characters if he had been writing now when there is an awareness of the political nature of domestic life and an acceptance that a writer can be political through the study of domestic subjects. Nevertheless, *The Unbending* belongs to the early fifties and reflects Waten's attitude to his own political commitment at the time.[22]

41

Hardy, Waten, David 'Forrest', Eric Lambert, and Walter Kaufmann (a German Jew who returned to Germany at the end of the fifties) all set their novels in times of major political crisis. Eric Lambert's *The Twenty Thousand Thieves* illustrated the value of socialist principles through the experiences of Australian soldiers in the Middle East during the Second World War. Lambert's robust story did not demand too much political consideration; the adventure of war and the appeal to national pride carried his politics lightly. 'Forrest's' novel of the Kokoda Trail, *The Last Blue Sea* offered a much more convincing portrayal of the experience of war but at the same time its interests were similar to those of T.A.G. Hungerford in his novel of New Guinea warfare *The Ridge and the River* (1952), and socialist realism did not seem to offer any greater insight than Hungerford's qualified nationalism.

In practice, the Australian socialist realists seemed to be evolving their own version of the theory. Their task was to bring home to their Australian readers the significance of moments in the recent past both at home and abroad (Kaufmann's *Voices in the Storm* vividly portrayed his experiences in Germany before the war; Ralph De Boissiere's *Rum and Coca-Cola* and *Crown Jewels* were based on his experiences as a West Indian). These significant moments were crises where struggles for survival gave urgency and excitement to the novels and this urgency reinforced their political aims. The novels rarely examined the nature of postwar life in Australia in order to express political commitment; instead they recovered Australian and world history in order to teach readers about the nature of political struggle.

Both Lambert's and Hardy's novels were popular successes and both offered the strong narrative and sensational elements—battle scenes, mild sexual adventure, criminal activity—which are often features of contemporary popular literature. In theory, socialist realism was not a technique which sought out adventure or the most exciting elements of life but one which looked steadily at the contemporary conditions of life for most people. By writing about war, corruption among the wealthy, or the most extreme cases of hardship, these socialist realists also evaded questions about the nature of postwar Australian society. One of the difficulties confronting writers who wished to write about postwar Australian life was the boredom of actual existence for most people. Patrick White stated the problem most openly, but the socialist realist writers, by turning so consistently away from contemporary 'typical' life in Australia (despite the demands of their theory), acknowledged this boredom by the absence of contemporary life from their work. Australia, as much as any modern Western society, is the land where nothing happens, but in the novels of the socialist realist writers things happened all the time. The novels sought out the experiences of the minority—the poor, Aborigines, Jews, criminals, those fighting wars—rather than observe the conditions of life for the majority of postwar Australians. Gavin Casey, a fellow traveller rather than a communist, drew attention to these in his *Amid the Plenty* (1962) but his analysis of fifties suburban life merely scratched the surface of the suburban malaise.

As a result of the socialist realists' concentration on people in crisis at exciting moments of history, their writing moved away from realism towards romance. That is, rather than 'seeking out the actual conditions of life' and so examining the relationships between classes in their society, the writers sought action and adventure and they romanticised the oppressed in order to provide a glamour for their work. Of course, there were exceptions to this— *The Unbending* is largely free from such romanticism—but the ironic result of socialist realism in Australia was the revival of a nationalist romanticism. In much socialist realist writing the Australian national character was represented by that romantic figure the easygoing, generous Irish-Australian and the poor were represented by the equally romantic working-class mother, keeping her children and house clean while her husband is out of work.

Among all the socialist realist novels published in the forties and fifties Dorothy Hewett's *Bobbin Up* is distinguished by its interest in Australian city life after the war and by the way Hewett tackled the task of considering both the individual and the whole range of society. Hewett concentrated on the lives of the women working at an Alexandria (Sydney) spinning mill for two days in 1956. Instead of following the life of one character through its length, each chapter of the novel examined the domestic problems of one or other of the women working in the mill: Shirl the promiscuous girl who longs for marriage, Dawnie who disguises her fear and innocence in obscene language, Beth the young married woman searching for a home, Mais the desperate seeker of security who works double shifts, Nell the communist organiser. All of the women are poor and badly educated. Some are pregnant, some old and physically ailing. All are slaves to the exhausting, grinding routine of the mill but need work to sustain their hopes of suburban happiness and their miserable livelihoods.

Hewett did not express the typical through one deeply realised character but through a pattern of life over a whole range of characters, and some of the women seem worthy of greater attention than Hewett gives them—Nell, in particular, whose marriage has suffered as a result of her communist enthusiasm and who has been called a 'careerist', or Mais, who offers the beginnings of a study of demoniac willpower in the service of worthless ideals. The novel came to a familiar socialist realist crisis and resolution: when the factory boss dismisses the old and the married women Nell organises a sit-in strike and the women band together in solidarity and hope. Yet the optimism at the end of the novel is difficult to share when it is based on an unlikely reform of the factory at home and the inspiring symbol of the Russian sputnik overhead.

As well, Hewett's very skill in creating the culture of the working women's lives suggests doubts about their future. Hewett wrote vividly about the city and unlike many of her comrades she refused to romanticise the daily routines of her working-class women or indulge in too much sentimentality about their attitudes to their children. Hewett was not a modernist but throughout the novel she sought objects, sounds, visual images, which could represent the nature of the lives the women led. Neon signs and advertising jingles, bits of pop songs and fashionable (yet tawdry) items of clothing recur through the novel, suggesting the kind of dreams which keep the women at their work. Hewett breaks up the narrative through the device of exploring two days in the lives of a group of women and she also offers a sense of the fragmentation of each life through her energetic descriptions of popular culture. The novel can be called experimental only by comparison with other socialist realist work but the degree to which it experiments is notable.

Bobbin Up recognises the boredom and hollowness of modern city life even while it asserts the possibility of a socialist future. Hewett presents city life as enclosed and even hopeless. She builds up a picture of the dismal life around the mill by listing the small details which make up the broad culture of the women she portrays—the pop songs of Frank Sinatra and Elvis Presley, nylon frills and chenille bedspreads, the slang of bodgies and widgies.

Against such overwhelming squalor Hewett offers the sympathy and kindness which the women give each other, the consistent values of Dawnie, Beth and Nell, the lyrical lovemaking of Beth and Len and the appearance of the sputnik:

'It's a man-made star. The workers put it there,' Stan said. O! little star
of Nellie Weber. O! little star of Stan Mooney, of Tom Maguire, his
brown-eyed wife, and his brown-eyed daughters. O! little star of Shirl
and Dawnie, Beth and Alice, Jessie and Lil. O! little star that whirls
through space and carries all the dreams of man. Sputnik grew fainter,
glimmered in the distance and disappeared over the rim of the
world. [23]

In retrospect, this dream of a Soviet heaven has some pathos and
one might be tempted to consider *Bobbin Up* as a document of
the attitudes of a communist working woman in the fifties, in a
similar way to Lindsay's view of Hardy's *Power Without Glory*.
Few people, even among communists, could read the novel on its
own terms today. However, the novel gives much more attention
and energy to the cultural emptiness of urban working-class life
than it does to socialist possibilities for the future, and it seems
to be moving towards techniques and interests which are more
modernist than the notions of Marxism current in the fifties.

Like other socialist realist novels of the time *Bobbin Up* did not
meet the demands of the more sophisticated versions of socialist
realist theory—it examined the role of the working class in contemporary Australia but it did not do this through the close
examination of individuals, nor did it show the class struggle
beyond a very limited part of society. Where Lukács, for example,
offered Balzac as a model of realism and rejected Zola's naturalism,
Hewett admitted to modelling the novel on Zola. At the same
time, the Australian writer she admired was Kylie Tennant, and
Hewett's method of working in a textile mill to collect material for
her fiction followed the example of Tennant who, on one occasion,
managed to be arrested for soliciting in order to gather material on
the lives of prostitutes. Nevertheless, of all the socialist realist
writers Hewett came closest to confronting the realities of Australian
urban postwar life, and in doing so, she raised an issue which had
been neglected by communists—feminism. This issue, particularly female working conditions and poverty, has emerged as a
continuing problem amid the prosperity of Australian life.

Admirers of Dorothy Hewett's later work must find *Bobbin Up*
a fascinating early indication of her interest in female experience
and her extraordinary skill with language. *Bobbin Up*, like her
later plays, was based on her own experience but it was an
experience artificially designed and the novel worked to equally

45

artificial constraints. Hewett's later writing has revealed that during the fifties she was entangled in a maze of domestic and romantic crises. *Bobbin Up* was written on the kitchen table in a Sydney suburban house despite the demands of three small children and an antagonistic man. In some ways, the novel represents the period of Hewett's life when she was most bound by masculine definitions of female life and art. Ironically, Hewett's resistance to current feminist prescriptions for literature comes from her experience and later rejection of the communist prescriptions of the fifties.[24]

The political commitments of the writers who called themselves socialist realists influenced their writing in a number of ways. For many of them, communism offered a reason to write and gave them the confidence to attempt novel-writing. Several of these writers, including Frank Hardy, could call themselves genuine 'worker-writers' in that they came from a poorly educated working class which rarely produces literary writers. By providing a place for literature in the revolution, communism gave these writers a sense of purpose which overcame their doubts about their own abilities. But at the same time that it gave the writers an urgent reason to write, socialist realism also attached literature to immediate political goals and led some of the writers to communist propaganda. It was the writers such as David Martin, John Manifold and John Morrison, who had found their way to literature without the programs of the Party, who were most able to ignore the Party's demands for overt political writing.

Throughout the years after the war there was a growing distrust of the use of literature for ideological purposes. Stalin's depiction of writers as 'the engineers of souls' suggested that writers were merely the tools of political manipulation, and most current formulations of socialist realism reduced writers to the status of servants of programs which had been decided at higher echelons of the Party. This denied the writer a role in exploring the possibilites of literature and, perhaps, contributing to the understanding of Marxism. It demanded overt displays of commitment from writers rather than accepting that literature is always an expression of ideology and that expression (as Engels claimed) may be all the more powerful for not being immediately apparent. Since the fifties it has become rare for a writer to believe that literature can change the world, and this loss of belief in literature as a political force may be traced to the experiences of the twentieth century when literature and language have often been misused for political purposes. In Australia communist writers who left the Party after 1956, including Hewett and Hardy, later expressed bitterness about the misuse of their talents.

However, Australians were most often attracted to socialist realism because of the future it offered to nationalist art rather than for its Marxist goals. The writing by socialist realists during the fifties added to the nationalist work by Palmer, Cusack, Tennant and others and it identified the difficulty which much of the nationalist writing faced. It was realist writing which was not particularly real in its depiction of Australian life. Socialist realist criticism of Ruth Park's work, for example, noted that she was sentimentalising the national tradition and that her 'kitchen-sink' novels exploited the poor rather than liberating them. Nevertheless, the socialist realist writers themselves were unable to avoid romanticising the workers, though the best of their novels— Waten's *The Unbending* and Hewett's *Bobbin Up*—overcame this tendency.

The Australian national tradition in the fifties, though it was most often described as a realist tradition, in the hands of writers such as Cusack, Palmer, Park, Cleary, and in the work of socialist realists, had become a romantic tradition where the poor were honest and caring while the rich were brutal, where the Australian character was represented in hard-fighting males with hearts of gold, and in their female counterparts, warm-hearted, rough-mannered mothers and working girls. Like communism, nationalism of this kind was also due for reconsideration by the end of the fifties, and even writers who had embraced it in the early fifties could be found criticising the national character for its racism, xenophobia and anti-intellectualism by the end of the decade.

Socialist realism, like nationalism, placed limits on the writers who pursued it and these limits derived from the way in which different literary styles had been perceived as expressing specific political commitments. To nationalist critics in the forties and early fifties, it was inconceivable that experimental writing might express a commitment to Australian cultural independence and democracy. To experiment was to be more interested in technique than subject and it suggested that the writer was exploring the self rather than the social world. Similarly, writing about the lives of the wealthy or those with close ties to Britain (such as the writing of Martin Boyd) was interpreted as unAustralian despite the fact

---

that Boyd's experience as an Australian was reflected with some accuracy in his novels. The subjects and styles by which a writer could express left nationalist views had been laid down on the basis of a fairly superficial reading of Lawson and his contemporaries. Though the idea of a national tradition may have helped new writers by giving them a sense of belonging to a strong national culture, in the long term it also placed limits on the kind of writing which could be termed nationalist.

Where nationalist critics such as Palmer and Phillips offered very general notions of the tradition to postwar writers, socialist realism defined the way in which political commitment and literary style were linked. Because socialist realists were convinced that modernism was a commitment to despair, to a preoccupation with the self and to an elitism, they were inclined to see all experiment as reactionary. This meant that socialist realist writers were wary of attempting new styles and subjects and most of them were content to rework the ideas of the past. In novels such as *Bobbin Up* and *The Unbending* the tension between the conventions of socialist realism and the writers' interest in new approaches is very evident.

The linking of certain political commitments to specific literary styles and subjects was not limited to the left in postwar Australia. During the period of the Cold War, in particular, both ends of the political spectrum were eager to interpret literary work as an expression of clearly identified political positions. To the left, experiment indicated reaction; to the right, it demonstrated anarchy. Both political extremes advocated the return to tradition, whether to the national tradition of the left or to the older European traditions of the right.

In examining the way in which particular literary styles were identified with political positions, I do not mean to suggest that literature is not political. Obviously, all writers express ideology of some kind in their work. However, the simple equating of particular literary approaches with particular political approaches has distorted the reading of some Australian literature, and it placed significant limitations on writers in the Cold War years of the early fifties. In the case of the socialist realist writers these limitations are difficult to ignore because a communist political commitment obliged writers to follow the conventions of an established tradition and denied them the opportunity to experiment. Socialist realism did not emerge naturally from a communist commitment but it was a convention by which such commitment was overtly expressed.

At the same time that nationalism and socialist realism were adopted by writers committed to the political left, other writers sought conventions which would express commitment to the political right. In particular, the conventions of the left—the realist narrative with a nationalist subject—came under fire from writers who rejected the politics of nationalism or communism. The emergence of an Australian Association for Cultural Freedom with a literary journal of its own demonstrated that in the early fifties the right, like the communists, saw literature as a powerful political force.

Just at the time when the Communist Party of Australia had begun to collapse as a base for writers, the anti-communists had managed to organise themselves as cultural opponents. The history of the founding of Cultural Freedom in Australia reveals the way in which writers and writing were perceived as central to the political conflicts in Australia at the time.

2

Cultural Freedom and *Quadrant*

When, after 1956, some Australian communists began to accept the truth about the Stalinist Soviet Union and left the Communist Party they were reviled by the faithful as traitors to the working class. Stephen Murray-Smith and Ian Turner were called 'revisionists and deserters' who had been offering a middle-class, democratic bourgeois approach to literature through *Overland* magazine.[1] In 1959, Murray-Smith wrote an editorial for *Overland* which lamented the Australian labour movement's distrust of ideas: 'The intellectual, be he from the ranks of the working class or not, is generally despised and rejected; and, what is worse, mistrusted. Probably no labor movement in the world has spurned ideas, particularly new ideas, as the Australian labor movement has.'[2]

This created a controversy in the pages of *Tribune*, with Rex Chiplin changing *Overland*'s motto 'temper democratic' to 'temper bourgeois democratic' and attacking David Martin's and Laurence Collinson's contributions to that issue as revisionist and, in Collinson's case, 'disguised pornography'.[3] Chiplin was the editor of *Tribune* rather than a writer and his attack was answered by a number of writers still in the Party. John Manifold, Katharine Susannah Prichard, Frank Hardy and Ralph de Boissiere all saw *Overland* as valuable to the labour movement despite its editor's 'political deterioration' (as Hardy put it). Most felt there was some

truth in Murray-Smith's comments on the gap between the worker
and the intellectual, though the fault might lie with the intellectual.
To these writers *Overland* was not anti-working class and certainly
not anti-communist. The real cause for anguish was its failure to
attack the true enemy—the pro-American forces of reactionary
capitalism. De Boissiere asked 'why is *Overland* standing in some
sort of Never Never throwing bouquets to the enemy whose
resources are so much greater than ours?'[4]

By 1959, these writers could discern a clear enemy: the forces
of anti-communism had organised themselves against the literature
of socialist realism. At a time when the Communist Party of
Australia was losing membership and when communist writers
were themselves beginning to reject the more rigid features of
socialist realism, the right had emerged as a rival promoter of
Australian literature.

But the move against the communist writers did not come from
other writers. Where in Britain, the USA and Europe a growing
number of writers had turned away from communism and joined
the ranks of the anti-communists by the early fifties, in Australia
such a move away from communism did not occur until the late
fifties. In the USA and Britain it was often the ex-communist
writers who were the most vocal anti-communists after the war.
This did not happen in Australia partly because the communists
were strengthened by association with nationalism and partly
because the experience which disillusioned so many British and
European communist writers—the Spanish Civil War—had been
so distant. Australian writers who were nationalists found common
ground with communist writers; in the early fifties, the left seemed
to be the only group that cared about Australian writing at all.

Politicians, not literary critics or anti-communist writers, were
the first to raise the issue of communism among Australian writers.
In 1952 questions were asked in Federal Parliament about the
Commonwealth Literary Fund (CLF) grants to communist writers.
Standish Keon, the Labor member for Yarra, accused the government of allowing the fund to be used to support various communist
activities by writers. W.C. Wentworth, from the other side of the
House, joined Keon in denouncing the Fund's Advisory Board as
communist sympathisers. Vance Palmer, as chairman of the Board,
was accused of distributing the Fund's largesse for the promotion
of communism.[5]

The alliance between these two politicians represented a new arrangement of social interests in Australia. Standish Keon was a Catholic member from a largely Catholic working-class electorate in Melbourne; his attack on communism stemmed from his strong sense that communism crushed religious freedom, and persecuted Catholicism in particular. W.C. Wentworth, the direct descendant of the early politician and explorer, represented Sydney wealth and the capitalist interests which would also suffer under a communist regime.

Keon was active in the Catholic lay society known as the Movement which organised the Labor Party's industrial groups in the late forties and early fifties. During the same period Wentworth had been active compiling information on communists working in the public service, universities and the media. By the early fifties, the communist strength in the Australian trade union movement was waning largely through the efforts of the Movement's industrial groups which had fought union elections against communist candidates. So the communism which had threatened to control the political institutions of the working class—the trade unions and the Labor Party—was all but defeated by the strength of Catholics, working-class anti-communists. With the union threat under control, Keon could afford to join Wentworth in searching out communists among the professional and intellectual classes. In 1952, writers were now due for attack on the basis of the flimsy Government support some of them received.

But the alliance between Keon and Wentworth had wider implications for Australian politics; it prefigured the formation of the Democratic Labor Party and its alliance with the conservative Liberal Party. About this time, the success of the Movement had generated fears among some Labor Party members that it would use its power within the Party to promote the ideals of a conservative and clerically ruled Catholicism. In 1955, the growing power of the Movement culminated in a split in the Australian Labor Party (ALP) with the Democratic Labor Party (DLP) being formed from the Movement remnants. Though the DLP was a working-class party, its denunciation of communism in the ALP meant that it helped to keep its apparent social enemies, the Liberal Party, in power.

Wentworth's and Keon's attacks on writers were probably useful to the Prime Minister, R.G. Menzies, because they called on him to intervene in the CLF grants without taking a virulent public anti-communist stand himself. Similarly, the DLP's attacks on communism performed the task for the Liberal Party while allowing

Cultural Freedom and Quadrant

powerful Liberal Party politicians to remain aloof from Catholic anti-communist hysteria.

Those wishing to establish a cultural alternative to the activities of the Communist Party faced two major problems. One was the widespread identification of Australian writers with the left. As Keon and Wentworth found, Australian writers such as the writer they named, Kylie Tennant, might not be members of the Communist Party but very few of them could be called anti-communist. To be an anti-communist writer was close to being an anti-nationalist writer at a time when most of the support for writers came from nationalists. Keon and Wentworth accused the wrong writers of communist commitment, and their attack on the innocent could win them few friends among writers.

The second problem was the identification of anti-communism with Catholicism. Because Catholics had fought longest and hardest against communism in the unions, anti-communism came to have a sectarian element. Any new arrangement of cultural forces must establish itself as non-sectarian and non-Catholic if it hoped to gain respectability. Anti-communists believed that a supportive organisation for non-communist or anti-communist Australian artists and intellectuals was needed, but it was apparent that such an organisation would not spring spontaneously from the efforts of the artists themselves. Such a need was purely political and it was the politicians who set about the task of creating it.

In 1950, an international conference of writers in Berlin had set up the International Congress for Cultural Freedom to defend 'intellectual liberty'. It would not have taken great perception to see that the existence of such an organisation was in the interests of the US government which supported the sponsors of the conference, the German magazine *der Monat*. In the aftermath of the Second World War the USA was concerned to offer resistance to both communism and lingering nazism in Europe, and it saw that intellectual resistance was as important for its long-term success as political resistance. Nevertheless, the writers who joined the International Congress, including Arthur Koestler, Upton Sinclair, John Steinbeck, Robert Penn Warren, André Malraux, Malcolm Muggeridge, Raymond Aron, were genuinely concerned by the continued totalitarianism in Eastern Europe and shared the anti-communist views of the US government. The Congress was not simply a US government construct; it harnessed the concerns of a range of artists, many of them former communists.

In the early fifties, US and British Committees of the Congress were set up and the journals *Partisan Review* (US) and *Encounter* (U.K.) began to promote intellectual discussion of the dilemmas of a world disillusioned by ideology. In Australia, in the early fifties, a similar group of ex-communist, anti-communist writers did not exist, but several anti-communists saw that an Australian Committee of Cultural Freedom might offer a useful alternative to the left-nationalist groupings of writers and intellectuals.

The principal agent in the establishment of an Australian Committee was Richard Krygier, a Pole who had escaped Europe during the war. Krygier's anti-communism, like that of many Eastern European migrants to Australia, came from his own experiences of prewar Europe and his concern for the fate of his homeland. In his letters, he described himself as a lapsed Jew and a former communist. During the forties, Richard Krygier worked for W.C. Wentworth's private campaign against communism before establishing himself as an importer and distributor of foreign literature. He was a member of the Liberal party and the Australian Institute of International Affairs, and when Salvador de Madariaga visited Australia for the Institute in 1951 Krygier learnt about the International Congress for Cultural Freedom. He contacted the organisation and proposed that a Committee be set up in Australia.[6]

The papers of the Australian Association for Cultural Freedom reveal the impressive way in which Krygier went about forming his organisation. He began by providing selected members of Parliament with copies of his own newsletter *Free Spirit* which offered a digest of overseas events and revelations about communism in Europe and China. Many Australians in public life responded with gratitude to Krygier's contact. From these initial contacts Krygier's circle of sympathisers grew so that, by 1954, he could select possible members for his Committee. By then he also had secured Sir John Latham's services as president of the Committee.

Latham might be remembered as the only High Court judge to vote in favour of the Bill to ban the Communist Party in 1951. But he was much more than simply an anti-communist judge. He had been leader of the United Australia (later Liberal) Party in the thirties and he was a founding member of the Rationalist Society in Australia, only leaving it when he believed it to be infiltrated by communists. He provided a perfect antithesis to the Catholic, sectarian face of anti-communism. Men like Latham demonstrated

54

that anti-communism could be an intellectual position, not simply the hysterical response of the priests of Rome.

Latham's first act on being approached by Krygier was to contact R.G. Casey, the Minister for External Affairs, for assurance that he was not being seduced into a communist front organisation. Such was the nature of the times. But Latham also refused Krygier's suggestion that he vet prospective members through the government security services—clearly, his friendship with Casey meant that he could have done so.[7]

Once convinced of the organisation's good intent, Latham invited a range of public figures to join the Australian Committee. At its first meetings the Committee decided not to impose a membership fee and members were not even charged postage for their copies of *Free Spirit*. As entry was only by invitation and membership required no real commitment, it was probably difficult to refuse Sir John's offer.

Yet the Committee was hardly artistic or particularly intellectual. Those invited to join the first Australian Committee for Cultural Freedom were all important or powerful men rather than artists or writers. The first executive consisted of Sir John, Professor J.C. Eccles, a scientist from the ANU, Eugene Goossens, the composer and musician then at the Sydney Conservatorium of Music, D.A.S. Campbell, the publisher and businessman, J.J. Maloney, a Labor politician, and Justice T.M. Barry, a Brisbane judge. They could well have been the members of an exclusive dining club. Potential members were likely to be flattered by the prospect of joining such company. The Vice Chancellor of ANU, Sir Leslie Melville, for example, felt he should join simply because of the reputations of the executive members. Walter Murdoch felt obliged to accept despite his desire to collapse into old age.[8]

When the Committee announced its existence in 1954 Clem Christesen immediately published an article in *Meanjin* by Hugh Trevor-Roper suggesting that Cultural Freedom was backed by funds from the CIA. Sir John Latham also had been the Chancellor of the University of Melbourne and Christesen saw an opportunity to air his problems with the University. In July 1954 he wrote to Latham pointing out that there was only one subscriber to *Meanjin* on the Cultural Freedom membership list—Sir John himself. In Christesen's view any important cultural figure in Australia would subscribe to *Meanjin*—where were the writers in Cultural

Freedom? In November, he even provided Latham with a list of writers who might be considered. Vance Palmer, Frank Dalby Davison, Kenneth Slessor, Judith Wright, A.D. Hope and several others were listed.[9]

In the same year Stephen Spender, the editor of *Encounter*, the British Cultural Freedom journal, toured Australia. He was subjected, among other things, to a writers' lunch where David Martin read a poem denouncing Spender's treason to the left. Despite the attack Spender ended his tour by asking the Australian Committee the same question Christesen had asked: where are the writers? Ironically, the Committee used Christesen's list to select some new members, among them A.D. Hope and Wesley Milgate. James McAuley was approached through A.D. Hope.[10]

It should not be supposed that every prospective member leapt at the opportunity to join the Committee. Some had noted the propaganda elements of *Free Spirit*, others had heard of the US State department's interest, others suspected the Committee of religious affiliations. When the title *Crux* was suggested for the Committee's proposed magazine, Latham intervened immediately for fear of any religious association. If Cultural Freedom was to be intellectually non-communist, neither would it promote the anti-communist propaganda of the Catholic Church.

Australian Cultural Freedom did not spring out of writers' and artists' dissatisfaction with communist interpretations of art or their concern with the political influence of communists among them. It was an organisation created largely by the work of one devoted anti-communist, Richard Krygier, who was not a writer nor, at that stage, a friend of writers. The first membership consisted of a group of men powerful in their own right, many of them elderly, retired or nearing retirement. They were members of Australia's establishment: chancellors and vice-chancellors of universities, judges, publishers and professors rather than novelists, poets, painters, composers or young critics and journalists. In other words, Cultural Freedom was not a new voice, nor a new bid for power but a rearrangement of existing voices and powers.

The source of Cultural Freedom's prestige was the prestige of its individual members rather than vice versa. This was graphically demonstrated in 1956 when customs officials discovered 'indecent' photographs in Eugene Goossens' baggage when he returned to Australia from a trip. Goossens was the single cultural practitioner on Cultural Freedom's executive, while the Customs department at the time was notoriously part of the patronage of a Catholic network. Most customs officials were Catholics, so that the Goossens' humiliation might have been seen as a demonstration of the difference between Cultural Freedom's liberal views and the rigid morality of Australian Catholicism. The freedom of an artist to live his private and sexual life as he pleased might have been a principle which Cultural Freedom could fight for. Not so. Goossens was immediately asked to resign lest Cultural Freedom's own name be besmirched by the incident. It was a matter of what Goossens could offer Cultural Freedom, not what it might do for Goossens.[11]

What did Cultural Freedom do? As secretary, Krygier sent a vast correspondence to the Cultural Freedom general secretary, Michael Josselson, in Paris. Krygier's monthly reports to Josselson provided a detailed account of politics in Australia, complete with brief sketches of the political colour of each participant. Krygier stressed to Josselson that communists were many and powerful in the newspapers, universities and public service and that Cultural Freedom was recruiting in these specific areas.

Josselson was sceptical. The Central Congress for Cultural Freedom provided Krygier with money to cover mailing expenses and printing. It saw itself as a 'cultural' organisation, principally of writers, which aimed to counter the well-organised communist writers and artists. He was supporting Krygier's organisation financially without evidence that writers were committed to it or that communism endangered creative life in Australia.[12]

At first, it seemed that there was little which Cultural Freedom could do to promote intellectual freedom in Australia. In 1954 Neil Glover, an Anglican clergyman, asked Cultural Freedom to help him obtain a passport to attend the World Council of Peace in Stockholm. Most of the executive Committee members believed that the Government had been perfectly justified in denying a passport to attend an international meeting of a communist front organisation. But Sir John Latham insisted that they help Glover on principle. Then, overseas members of Cultural Freedom began to suggest cases which the Australians might pursue. In 1956, a member of the International Science and Freedom Committee, Professor Polanyi, took up the case of Professor Sydney Sparkes Orr and forced the Australian branch of Cultural Freedom to investigate.

The University of Tasmania had dismissed Professor Orr from his academic position on the grounds of alleged misconduct with a student. But Orr had been critical of the University administration and the manner of his dismissal suggested that the charges may have been concocted to remove a troublemaker from a position of influence. Polanyi thought this was a clear case of the suppression of academic freedom and so, at first, did some members of the Australian Cultural Freedom organisation. The lawyer Hal Wootten found a number of anomalies in the way the University had mounted its case against Orr but there were obvious difficulties in an organisation headed by a former chancellor of one Australian university criticising the administration of another Australian university.[13]

On the one hand, Orr was an intellectual suffering at the hands of a conservative, narrow-minded university administration. On the other, Cultural Freedom represented university administrators among its 'intellectuals'. The case threatened to split Cultural Freedom. John Kerr and Wootten went to Tasmania to interview the main participants in the affair and, on their advice, Cultural Freedom withdrew its support for Orr.

These incidents show some of the difficulties which Cultural Freedom was found to have as a result of its conservative, establishment membership. It is easy to miss the fact, though, that the Australian branch of Cultural Freedom was much more conservative, and much more anti-communist, than its counterparts in Europe and the USA. Michael Josselson, later to be 'exposed' as a CIA agent, constantly begged Krygier to tone down his propaganda. He insisted that the organisation was cultural not political, that ideas such as a campaign to persuade Eastern bloc athletes to defect at the Melbourne Olympics could not be part of its charter.

The International Congress for Cultural Freedom had a large proportion of members who had been communists in the thirties and had changed allegiance because of their discoveries about Stalinism after the war. They were much closer in interest and experience to the Australian communist writers who left the Party after 1956. If Australian communists had accepted the facts about Stalin ten years earlier an Australian Cultural Freedom body might never have existed—or if it did, it might have had Stephen Murray-Smith, Ian Turner and even David Martin as its leaders.[14]

These differences show that the notion that the CIA was using an innocent group of Australians for subversion and propaganda is an exaggeration. Humphrey McQueen has conjured up the spectre of US manipulation and John Docker refers to the 'murky depths' of the CIA as if Australians must be innocent of political plotting.[15] But all the subversion and propaganda initiatives came from Australia, while the CIA agent suggested less enthusiastic programs. Josselson footed the bills while lamenting his own lack of control over the Australian organisation. The CIA gave its funds on the premise that Australian Cultural Freedom represented a group of non-communist and anti-communist writers who needed help in promoting their work. In fact, Cultural Freedom did not represent such a group of writers or artists; instead, it used CIA money and the reputations of writers to give credibility to virulent anti-communist views.

Despite the clearly political nature of its origins Cultural Freedom did become a significant influence in Australian cultural life. From its first meetings Cultural Freedom aimed to produce a journal along the lines of the British *Encounter* magazine, to rival *Meanjin* which, until then, had the broad social, literary and cultural field to itself. Members gave full support to this idea; most were delighted at the prospect of a journal which would express an intellectualism free from *Meanjin's* nationalist pre-occupations. In early discussions with members, Menzies even indicated that he would be very pleased to withdraw *Meanjin's* CLF grant and bestow it on the new rival.[16] However, the timely appearance of *Overland* in 1954 kept Menzies from this act of generosity—he could favour a conservative journal over one radical journal but to do so at the expense of two radical journals would look like bias.

Cultural Freedom's journal gave it a new impetus at a time when Michael Josselson was threatening to cut its funds completely. And the choice of editor for the journal pulled the organisation in a direction which many had not foreseen. The organisation considered three proposals for the editorship: one from Roger Covell, then a journalist working in Brisbane, one from the poets and journalists Kenneth Slessor and John Thompson and one from James McAuley, poet and teacher of administration at the School of Pacific Administration.

The first two proposals were essentially liberal in their approach to cultural matters. Covell suggested fairly exclusive literary and cultural interests; Thompson and Slessor declared themselves to be political moderates who would not use the journal to score political points. McAuley prepared a long and detailed proposal, claiming that the journal's aim should be to give prestige to 'schools of thought' independent of, or opposed to communism. When members queried McAuley's lack of liberalism, he pointed out that the kind of liberalism represented by the Association was so diverse as to be feeble. McAuley did not represent the views of the majority of Cultural Freedom members but he was combative and sure in his beliefs. McAuley offered a strong, committed voice rather than the vague ideals of liberalism.[17]

McAuley became the editor of *Quadrant*, and the public face of Cultural Freedom became that of a vociferous anti-communist. The choice of editor is at first sight an anomaly. McAuley had worked with Krygier on *Free Spirit* and he was obviously Krygier's candidate for the editorship. Nevertheless, McAuley was that creature studiously avoided by Cultural Freedom in its early days, an anti-communist Catholic. Krygier had not offered membership to B.A. Santamaria or Standish Keon precisely to avoid association with Catholicism, and Cultural Freedom had even tried to hide Malcolm Muggeridge's meeting with Santamaria in 1955 lest it damage the organisation's liberal image. But in choosing McAuley, Cultural Freedom had set its sails in the direction of the DLP. Sir John Latham's willingness to preside over this cannot be fully explained by McAuley's impressive personality and standing as a poet.

The explanation lies presumably in McAuley's background. Unlike many cradle Catholics McAuley had had the benefit of a Fort Street Boys' High and University of Sydney education. His university friends included men such as A.D. Hope, Donald Horne and Alfred Conlon, who were known for their independent views, and he joined Conlon's military intelligence unit during the war years. After the war, he continued to work with Conlon and important Cultural Freedom members such as John Kerr. McAuley's Catholicism did not interfere with a general perception that he was a University of Sydney graduate who might even be called an Andersonian.

With the help of A.D. Hope, McAuley convinced Manning Clark, Joseph Burke, Leonie Kramer, Roger Covell, Wesley Milgate, Norman Jeffares, Alec King, J.C. Eccles and O. Rapoport to join them on *Quadrant*'s advisory board. Where McAuley might have been less than liberal, these advisers, in the main, were noted for the independence of their views. And the reputations of several—Leonie Kramer, Roger Covell and Manning Clark, for example—would grow considerably in the coming years. Joseph

Burke had initially refused membership of Cultural Freedom because, as the only professor of Fine Art in Australia, he did not wish to seem partisan; acting as a journal adviser was a different matter. Leonie Kramer, Wesley Milgate and Norman Jeffares taught English literature in various Australian universities and were friends of Hope. Manning Clark welcomed the arrival of a new journal which might free writers and critics from Clem Christesen's idiosyncrasies. And there can be little doubt that these advisers admired McAuley as a poet and had the vaguest understanding of his politics.

Furthermore, McAuley was careful to absolve his advisers from responsibility for the journal's policy. In the second issue he stated:

> the editor chooses his own path, his own comments, and does not commit those well-known and diversely-minded people who have consented to be editorial advisers. Just as they are not interested in binding or limiting the editor in his task, so they are not to be regarded as responsible for the pattern that *Quadrant* assumes as a result of the editor's temperament and the independent activity of contributors.[18]

Here was an editor as forceful and independent as Clem Christesen of *Meanjin*.

McAuley's first editorial, though, states his own answer to literary nationalism in a document ringing with Cold War rhetoric. McAuley stated the journal's aims:

> To be Australian in our orientation, quite naturally, because we are interested in this country, its people, its problems, its cultural life, its liberties, and its safety;
> To publish work of interest and merit on any topic without regard to the affiliations or repute of the author, the sole requirement being that the material should be worth reading;
> To be guided, when an editorial attitude is called for with regard to questions of civil liberty or public standards, by the principles underlying the parliamentary institutions of this country and the Common Law—than which we know no better school of freedom and civility and prudence, in the old sense of those words; for to be a good Australian is to be a local variety of that 'free and lawful man', the traditional ideal of Western civilization.
> Our aims and hopes may perhaps be further illuminated by making clear some of the things we do *not* intend to do or be:

We shall never, we hope, confuse the Australian regionalism and proper pride with the ugly nineteenth-century vice of cultural nationalism, which imposes 'Australianity' as an anti-intellectual criterion, limiting the scope of the mind and serving only as a means of giving a false value to mediocrity. We shall try to be up-to-date, lively, and receptive, without the superficial cultivation of mere *chic*, intellectual or aesthetic; and without feeling obliged to grovel before a decayed *avant-garde* mentality which is actually living in the past. We shall try to be liberal and progressive, without falling into the delusion that to be liberal and progressive means to rehearse with childish obstinacy the rituals of a sentimental and neurotic leftism. We shall remain suspicious of the idea that the totalitarian Beast from the Abyss is really a big woolly bear which the little men who have had a busy day in this country can safely cuddle as they sink into the dreamland of Peaceful Co-existence. [19]

Here were the fundamentals of McAuley's literary and political position. He was nationalist only in the sense that he was naturally an Australian and to be Australian was to be a member of Western civilisation. Nationalism to McAuley had come to mean anti-intellectualism: his journal would be unashamedly intellectual. At the same time, he shared the left nationalists' scorn for modernism as being empty and superficial. The editorial was as much concerned with the things *Quadrant* would not be as what it would be. McAuley confronted *Meanjin* and *Overland* from the beginning.

Quadrant's first issue offered George Molnar on street architecture and A.D. Hope on the long poem alongside Denis Warner on 'The Communist Conspiracy in Asia'. The mix of the editor's views, at least one strong anti-communist or anti-radical nationalist piece with good short stories and poems and seemingly independent critical articles, was apparent. McAuley refused to publish experimental poetry, perhaps in fear of a reprisal for the Ern Malley hoax, but he could support his anti-modernism by reference to Hope and the rise of traditionalism among poets in the USA and Britain.

To the casual observer *Quadrant* may have looked like the spontaneous work of a group of right-wing Australian intellectuals. But James McAuley did not have a close group of literary supporters; his anti-liberalism prevented even conservative writers from fully endorsing his opinions. Many admired his poetry, however, and some found McAuley an attractive personality although they did not share his passions.

Cultural Freedom and Quadrant

Many writers responded to the new opportunity for publication offered by *Quadrant* and in the first few years some important poetry and criticism appeared in the journal. A.R. Chisholm wrote on Brennan in the third issue, Robin Boyd produced 'Austerica' for the sixth issue and Vincent Buckley's 'Utopianism and Vitalism in Australian Literature' appeared in the tenth issue. Poetry by Judith Wright, Evan Jones, Douglas Stewart, Rosemary Dobson and others appeared on *Quadrant's* pages. These contributors were not virulent anti-communists or DLP stooges; they simply responded to a new outlet for their work, and, perhaps, were pleased not to have it wrapped in nationalist clothing. One example of the differences between McAuley and his contributors and advisers came in 1960 when McAuley reviewed Manning Clark's account of his visit to the Soviet Union, *Meeting Soviet Man*. McAuley urged Clark to abandon left-liberalist cliché and allow himself to perceive religious truth—a path which McAuley himself had followed.[20]

Quadrant's appearance at the end of 1956 meant that it was well positioned to receive the intellectual defectors from the Communist Party after the Soviet invasion of Hungary. Stephen Murray-Smith clung to *Overland* and moved it out of the Party with him, but Cultural Freedom made friendly overtures to Murray-Smith and his supporters. By 1960 writing by David Martin and other defectors from the Party was beginning to appear in *Quadrant*. In the sixties *Quadrant* was able to draw on a much wider range of contributors than might have been foreseen in the mid-fifties.

Just as Cultural Freedom became prestigious by winning prestigious members, *Quadrant's* reputation grew because of the reputations of its contributors. The same, of course, might be said of any journal struggling to establish itself. Innocuous or apolitical articles, poems and stories appeared alongside editorials which expressed extreme views or discussions of the evils of communism. Sometimes, however, the contributors supported the editorial view more than they may have realised. Douglas Stewart's poem 'Rutherford' might be read as strongly supporting atomic research in a journal which had published Ernest Titterton's plea for the West to keep ahead of the Soviet Union. Certainly, A.D. Hope's poetic questioning of the academic's relationship to art and life, 'Meditation on a Bone', sits oddly beside McAuley's attack on philosophical agnosticism and academic freedom in the third issue.

There were anti-communists in Cultural Freedom from its inception, but the majority of its membership in the late fifties and sixties could be described more accurately as conservative liberals. Manning Clark, Donald Horne, Henry Mayer, John Gorton or Tom Inglis Moore could hardly be accused of right-wing extremism. Nor would they be likely to agree with the editor of *Quadrant* when he praised the British monarchy for upholding family values or attacked Bertrand Russell for his irreligion. Yet so unrepresentative a member as McAuley was allowed to become the public voice of Cultural Freedom. Similarly, Richard Krygier dominated the daily business of the Association. In Cultural Freedom's history the voices of men such as McAuley or Krygier have often been heard loudest. Perhaps this was due to the very weakness of liberalism which McAuley deplored: its tolerance of a range of views.

But McAuley's voice became more muted as Cultural Freedom moved into the sixties. In 1964, after McAuley moved to Tasmania, Donald Horne became co-editor of *Quadrant*, leaving McAuley responsible only for the poetry contributions. This change meant that *Quadrant* moved closer to the kind of liberal intellectual journal which many members (and its CIA sponsors) had wanted in the first place.

Some idea of the attitudes of other Cultural Freedom members can be found in Peter Coleman's collection of essays, *Australian Civilization*, published in 1962. At least half the contributors to the collection were, like Coleman, Cultural Freedom members. Yet here they were prepared to rail at the narrow-mindedness and prurience of Australian society. Douglas McCallum attacked the limited definition of freedom in Australia, even using the Orr case as an example of the timidity of Australian academics when confronted with an attack on their independence. McCallum and others saw Australian life as puritanical and dull, with restrictive drinking, entertainment and censorship laws. Vincent Buckley attacked Australian academics for their failures as intellectuals. Clark contributed his famous essay on 'Faith' which argued that the two faiths at war in Australia were not Protestantism and Catholicism but a democratic secularism and an elitist libertarianism.[21]

Coleman's introduction made it clear that he viewed Australian culture rather differently from the opposition, *Meanjin* and *Overland*. Coleman, obviously, was not one of those who had read

Australian literature of the nineteenth century, as he was prepared to accept that it was neither rich nor serious. Coleman saw the principal heritage of the Australian legend as naive humanism, the ideal of 'innocent happiness' supplemented by a nihilism. It was an idea of nationalism already suggested by Vincent Buckley's essay, 'Utopianism and Vitalism in Australian literature', and reiterated in Manning Clark's contribution to the book. Coleman concluded that these elements of 'Australianism' led to contempt for high achievement and beauty, and so were essentially anti-civilisation.

This was a more reasoned statement of Cultural Freedom's rejection of nationalism than the obvious anti-communist stand. It placed the interests of the intellectual and the artist together, and argued that democratic humanist ideals undermined the ability of the intellectual and artist to pursue excellence. Furthermore, it was only this pursuit of excellence by intellectuals and artists which would establish civilisation in Australia.

This kind of logic exacerbated the dilemma of democratic nationalists like Stephen Murray-Smith. By the end of the fifties, they also came to believe that the Australian working people were anti-intellectual. Even the writer devoted to the cause of democracy found himself ignored by the people whose interests he served. But for these writers and intellectuals to accept an unalterable schism between the intellectual and the people was to negate the purpose of literary culture. What was the point of civilisation if it existed only for the elite?

In 1962 *Overland* published its own discussion of the state of Australian art, called 'The Legend and the Loneliness' with Albert Tucker (the painter), Tim Burstall (the film-maker), Phillip Adams, David Martin and Stephen Murray-Smith taking part. All of the participants were ready to bury left nationalism and socialist realism as having served their purpose. They saw Patrick White, Randolph Stow, Albert Tucker and Sidney Nolan as offering a new and important direction for Australian art. But they were bemused by the way in which real Australian life—the actualities of suburbia—remained beyond the interests of these artists. White's *Voss* and *The Tree of Man* took up the old national figures, the explorer and the settler. The realist city novel was as distant as ever. Martin still hoped for a realist novel which was broad enough to encompass the interests of a writer such as White and which could express the full nature of modern Australian life. Burstall dismissed this as too utilitarian a view of art: the real task was the education of the philistine Australian public.[22]

Despite the left intellectuals' lingering ideal of an art which was humane and concerned about ordinary people, they shared a growing range of attitudes with the *Quadrant* intellectuals. Given the fact that *Quadrant* had been set up to combat the influence of the left through *Meanjin* and *Overland* it was understandable that loyal communists might see this as 'throwing bouquets to the enemy'.

In the mid-sixties *Quadrant*'s origins as an anti-communist voice might have been forgotten as men such as Peter Coleman and Donald Horne became more prominent in the Association. In 1962 Sir John Latham retired and an election for president revealed that Cultural Freedom was far from a unified or monolithic group. Lloyd Ross won the election over John Kerr and a number of members left because they believed Cultural Freedom would become less liberal.

However, the pattern of liberal attitudes shared between some Cultural Freedom members and some members of the old left continued through the sixties. *Overland* and *Meanjin* had argued strenuously against censorship in the late fifties and censorship was an issue taken up by Cultural Freedom liberals in the sixties. The legal difficulties of Australian Aborigines was another area of shared concern. It was not until Australia became involved in the Vietnam war that Cultural Freedom once again fell under the shadow of extreme anti-communism. Where in 1962, McCallum could attack the Returned Services League (RSL) as one of the forces of puritanism in Australia, by 1966 Cultural Freedom identified itself with the Liberal government of Australia and *Quadrant* did its best to provide intellectual justification for the government's military decision.

By supporting involvement in Vietnam *Quadrant* cut itself off from many of the younger generation of intellectuals beginning to emerge from the universities. It should not be supposed that all members of this younger generation disagreed with Australia's participation in Vietnam; Catholics were one group in Australia who still considered communism to be the greatest threat to religious freedom and many were prepared to support a war against communism in Asia. Other Australians, even of the postwar generation, accepted the 'domino' theories of communist expansion.

However, the anti-Vietnam movement attracted a broad range of younger intellectuals who might otherwise have found much in common with Cultural Freedom members. Cultural Freedom made itself an opposition to a new kind of radicalism and *Quadrant*, once again, became the voice of reaction.

More damaging than this was the revelation at the International Congress in 1967 that Cultural Freedom, and *Quadrant* in particular, had received funds from the CIA. I have argued that the CIA did not manipulate James McAuley or Richard Krygier for anti-communist ends. McAuley was quite right when he claimed never to have been bribed or pressured by the CIA; his enthusiasm for anti-communism made this unnecessary. However, the implications of US government interference in the culture and politics of another nation were much more serious. It was perhaps a sign of McAuley's naivety and political blindness that he could not see that without CIA money his journal would not have come into existence. McAuley's extremism might never have been heard without US funds. Certainly, it might never have become so respectable. The revelations showed that *Quadrant* and Cultural Freedom were an artificial development in Australia. One can only speculate whether a magazine like *Quadrant* would have come into existence without the Cultural Freedom organisation and the US government funds. By 1960, there were other outlets for most of the *Quadrant* contributors: Donald Horne and Peter Coleman exchanged places as editors of *Quadrant* and the revamped *Bulletin* in the early sixties and surely would have published some *Quadrant* discussion in the *Bulletin*. As well, several universities had begun to publish cultural and literary journals in the early sixties; *Quadrant*'s academic contributions could have found more specialised publishers.

Cultural Freedom did not represent a literary ideology for writers; in practice it hardly represented writers at all. The organisation was able to claim a cultural role because Australian writers who were not communists or enthusiastic nationalists found an outlet for publication in its journal, *Quadrant*. In this way, the writers helped to dress a right-wing organisation in the respectable clothes of a literary and artistic support group. Cultural Freedom and the right did not offer any positive alternatives to the socialist realist theories or radical nationalism. Where the Communist Party of Australia had offered both a political and a literary approach to contemporary Australian life, Cultural Freedom was interested only in political power and was quite prepared to exploit writers to maintain the appearance of a liberal and independent position.

Essentially, *Quadrant* under James McAuley's editorship promoted poetry rather than fiction as literary art. This accorded with McAuley's view that poetry was the highest form of literature. Furthermore, the journal published a particular kind of poetry which conformed to traditional form, diction and subject. Poets such as Evan Jones, Rosemary Dobson, Gwen Harwood and Vincent Buckley, with McAuley and A.D. Hope, were the most frequent contributors in the first years of the journal. Their poetry did not express obvious conservative political ideas or commitments, but it did confirm McAuley's view that poetry should be 'above politics'.

By the mid-sixties the occasional fiction pieces in *Quadrant*—most often realist stories by writers such as Brian James, E.O. Schlunke or Hugh Atkinson—had been subsumed under the headings 'narrative' or 'fiction and memoirs'. The journal began to commission autobiographical pieces from both fiction and its general contributors. *Quadrant* favoured experience over imagination and encouraged the genre of autobiography, a genre pursued by its new joint editor, Donald Horne.

Quadrant's prose stressed the authority of experience just as its poetry stressed the authority of tradition. It was an emphasis which aligned itself with the political ideas the journal promoted. McAuley saw his political ideas as a defence of poetry; by defeating the ideologies of the left he was preserving poetry's freedom from politics.

Many of the poets and prose writers who contributed to *Quadrant* in the late fifties and early sixties did not share McAuley's commitments and it is mistaken to group them together as a *Quadrant*, anti-communist group. Most of these writers considered themselves to be independent of the editor's opinions and this independence, of course, was cited as evidence of the literary freedom promoted by the journal. However, the poets in particular wrote within the traditions of Western civilisation; they chose forms, diction and subjects which conformed to expectations of 'good' poetry. It was decorous poetry which bore all the traditional marks of high art.

These writers may have shared McAuley's commitment to the values of Western civilisation but few of them endorsed his beliefs about the political means of defending these values. Many of the poets were not committed to political positions and some, like A.D. Hope, prided themselves on their freedom from ideological commitment. McAuley, as editor of *Quadrant*, marshalled these uncommitted writers under the banner of his own political beliefs.

Australian writers in the fifties and early sixties cannot be categorised into simple ideological positions of left and right, nationalist and anti-nationalist, anti-modernist and modernist. As changes occurred in Australian life writers expressed changing ideological positions. These complex responses need to be closely considered in the case of individual writers.

Because James McAuley was the single important writer with strong anti-communist views and, through *Quadrant*, exerted a degree of literary influence, he is an obvious place to begin such a consideration.

3

James McAuley's Quest

If *Quadrant* and Cultural Freedom became a genuine cultural force in Australian life, it was due to the efforts of one man: *Quadrant*'s editor, James McAuley. In 1954, when Cultural Freedom was set up, McAuley's reputation as a poet was by no means secure. He had published only one book of poems, *Under Aldebaran* (1946), and was notorious as part of Ern Malley's alter ego. His contemporaries at the University of Sydney knew him as one of many campus personalities. However, in the Australian literary community at large he was a relative newcomer.

James McAuley had missed the chance to become a literary academic; his Master of Arts thesis had not given him the University of Sydney position he expected. *Quadrant* gave him the opportunity to become an important voice in the literary world from outside the universities. In this way, McAuley made *Quadrant*'s reputation and *Quadrant* established his.[1]

McAuley's background was not socially privileged like that of Patrick White or John Manifold. His father had been a stock inspector in northern New South Wales but had settled in Sydney to build houses and live off their rents. James lived as a child in the western suburbs of Lakemba and Homebush. But he followed the path which led many clever western suburbs boys to education and prominence: he attended Fort Street Boys' High and won a scholarship to the University of Sydney.

As poet and critic, James McAuley was always committed to art which promoted the welfare of society. Though his poetic career presents many paradoxes and apparent changes of direction, he remained interested in the poet's responsibility to his own culture. It is this interest which often leads him surprisingly close to the ideas of his avowed enemies, the communists.

As a student in the late thirties McAuley became interested in the French symbolists and in the poetry of their Australian counterpart, Christopher Brennan. He admired their poetry but was dissatisfied with their interpretation of the role of the poet in society. When McAuley extended his researches into the beginnings of the Romantic movement he believed that he had found the source of the difficulty. The poets he admired—Blake, Novalis, Rilke, Hölderlin, Brennan and Yeats—formed a movement away from society into the realms of 'pure' poetry and, often suspect, metaphysics.

In McAuley's view, the political and social changes to European society at the end of the eighteenth century had isolated the poets.[2] McAuley believed that rather than taking their place in society as part of an integrated social, religious and political system, poets increasingly had been forced to find a role outside the limits of their society. He concluded that as the nineteenth century progressed important poets began to seek a 'pure poetry' which had little reference to the social order. They had eventually attempted to use poetry as a means of exploring the metaphysical world and of conquering the Absolute. As the importance of Christian religion declined, poets had attempted to substitute their own metaphysical experiments for the spiritual knowledge which once was the prerogative of the Church. McAuley admired their achievements but came to the conclusion that the use of poetry as a substitute for religion was futile. Poetry was a human art and poets could not aspire to divinity.

Such a summary of McAuley's intellectual discoveries hides many complexities. McAuley's admiration of the romantic-symbolist poets obviously influenced his own writing. He was a romantic poet in the tradition of romantic poets and, at the same time, distrustful of the romantic concern with the self. He believed in a spiritual world but feared the consequences of an individual search for spiritual knowledge. McAuley cared about his society and wished to have a creative role within it. But the poets he admired seemed intent on cutting themselves away from their society. The problem which McAuley identified quite early in his career was

71

how to lead the poetic tradition back into the human and social world.

To many observers the rise of Hitler demonstrated graphically the evils which followed a deformed romanticism. For Hitler called the German romantic tradition to the defence of anti-Semitism, murder and inhumanity of the most savage kind. McAuley graduated to a world at war and believed his concerns about poetry were entangled in the philosophies of the warring parties. Just as in the First World War Brennan renounced the Germans whose tradition he had absorbed, McAuley confronted the tragic and distorted end of the poetic philosophies he admired.

Several critics have commented on the apparently contradictory changes in James McAuley's allegiances over the years.[3] They identify a radical and even fellow-travelling McAuley at the University of Sydney, a conservative Catholic McAuley during the fifties and a mellowed and tolerant McAuley in the late sixties and seventies. But his changing political, cultural and religious commitments were part of a single-minded search for an appropriate role for the postwar poet, a role for McAuley himself.

Looking back on his life McAuley liked to emphasise the radical nature of his student days. In the fifties he claimed to have danced to the tunes of 'ideological pipers' in his youth.[4] Donald Horne remembers him writing songs for a revue put on by the communist New Theatre League called 'I'd Rather be Left'. This, of course, hardly amounts to a communist commitment.[5] At the same time that he played the piano for the communists he was playing the organ and training the choir at his local Anglican parish church.[6]

The influence of John Anderson, Professor of Philosophy at the University of Sydney may have been more important, though the extent to which McAuley can be called an Andersonian is debatable, especially since Anderson's supporters split into two groups in the fifties. McAuley attended Anderson's exciting philosophy lectures and clearly accepted Anderson's challenge to the intellectual—to criticise every theory and convention in order to find truth. When McAuley later described himself as 'inclining to the radical and libertarian side' he was no doubt referring to his early contact with the Andersonians.[7] He thought of himself as a man of independent mind who was ready to challenge conventional wisdom. As a young man, he had certainly taken an anti-clerical stance in a piece called 'Work in Protex' for *Hermes*, he had contributed with Harry Hooton, A. D. Hope and Oliver Somerville

to the *First Boke of Fowle Ayres* and he had listened to Harry
Hooton's peculiar version of anarchism.[8]

But if McAuley was a radical at this time it was not a radicalism
of the political left. It was rather the iconoclastic activism of a
questing intelligence. Peter Coleman tells us that McAuley gave
up his teaching job at Shore in 1940 because he could not follow
the school's tradition of unquestioning patriotism—he did not
wish to enlist.[9] This may be taken as further evidence of a radical
frame of mind but it should not be forgotten that in Australia there
was little enthusiasm for enlistment in the early years of the
Second World War. It was not until Japan entered the war that
many Australians felt they should offer themselves for service. For
McAuley's generation the First World War and the depression
had robbed war of its glamour.[10]

McAuley was one of many who accepted the inevitable after
Japan's entry to the war and he did not object to his own con-
scription in 1943. Furthermore, Alfred Conlon commandeered
McAuley for his Army Directorate of Research and Civil Affairs.
This vague title covered a group of men who reported directly to
the commander-in-chief of the armed forces, General Blamey. As
the war was being won, Blamey had increasing problems with
various civil authorities, especially with the Department of External
Territories over the administration of occupied New Guinea. The
Directorate advised Blamey on dealing with these authorities and
became a powerful liaison between the army and the civil powers,
including foreign governments.[11]

It is difficult to underestimate the effect of this wartime experience on McAuley. Without even taking part in any fighting he
learnt about army politics at the highest level, he discovered New
Guinea and the Pacific and he emerged as an expert in the
administration of Pacific territories. Before the war McAuley was a
disappointed literary academic who had fallen back on school-
teaching to sustain his writing; after the war he became a teacher
of Pacific administration at the school set up to train Australian
patrol and administrative officers for Papua and New Guinea. He
remained a poet but he now had contacts and interests in the
political world. No one has given much attention to James McAuley's
professional attitudes to Papua and New Guinea but it is clear
from both his poetry and his prose that his concern for the native
people was genuine.

McAuley's first book of poems, *Under Aldebaran*, was not published until two years after the perpetration of Ern Malley's poems. This hoax is now well known, kept alive by the argument of Max Harris and others that the poems remain genuine works of art. In 1944 McAuley and Harold Stewart, another member of the Army Directorate, invented a dead motor mechanic whose sister had found several poems when clearing out his room. Ethel Malley sent Ern's poems to Max Harris, the editor of the journal *Angry Penguins* and Harris greeted them as the work of a genius.

The poems were published complete with a critique by Harris and, worse, they led to Harris' trial on charges of indecency. I do not wish to give a detailed discussion of Ern Malley's poems here, nor enter the debate about their literary value. However, the hoax reveals several important features of McAuley's literary personality as well as the nature of Australian society at the time. McAuley and Stewart believed that the poetry which Max Harris and his Adelaide friends published in *Angry Penguins* was modernist nonsense. McAuley objected to the intuitive nature of modernist poetry; he saw it as irrational, non-intellectual and limited to the poet's own consciousness rather than related to society. It was an extension of the romantic excesses to which McAuley objected even in the great poetry of Yeats or Verlaine.

McAuley was good at writing modernist poetry. He had studied T.S. Eliot and adopted several modernist techniques in his own work. Ern Malley's poems, with all their nonsense, were clever poems and not simply random phrases or prose. The 'Sonnets for the Novachord', for example, followed a strict, if not classical, sonnet rhyme scheme. Many of the images, phrases and the arcane vocabulary of Ern's work can be found in McAuley's own verse; the 'black swan of trespass' of 'Durer: Innsbruck, 1495', for example, is a close relative of the black swans of 'Mating Swans' and 'Tune for Swans' in *A Vision of Ceremony*.

The Ern Malley hoax revealed the way in which McAuley's conservatism emerged in the larrikinism often seen as essentially radical. It also showed that the society beyond the literary circles of McAuley, Stewart and Harris was confined and intolerant: Ern Malley's poems were nonsense and mostly unintelligible but they could still offend standards of public decency.

After the public demolition of Max Harris and his modernist offerings McAuley presented his own poems for comparison. *Under Aldebaran* contained several poems which revealed the enthusiasms of McAuley's youth. 'When Shall the Fair' had overtones of Eliot, 'Gnostic Prelude' paid its respects to Blake, 'The Incarnation of Sirius' recalled Yeats' 'Second Coming'. Rilke was honoured in 'Autumn', Brennan in 'Revenant'. And there were other formal debts—a traditional dialogue between mother and son, the sharp satire of 'Jindyworobaksheesh' or the Augustan games of 'The True Discovery of Australia'. Yet McAuley put each of his borrowings to an original poetic use. His voice was his own—though in some poems such as 'When Shall the Fair' its tones resembled Ern Malley's tentative gropings.[12]

The most impressive aspect of *Under Aldebaran* was McAuley's ability to relate his romantic concerns to the world of the forties and the realities of Australian life. 'Envoi' remains a disturbing conjunction of the landscape of Australia and a desolate state of mind: 'And I am fitted to that landscape as the soul is to the body'. It was an idea which Patrick White made central to *Voss* ten years later. It could be found in 'Terra Australis', too, where the physical features of Australia became part of a surreal dream, or in 'Landscape of Lust' where the mythical pleasureland was clearly the un-European landscape of Australia:

And the writhing limbs of trees
Are like our smiling energies.

The very barrenness and waywardness of Australian natural life matched the subject far better than European Cythereas had ever done.

McAuley wrote of isolation, despair, the emptiness of modern existence quite as much as any modernist. But the despair was not simply personal: the chimney stacks and 'sacred turbines' of 'The Blue Horses' turned a whole nation away from beauty and love 'to furnish the supplies of war'. It was a vision both horrific and, at the same time, related to contemporary realities.

McAuley in *Under Aldebaran* was unashamedly a romantic but a romantic deeply concerned about his own society. The satirical pieces were shrewd and clever; 'The True Discovery of Australia' turned one of McAuley's favourite themes to fun. In later years, McAuley's concern about the world grew dominant and he began to set himself impossible poetic tasks. But *Under Aldebaran* stated his interest in both the romantic quest for mysterious knowledge and the more material concern for the social world. His search was for a reconciliation of the two.

During the war McAuley met the Catholic bishop Alain de

Boismenu in New Guinea and came to admire him. He learnt of
the life of the New Guinean missionary, the saintly Marie-Therese
Noblet, and heard some accounts of her ability to work miracles.
This evidence of Catholicism in action, helping the people close to
his own heart, supported McAuley's intellectual attraction to the
faith and he was baptised a Catholic in 1952. McAuley's father
had been a Catholic and some of his friends saw it as a return
rather than a conversion. Whatever the personal circumstances of
McAuley's conversion, his new faith appeared to provide him with
some solutions to his poetic predicament. Catholicism asserted the
existence of a spiritual world while providing an intellectual and
social order. As a Catholic poet, McAuley could celebrate and
explore the spiritual world without adopting an irrational and
subjective position. Catholicism offered both a sense of the spiritual
and a justification of it.

McAuley's letters and comments on Catholicism show that he
was interested in cases of metaphysical intervention in the material
world. The Catholic Church's secure knowledge of the ordering of
the spiritual universe and the accounts of miracles and saints
fascinated him. He was an intellectual man who demanded rational
attitudes to the social order but, at the same time, had a romantic
interest in the intervention of higher forces.

McAuley's considerations and conclusions after his conversion
to Catholicism are displayed in his collection of essays, *The End of
Modernity: Essays on Literature, Art and Culture* (1959). The title
of the collection refers to Daniel Bell's *The End of Ideology* (1952)
which argues that the postwar period had brought an end to the
ideological commitments of American intellectuals which had
marked the twentieth century.[13] McAuley's book was also about
the failure of ideology but he was more interested in the modern
literary developments associated with ideological causes. McAuley
took as his starting point for several essays the work of another
American, Lionel Trilling, who (like Bell) was a member of Cultural
Freedom in the fifties. Trilling's *The Liberal Imagination* (1951)
noted that the praiseworthy tenets of liberalism had not produced
the great literature of contemporary times. Trilling believed that
this literary failure reflected poorly on liberal ideology; he concluded that there was 'no connection between the political ideas of
our educated class and the deep places of the imagination'.[14]

McAuley took this further. He identified an 'anti-metaphysical
and un-religious modern mentality' which appeared either in the

76

liberal mood, noted by Trilling, or in a totalitarian mood. McAuley argued that the writer who cut himself off from the absolute committed artistic suicide; poetry, in particular, relied on perennial metaphysical and religious principles. In McAuley's view the poet who committed himself to materialist ideology gave up his ability to understand the metaphysical which was part of the poetic function.[15]

At the same time McAuley rejected the role of poet as secular prophet, which he regarded as a feature of modernism. In his 'The Magian Heresy' (1957) he traced the modern poet's flight from the 'completely secularized and anti-metaphysical gnosis of the Enlightenment' to a 'new poetic' gnosis 'fed. . . by the underground streams of European occultism, cabbalism and theosophy'. In McAuley's view this development culminated in Surrealism with the reduction of metaphysical understanding to 'purely inward and senseless subjectivity'.[16]

Under Aldebaran, of course, had surreal elements, but these could not be called part of a 'purely inward' subjectivity. McAuley himself had demonstrated that this was not necessary. But he spent the fifties rule-making. He wanted a metaphysical or spiritual role for poetry which also satisfied the demands of intellect and order. He believed that his own religious faith had offered him these essential poetic bases.

McAuley followed many other Western liberal intellectuals in becoming anti-communist after the war. Trilling, Spender and Bell are but a few of a large number of intellectuals who believed in the fifties that Stalinist totalitarianism threatened world peace and individual freedom. But, as *The End of Modernity* attests, McAuley did not see communism simply as a threat to humanism but as an assault on the spiritual understanding which was the source of poetry. As a poet and as a Catholic who believed in a Divine order McAuley saw totalitarianism as a formidable pagan force which would destroy art, the spiritual connections which gave life meaning and the moral values which made civilisation possible.

In taking this extreme position McAuley showed a habit of mind which preferred large general issues to the particular. Strictly speaking, totalitarianism could not destroy poetry nor even spiritual understanding so long as individual poets continued to have this understanding. McAuley had determined his own individual opinion on the role of poet but then generalised so that he began to demand that all poets should adopt his own approach. In this way, large 'isms' came to dominate McAuley's critical writing rather than discussion of individual poets and their different assessments of contemporary times. 'Modernist subjectivism' became, in his eyes, an external force acting on poets like a disease rather than a quality emerging from highly individual poetic efforts.

A similar habit of thought is evident in McAuley's attitude to communism; in his eyes, it was not a political system supported by various groups of people but an external thing, a Dragon, a 'Beast from the Abyss'. Once communism was seen in these terms the wars against it could become crusades, romantic battles against a monstrous evil. When *The End of Modernity* appeared in 1959 it was attacked on several sides and the new literary journal (produced by Max Harris' friend Geoffrey Dutton) *Australian Letters*, devoted a whole issue to attacking its sweeping condemnations. [17]

Because of this book of essays and because of McAuley's identification with the forces of reaction in the fifties, sixties and seventies the importance of his early perceptions has been largely ignored. McAuley knew that if poets continued to turn inward and away from the social world they would lose any place in their own societies. He also recognised that the romantic tradition, the strength of modern poetry, tended increasingly towards inwardness.

At this stage of his life McAuley rejected the possibility that the most personal might be the most universal. Like the socialist realist poets he believed that the poet should take a public role and struggle to regain a place among the people. At the same time, he clung to the primacy of a spiritual order rather than the material one of the socialist realists. He saw the failure of the contemporary poet to reach an audience as a result of the 'inwardness' of modern romanticism.

Though McAuley's diagnosis of the postwar poet's dilemma might be endorsed by a number of his contemporaries and by many younger poets and readers, his dogmatic exposition of the solution was less acceptable. When Irving Kristol, the former editor of Cultural Freedom's British *Encounter* magazine, read *The End of Modernity* he was astonished at McAuley's notion of the poet's role. Kristol thought that surely this was the opinion of an administrator, or, at least, a teacher of administration. [18] And McAuley's profession in the fifties must have influenced his poetic path quite as much as his dogmatic approach to his new religion.

In 'The Blue Horses' McAuley had declared himself with Blake in seeing industrial society as a monster devouring humanity: 'For some shall work and some possess'. Ten years later he could be found defending United States militarism and the prosperity government of Menzies. The monster of war and industrialism in the early poem had changed and become a simpler creature in the process. Communism was now the enemy of a modern crusade. McAuley's romanticism allowed him to see the United States as a Defender of the Faith.

In 1955, McAuley met with B.A. Santamaria to discuss the political crisis in the Australian Labor Party. As a result of these discussions McAuley committed himself to Santamaria's Catholic Action program and he became a member of the Democratic Labor Party when it was formed in 1957. Although McAuley never took public office he organised the Party's first meetings in Sydney, wrote speeches for Jack Kane, its leader, and championed it in public from time to time. He was even prepared to argue publicly with the Archbishop of Sydney, Cardinal Gilroy, who refused to support the new Party. The spiritual rewards of Catholicism seemed to pale beside the call for political action in the material world.[19]

It is difficult for those who did not know McAuley to understand how he became so influential. McAuley's temperament provides some of the explanation of his ability to win affection from other Australian intellectuals such as Leonie Kramer, A.D. Hope or Gwen Harwood. McAuley loved controversy and rose to its demands, and his conservatism remained radical in its expression. Several of McAuley's editorials for *Quadrant* have an element of self-mockery, a recognition of McAuley's own enjoyment of the extremes of argument. Thus, he repeats his opponent' description of himself as 'a reactionary clerical-fascist hyena' or calls totalitarianism the 'Beast from the Abyss' mistaken for a 'Woolly Bear'. In his obituary for McAuley, Donald Horne commented on McAuley's pleasure in setting up exaggerated positions; he recalled that McAuley always believed what he said he believed though he sometimes expressed these beliefs in extreme or aggressive ways. Peter Hastings, who worked with McAuley at the School of Pacific Administration, has recalled that McAuley was 'intemperate' in his convictions and that his political views were inspired by 'a blind and zealous innocence'. He claimed that McAuley had a 'knack for absurd political romanticisation. Did men and women really act in the way he claimed, say the things he believed they said? This was his Catholic romanticism'.[20]

McAuley's outlook was idiosyncratic but he was far from alone in deriding modernist poetry. In Australia, writers as diverse as Douglas Stewart, R.D. FitzGerald and Frank Hardy also saw modernism as an abomination. In the fifties Australian literary figures rejected obscure, self-indulgent or disorganised poetry almost universally. But McAuley's solution to the dilemmas of the modern writer was not so acceptable. By the mid-fifties, he believed that the hope for society and its literature was a return to tradition, admittedly a more flexible tradition than that before the nineteenth century. The essential element in this tradition was the belief in a metaphysical world, in the importance of a spiritual order within which activities of all kinds could be pursued. In McAuley's view this must be a Christian spiritual order, for the gnostic undercurrent in the West denied the value of the human individual. But McAuley's solution gave little help to the unbeliever; faith could not be acquired at will in order to assist the writing of poetry. In his introduction to *The End of Modernity*, McAuley admitted the futility of this: 'it would be grotesque and ridiculous—also *impossible*—to adhere to religious doctrine simply as an antidote to the inanities and vulgarities of modern secularist humanism'.[21]

Thus, McAuley's solution in the fifties to the problem of the modern writer's need for spiritual understanding was a solution for himself alone. When John Thompson interviewed McAuley in 1965 he answered a question on the poet's need for Catholicism as the basis for his art as follows:

> Without a certain concern—a metaphysical sense—a sense of the ultimate issue—the mystery of being—I don't think poetry can have depth and resonance. I think it dies—becomes trivial—unless there is this. Now, normally a religious background in one's consciousness may be the guarantee of this, but I wouldn't want to be more dogmatic, in respect of poetry, than that, I think.[22]

He maintained that important poetry required a 'metaphysical sense', though at this stage of his career McAuley was wary of prescribing beliefs for other poets. *The End of Modernity* had offered a more definite order of things: liturgical poetry and sacred poetry were of a higher order than secular poetry, the novel was a lesser form of art than the poem, personality should be subdued to the demands of intellect.

The poems which put McAuley's theories into practice were published in *A Vision of Ceremony* in 1956 and as *Captain Quiros* in 1964.[23] *Captain Quiros*, in particular, was written as an act of piety and absorbed most of McAuley's creative energy in the late fifties. In these poems, tradition would be upheld and the intellect would rule emotion. McAuley would not indulge in the 'self-expressive art' of the modernist.

In *A Vision of Ceremony* McAuley stated his purpose in the poem addressed to Vincent Buckley, 'An Art of Poetry'. McAuley intended to follow the example of Christ by providing spiritual insight through simple imagery. The poem 'Jesus' celebrated Christ's role as scholar and poet. Though a scholar and poet in a different age, McAuley attempted to observe the strict rules of simplicity.

In some poems he managed to create suggestive images which gave new meaning to Christian belief. 'To the Holy Spirit', for example, transformed the Christian dove into a Bird of Paradise: Heaven's bird and the glorious living bird became one. McAuley enriched the Catholic call to 'Come, Holy Spirit, fill the hearts of your faithful' by the sustained image from nature: the fantastic reality of the Bird of Paradise dancing for his drab mate exemplified the role of the Holy Spirit in lifting the hearts of ordinary men and women.

Elsewhere, McAuley's insistence on austerity, simplicity and a narrow range of subject and imagery made his poems remote and even prosaic. 'Sequence' kept so closely to a liturgical litany that it offered little that was original. Reverence for his subject seemed to prevent McAuley from the surprising conjunctions which made his earlier work exciting. Even in a poem such as 'To the Holy Spirit' McAuley is least successful when he is most universal or liturgical: 'Engender upon our souls your sacred rhythm...'. At these moments he chooses the elaborate or archaic word rather than the familiar or even the most resonant. He dresses up simple notions in quite deliberately pretentious language; the words 'engender', 'incandescent' call attention to themselves as words rather than to their contribution to the poem. It is as if McAuley must employ a particularly pompous language when he comes closest to the mysteries of faith so that they are protected by reverent obscurity.

—

In 'New Guinea' McAuley moves so far from his liturgical, impersonal ideal as to introduce himself—'figures of my inmost dream'—and to recall the identification with Australia in 'Envoi', 'New Guinea' concentrates on the speaker's own experience of New Guinea, though it interprets this experience in terms of Christian insight. In the poem McAuley describes the extraordinary qualities of the New Guinea landscape and pattern of life. The island is a 'land of apocalypse' where men may be shaken and changed by the metaphysical mysteries it seems to offer. The actual landscape and natural life in New Guinea are like the poet's 'inmost dream', his own imagining of a metaphysical world. But New Guinea has a tradition without Christ, and 'stains of blood, and evil spirits, lurk' within its social patterns. In 'New Guinea' McAuley's experience of life and his wider opinions lead the poem away from a specifically religious function. He turns to the actual state of New Guinea and the problems posed for the white bearers of civilisation. Religion is the basis for McAuley's identification of New Guinea's problems but these are also social and political problems.

McAuley's views on New Guinea and the colonial responsibility are partly set out in his essay 'My New Guinea' (1961) where he describes his first encounter with New Guinea culture and his concern about the future of the new nation. In the essay McAuley rejects Western liberalism as a satisfying replacement for the rich pagan culture of the natives:

> Certainly, I decided, [the solution] was not our sterile secularism with its will to desecrate, literally, all departments of life; nor our disintegrated liberalism with its inability to rationally affirm or practically defend its own values; nor our mixture of shiftless hedonism with abstract and unreal U.N.-type clichés. These things were the late luxury products or parasitical features of a Western civilization which had been founded and formed and maintained by far other commitments and disciplines, enthusiasms and sacrifices...[24]

His religious beliefs are thus connected to his analysis of the social and political order. New Guinea natives do have a sense of the supernatural which will not be satisfied by the consumerism of modern Western society. The Christianity which has formed Western society must be offered as the source of its values. In both poem and essay, McAuley claimed that Christian values would provide a solution to the future of New Guinea and, in each, he referred to Alain de Boismenu as one man who had the faith to recognise this.

The poem 'New Guinea' demonstrates McAuley's ability to absorb the physical world into his spiritual vision. His suggestive descriptions of the New Guinea landscape are both physically accurate and convincingly part of McAuley's understanding of a cosmic order. Again, he falters only when he leaves detailed imagery for the large issues of 'untellable recognition' or 'wordless revelation'. And in one line, at least, he confuses the two scales: 'Like cockroaches in the interstices of things'. As in his critical writing, McAuley shows in his poem the tendency to move from the striking detail to much more general propositions. So, the white men with their 'grin of emptiness' are defeated by the vaguest of personified forces—'formless dishonour'. And the qualities by which such dishonour can be defeated are equally formless: 'splendour, simplicity, joy'. In a similar manner McAuley protects the mysterious nature of religious truth by shrouding it in abstractions.

Of course, McAuley's unwillingness to examine the nature of religious feeling was a deliberate decision to avoid the exploration of the self or even a type of magian heresy. The poems emphasise the political and social role of religion, or they adopt a celebratory role which presumes religious faith rather than illuminates it. The exploration of Christian metaphysics which one might have expected from a reading of *The End of Modernity* is not offered in *A Vision of Ceremony*. The questions of the unfaithful—How is religious faith achieved? Why do you believe? What does religion mean personally?—are not answered. Instead, McAuley points to the artistic, social and political advantages of religion.

McAuley's 'Celebration of Divine Love' is the most ambitious treatment of his Catholicism in the book. This poem has an auto-biographical base but McAuley contains the story of his life within the biblical history of man and maintains an impersonal attitude. The figure growing through the poem is not identified as McAuley himself. Yet the poem quickly distinguishes between the universal growth of man and the man at its centre. This particular man bears a tragic knowledge and is 'marked' with a particular 'inward flaw' which leaves him without vocation. The outline of McAuley's own life story is there: the childhood perceptions as remarked in 'Vespers', the undergraduate libertarianism, the listening to the ideologues, the Catholic faith and its importance to the ordering of McAuley's poetic imagination.

But, despite its clear reference to McAuley's own life history, the poem moves away from the personal by aligning this individual life with a larger Christian pattern. In particular, McAuley chooses a ritualised rather than a personal language to express the individual's experience. For example, McAuley's youthful pursuit of ideology becomes in the poem:

> Fled from his own disaster, he consults
> The learned magi casting horoscopes
> For the New Babylon...

The poem absorbs individual experience into a formal pattern which is part of the gift of Christianity. In particular, Catholic faith has provided the man at its centre with a sense of order, a confidence in his own goodness and a rich symbolic imagery.

The sincerity of McAuley's commitment to his faith in this poem cannot be doubted. At the same time, this faith allows no uncertainties about life: men may rest safe within the Christian order or drift in the monstrous world beyond it. The poem does not offer the kind of personal experience of faith which contemporary readers might expect. Perhaps its most contradictory element is the claim to celebrate Divine *love* when Divinity is held at such reverent distance.

But the most important difficulty in the poem appears to be McAuley's own self-discipline. He has decided that he will be a secular rather than a mystic poet. At the same time, he scorned personal and self-expressive poetry. This left McAuley in a middle ground where he could not pursue spirituality or his own experience beyond certain limits. In his essays 'Sacred Art in the Modern World' and 'A note on Maritain's View' McAuley argued that personalised artistic techniques obscured the meaning of relegous art.[25] This meant that the religious artist must restrict himself to the symbols of religious tradition. McAuley did not wish to tamper with these symbols; hence in 'Celebration of Divine Love' and other poems such as 'Sequence' they are recited rather than actively explored. In 'To the Holy Spirit' he added to these symbols successfully, but such a religious role for the poet was very limited.

The other task which McAuley set for himself was to observe the secular world in the light of his faith; but once more he refused to examine his own existence in any detail. This decision to avoid the personal was a deliberate decision but it meant that many of the poems in *A Vision of Ceremony* have a distant, unmoving quality; they are poems which Vincent Buckley described as 'remote from the human preoccupations'.[26] Although McAuley's faith was Christian, he was intent on the stylised rather than the human face of Christianity.

If he was to be a poet of the secular world while steadfastly avoiding personalism, satire was one option open to him. 'A Letter to John Dryden' continued the eighteenth-century style demonstrated in 'The True Discovery of Australia'. Intellect and order might be expected to find apt expression in the strict forms of Augustan satire and the studied objectivity of its criticism. Furthermore, McAuley's moral and political views gave a sure position from which a satirist could attack. McAuley's love of argument and interest in political affairs would seem to suit him for the satirist's task.

However, 'A Letter to John Dryden' does not dazzle with its incisive attack on folly and vice. Instead of concentrating on the stupidity of his opponents, McAuley presents his own opinions as unquestionably right. His opponents are not specifically identified because they constitute a general group: modernist poets, people who have attended government schools, academics, communists, progressives, positivists, Taoists, Buddhists, atheists, agnostics, divorcees, and the rest. The range of victims is immense, and McAuley is unable to take advantage of individual absurdities. Like the socialist realist poets, McAuley sets his own opinions up for attack rather than defeating others; he believes too strongly to control the direction of his satire.

In the last stanza of 'A Letter to John Dryden' McAuley writes:

Thus have I written, hoping to be read
A little now, a little when I'm dead.

But it is difficult to believe that he had a public in mind at all when he wrote the poem. For the question upon which the poet ponders in his letter to Dryden is how to write for the ignorant Modern Mind. That is, the bulk of the poem is an attack on McAuley's readers. McAuley may claim to be preparing the soil for faith but his argument never attempts to convince the reader/ victim that any one of the reader's commitments is intrinsically foolish or immoral. Nor does he offer any sympathy to the mass of mankind. 'Man cannot live by Oslo lunches merely' but McAuley refuses to contemplate the idea that those who eat Oslo lunches might also be able to think and understand spiritual life. McAuley's knowledge is exclusive; the arrogance proper to satire as a form becomes the virtue it promotes. Here, as in 'Celebration of Divine Love', his Christianity argued for perfection rather than human forgiveness.

'A Letter to John Dryden' canvasses most of McAuley's opinions on society and art. It also presents itself in the form of a question, 'How does a poet write in the modern world?' This was the question which continually puzzled McAuley; it accounts for the variety of his poetic work—the liturgical poems, modernist poetry (under the pseudonym of Ern Malley), his nature poems, satires, classical masques, lyrics and narrative poems. 'A Letter to John Dryden' also states that in the fifties McAuley's ambition was to 'show Christ forth'. It is this motivation which prevents McAuley from being constantly satirical in the poem and leads him to the celebration of Catholicism in the second last stanza. The poem shows the mixed nature of McAuley's poetic desires: he wanted to attack the elements in society which erred against his own notion of order and at the same time celebrate the glories of a private Catholicism and act as its missionary. The faithless cannot know the mysteries of faith and McAuley cannot give them faith. All he can do is attack the manifestations of materialism or misguided spiritualism and fall back on prayer and good works to 'touch Hearts'.

When McAuley undertook the writing of *Captain Quiros* in the latter part of the fifties he was still seeking a form to express both his Catholic faith and his beliefs about literature and society, particularly the problems in Pacific societies such as New Guinea. McAuley had written historical narrative before in his 'Henry the Navigator', published in *Under Aldebaran*, but in the historical figure of Captain Quiros McAuley found a more fitting vehicle for his own interests and problems. For Quiros, like McAuley, was a man of faith who had to contend with the scorn and blasphemy of his fellow Christians. Like McAuley in New Guinea, Quiros had to confront a native people living in a spiritual order which was nonetheless barbarous, knowing that members of his own more advanced society were impious and immoral. Quiros also hoped to find the South Land, later known as Australia, which he would establish as a society dedicated to God; this gives McAuley the opportunity to express his opinions on the state of Australian society and its future.

The narrator of *Captain Quiros* states that Quiros' quest is to find Terra Australis, 'land of the inmost heart'. The phrase is recurrent in McAuley's poetry. In 'Envoi' he wrote of Australia as a land within the mind; in 'Terra Australis' it was a land found by an inward voyage, a 'land of similes'; in 'New Guinea' the land was 'like the figures of my inmost dream'.

I have commented that Patrick White found a similar poetic image of the landscape in *Voss*, which was published in 1957. McAuley recognised this, and White's novel drew a sympathetic and almost envious response from McAuley. In an article in *Southerly* in 1965 McAuley wrote that his admiration for *Voss* had crystallised his resolve to write *Captain Quiros*.[27] *Voss* had taken on a poet's task and succeeded; McAuley saw it as a challenge to poets to attempt an equally ambitious narrative. McAuley saw that White was examining the possibilities of spiritual life in a society which had rejected a Christian God. This was also, of course, the source of his own preoccupation with the poet's role. But White remains equivocal about Christianity in *Voss* and clearly cannot accept a complacent and unquestioning approach to religion. McAuley had surer knowlege and *Captain Quiros* celebrated his certainties.

Captain Quiros is as pious as the Aeneid. Christianity is its base and, as A.D. Hope commented in his review of it, it demands a suspension of religious doubt in the reader. For his ambitious narrative, McAuley adopted a grand style which emphasised saint-liness rather than human experience. McAuley's poetry aimed to be as great as Quiros' own ambitions:

This Great Work must rise clear
Of the earth's dross, refined by heavenly fire.

In many ways, *Captain Quiros* is an engrossing narrative of exploration, but most criticism finds that its major fault is its lack of human concern. The poem is solemn except where McAuley himself intrudes in the final section to comment on the state of the contemporary world.

Captain Quiros examines several of the religious and social problems which absorbed McAuley's attention during the fifties. The first is the difficulty of bringing European civilisation to pagans who already have a developed religious and moral order. In *Captain Quiros* the bearers of white civilisation are Catholics rather than the secular liberals derided in 'My New Guinea'. But, despite

their faith, they are marked by greed, vanity, lust and murderous-
ness. Mendana's expedition demonstrates the tragic impact of
such 'Christian' civilisation on the Pacific islanders.

But Quiros survives the voyage with a renewed belief in the
importance of bringing his faith to these people and of founding
the South Land on Christian principles. Quiros' missionary zeal is
based on an understanding of the social meaning of Catholic faith.
Like McAuley Quiros believes that Catholicism can provide the
Pacific islanders with rituals and spiritual values so that they may
be enriched by the culture and technology of Europe rather than
be depraved by it. But the struggle to rise above the 'earth's dross'
does not end with the acquisition of faith, and human sinfulness
may distort the most pious ambitions. Religious faith does not
guarantee virtue.

The second major concern of the poem arises from its consideration of the failings of the Spanish Catholics. Quiros is disturbed by
the Father Commissary's deathbed lesson:

'That even perfection is a snare, I see;
Yet by the gospel word am I confounded:
Be ye perfect. Was it a fault in me
That with intense desire I sought to escape
This blind world's evil so far as to shape
Our labours to a secular liturgy?'

This is remarkable self-questioning not only for Quiros but for
McAuley. At the beginning of the poem there can be little doubt
that building 'a secular liturgy' is one of its purposes. The poem
itself is conceived as a work of piety, just as it gives an account of
pious secular endeavours. In this later part of the poem, McAuley
recalls the Christian lesson that the kingdom of Heaven is not of
this world. Attempts to achieve it such as Quiros' voyage are
doomed to failure. McAuley's own ambition to write a 'sublime'
poem, as perfect as he can make it, is also bound to fail because of
human imperfection.

This awareness creates a humility in poet and hero, and the final
part of the poem might have been expected to elaborate this new
insight. But Part Three finds Quiros with zeal undiminished plan-
ning for a third voyage. And McAuley openly presents his own
political beliefs and criticisms of the beliefs of others as part of
Quiros' experience. For example, McAuley's political opponent,
Cardinal Gilroy, appears as a Spanish cleric:

One was a churchman in the recent style,
Well suited to a failing age of drift,
A cold mean creature with placarded smile
Whom God to try the faithful had bereft
Of magnanimity and honour...[28]

This part of the poem is preoccupied with McAuley's assessment of the fifties. The dying Quiros prophesies the first discoveries of Australia and Cook's final mapping of the east coast. Quiros sees the convict settlement, then the establishment of 'common law and ordered liberty' as Australia gains colonial then dominion status. He goes further to prophesy a future yet to be seen by McAuley himself where 'colder, vaster systems rise instead', presumably totalitarianism. The 'ancient Dragon wakes and knows his hour' as Communist China rises to conquer Australia. Then Antichrist will rule the world and the faithful will be scorned and kept apart until finally the end of the world will come and they shall gain their rightful place in Heaven.

This is McAuley's own prophecy for Australia; it is the basis for his public political stance. Yet McAuley's emotional commitment to these views overrides the intelligent self-criticism evident at the end of the second part of the poem. In these last stanzas McAuley praises faith as the only source of virtue. The faithful will survive all the monstrous events that the future has in store.

Captain Quiros portrays that 'significant action', the physical and mental search for truth, which McAuley admired in *Voss*. But the truths in *Captain Quiros* have been decided at the outset, so that few genuine discoveries can be made. In fact, the most significant discovery of the poem—the necessity of human imperfection—is cast aside to make way for McAuley's opinions on the state of the world. Even the form of the poem and the reverent nature of its language seem to have been developed as a result of opinion rather than as part of McAuley's response to his material. McAuley proudly proclaims his obstinancy:

Therefore I have less care who shall approve;
For poems in this kind are out of fashion,
Together with the faith, the will, the love,
The energy of intellectual passion
That built the greatness which we have resigned.
I play a match against the age's mind:
The board is set; the living pieces move.

—

89

So with a flourish of bravado, McAuley defied the values of the world in which he lived. He later noted that *Captain Quiros* was the only poem written with a 'blind' confidence in his choice of form. At that same time, the doubts expressed at the Father Commissary's deathbed must be taken seriously—despite the way in which the poem casts them aside. For McAuley had begun to lose his enthusiasm for the religion he had championed so publicly. By 1961, he was writing to A.D. Hope about his disillusionment and his puzzling lack of interest in God.[29]

Captain Quiros, too, had exhausted him. The poem had absorbed most of his creative energies over a period of five or six years, yet the final composition had been a disappointment. Critics commented on the prosaic nature of the verse, on its lack of drama and colour.[30] McAuley's imaginative powers seemed to have faded in inverse proportion to his access of dogmatism. Yet even in *Captain Quiros* uncertainties about faith had appeared; it was simply that McAuley's pronouncements had become louder to drown them out.

There were other crises in his life at the end of the fifties. There had been unpleasantness about the retirement of Alf Conlon from the School of Pacific Administration, and McAuley wanted to leave the School. His hostility towards Cardinal Gilroy had not abated and McAuley applied to his academic friends and was offered a poetry fellowship at the University of Tasmania—an ironic and, perhaps, appropriate place to retire after Cultural Freedom's attitude to the Sydney Orr case. Within a few years he became professor of English, thus returning to his first career plan.

McAuley did not abandon his religion though he began to make public complaint about the reforms that came in the wake of the Second Vatican Council.[31] The religion which seemed to have been the last refuge from the weakness of liberalism now embraced liberalism with a will. Yet, with the support of Guildford Young, the Bishop of Hobart, McAuley settled down to write hymns for the new English mass.

This was a humble enough task for the author of *Captain Quiros*, but McAuley's readers were more surprised by the humility of his next book of poems, *Surprises of the Sun* (1969). This book contained poems such as 'Father, Mother, Son', 'Because' and 'Tabletalk' which examined McAuley's family life and the failure of human affection. McAuley was still writing religious poetry but now this took the form of a self-examination as in 'Confession' rather than the generalised symbolism of 'Celebration of Divine Love'. It is tempting to read a poem such as 'Released on Parole' as an admission that McAuley came to regard his self-imposed notions of discipline and order as imprisonment. His 'twenty years hard' may mean such poetic discipline but it may also mean more simply the burden of intellectual pursuits.

Surprises of the Sun showed a willingness to look at the actual state of man and, in particular, the human failings of the poet himself. In 1976, McAuley admitted that he was amazed at his turn to small lyrics in the sixties. He recalled that he had never been completely happy about his own traditionalism but that he had adopted it as an alternative to modernism or literary nationalism: 'More and more clearly I see any general critical views I would want to advance as being directed to keeping options open and resources freely available—for oneself as well as for others'.[32]

Modernism and literary nationalism had died as threats to the poet in the sixties. They had been paper tigers hardly worth the energy McAuley gave to demolishing them. In *Surprises of the Sun* he was born again as a poet who could make ordinary life and ordinary people touch the grandeur of myth. In 'Pieta' his own wife suffered the bereavement of Mary after the crucifixion; in 'Father, Mother, Son' he plays Seth to his father's Adam; in 'One Tuesday in Summer' Mr Pitt, the grocery man, takes on the mystical significance of an angelic messenger.

This identification of the contemporary world with the past was not new in McAuley's poetry. 'Celebration of Divine Love' had linked McAuley's own life with the stories of Cain and Abel, the tower of Babel and the Flood, and even Quiros was clearly an image for McAuley, the Catholic crusader—but the arrogance and righteousness had gone. McAuley, in these poems from *Surprises of the Sun*, now shared the doubts and the failures of his fellows; he could even celebrate these failures.

Furthermore, in his later poetry McAuley resisted the temptation to comment on every image but, more often than not, left his observations of the world to stand on their own. His poem 'Numbers and Makes' recounts McAuley's childhood pastime of noting the numbers of trains and makes of cars. The adult intellectual writing the poem wants to develop some theory from this but turns away with the question:

Why change the memory into metaphors
That solitary child would disavow?

91

McAuley always claimed that simplicity was the key to good poetry, but it was not until these late poems that he managed to control his penchant for 'messages'.

The later poems also return to the physical world with renewed attention. Where in the earlier poems, such as 'New Guinea', McAuley saw the real natural world as an image of the greater spiritual order, his later poems are content to seek any spiritual understanding through knowledge of the natural world. A poem such as 'In the Huon Valley' ventures no further than the simple wisdom 'Life is full of returns', and in the series of poems published after his death, A World of its Own, McAuley resists comment almost completely.[33]

It is, perhaps, ironic that McAuley is more clearly present as an opinionated, controlling voice in the 'impersonal' poems such as 'Celebration of Divine Love' and Captain Quiros than he is in poems about his own life such as 'Because' or 'Convalescence'. In the later poems, McAuley is intent on conveying actual, living experiences—his father turning from a childhood kiss, the children clattering off to school leaving the dying poet alone in bed. Such familiar details of domestic life do not end in personal revelation or the dreaded sterile inwardness. By dramatising his own life McAuley actually portrays a more general suffering humanity.

In 1970 McAuley found that he had cancer and it may be that his recognition of impending death made the physical world more precious to him. Certainly, the poems written in the last six years of his life celebrate the living world, the world of the senses rather than an abstract spiritual order.

However, McAuley kept to anti-communism to the last. He angered many of his students by his adamant support of the Vietnam war and, using Cold War analyses on a new generation, he formed an organisation called Peace with Freedom to (in Peter Coleman's terms) 'make war on the left in the universities and colleges'. It can be no wonder that the sixties generation disbelieved the tales of McAuley as a young university radical or an unwilling soldier in the Second World War. For all his declaration of concern for human life and freedom, McAuley refused to see that Vietnam threatened the lives of yet another generation of Australian men. And even cancer could not prevent McAuley from raising his voice in support of Sir John Kerr's dismissal of Gough Whitlam's government in 1975.[34]

James McAuley's struggles and experiments to find an appropriate poetic mode through the forties and fifties were the result of his interpretation of his times. He was never a poet cut off from the world; political and social crises absorbed his attention. McAuley read his times as demanding a new role for the poet, one which was both outward-looking and spiritual. In the fifties, McAuley thought that his Catholic faith could provide the answers to his poetic problems.

It now appears that, at least for a time, McAuley sacrificed himself to his own restrictive views of poetic responsibility. They were views developed under the pressure of the times: extreme positions seemed to be the only protection against chaos. In this respect, the similarities between McAuley's response in the fifties and that of the communist writers must be noted. They were at least as fearful of the meaning of modernism as McAuley; they also believed that the worth of the individual human life was at stake in postwar society. Communist writers, of course, never considered the option of Catholicism as a source of metaphysical understanding of art, but their own doctrines were as rigid as the Catholicism which McAuley embraced. The similarities between Stalinism and strict Catholicism have been noted many times and the observation that ex-Catholics were amongst the most dogmatic of Australian communists is commonplace. Both systems of belief provided a certain simplicity in increasingly complex times; each allowed its adherents a sense of belonging and of superior knowledge. Just as the socialist realist theory propounded by Australian communist critics simplified the nature of literary creation, so McAuley used his Catholicism to simplify the task of the contemporary poet. During the fifties McAuley found an order within Catholicism which explained both heaven and earth, and gave him the social and political role he desired while allowing him to feel part of a supernatural order. In his political and critical writing, and in many of his fifties poems McAuley was inclined to confuse the two orders so that his social and political beliefs took on the authority of spiritual truth.

I have tried to trace here the way in which McAuley's personality, experiences and observations of the contemporary world forced him to seek a conservative ideology and to express that ideology in his poetry. I have argued that the failures of many of the poems in *A Vision of Ceremony* and of *Captain Quiros* can be related to the disciplines which McAuley placed on himself in accord with his ideological beliefs. Most critics who have written about McAuley's poetry encounter some difficulties with the poetry of these two books, but it also remains impossible to separate the poetry from McAuley's public political and religious statements in the fifties and early sixties.

For this reason, most writers about McAuley's poetry have been friends or fellow-poets published by him during his editorship of *Quadrant*. Leonie Kramer, A.D. Hope, Vivian Smith, Vincent Buckley and Chris Wallace-Crabbe have written sympathetic criticism which, nevertheless, recognises the problems or limitations of his fifties poetry. On the other hand, John Docker has discussed McAuley's poetry from the viewpoint of a younger generation of leftist critics and Livio Dobrez has argued that McAuley's fifties poetry expresses a very selective and limited kind of Catholicism. The political and religious ideas behind the poetry are so strong that traditional, 'objective' judgement of it seems impossible, even thirty years after it was written.[35]

In a *Quadrant* article in 1976 Leonie Kramer argued that critics may mistake McAuley's 'firmness for dogmatism, and faith for certainty' and so overlook the constant struggle with himself which lies behind McAuley's poetry.[36] I have no doubt that McAuley did engage in such a struggle and I think this is most evident in some of the poems of *Under Aldebaran* and in his later poetry. Nevertheless, in his fifties poems McAuley seemed intent on hiding any personal doubts behind a formality of subject and style.

The question of McAuley's influence on other writers is also difficult to answer. Vivian Smith has suggested that McAuley's influence on other poets has been insignificant, yet McAuley, as editor of *Quadrant*, patronised a range of poets, including Smith, who practised the formal, lucid, decorous kind of verse which McAuley wrote himself.[37] He may not have converted these poets to Catholicism or anti-communism but he did encourage them to pursue traditional poetic forms, subjects and language.

It may be that because of his political associations, younger poets are unwilling to declare McAuley as an influence on their work. Since the sixties, McAuley's poetry has been included in the standard Australian poetry anthologies and is regularly set for study on Australian literature courses, so his work has been readily available to other poets and readers.

Rather than a direct influence on Australian poets in the eighties McAuley remains important as a focal point for the continuing commitment of some Australian poets to simplicity and clarity, and to a religious poetic function. Whatever McAuley's personal success as a Catholic poet, his conviction that poetry must have a spiritual role has been endorsed by several prominent Australian poets in the seventies and eighties. At present the Australian poet with the highest critical reputation is Les Murray, a poet at ease with nationalism and some of the techniques of modernism but determined to pursue a religious view which has similarities with McAuley's. Though Murray espouses a sympathy with ordinary people and their vernacular, his attitude as Catholic poet is in many ways as exclusive and superior as McAuley's.[38]

Ten years after McAuley's death, *Quadrant* supports and publishes a group of poets interested in a spiritual role for poetry. For those poets McAuley remains significant, not through a desire to imitate his poetic style but because he claimed and won a public recognition of religious poetry and because he established a conservative network to support it. As well, McAuley's successors as literary editors of *Quadrant* have been able to maintain the tradition of lucid, decorous poetry which McAuley saw as a bulwark against chaos, and this poetry has, in turn, continued to give credibility to the sometimes extreme right-wing views promoted by the journal. Australian poets may no longer see any link between these right-wing political commitments and the kind of poetry published by *Quadrant* but the journal itself continues to suggest that such rational and intelligent poetry comes from the same source as its political critiques.

4

Uncommitted Modern
Man: A.D. Hope

James McAuley's poetry, with its expression of a Catholic anti-communist commitment, is often discussed with the traditional poetry of his friend A.D. Hope. But though both poets adopted traditional form and despised modernist techniques and both derided the nationalism of the radical writers, there are important differences in their attitudes and in their expression of these attitudes in poetry. Far from committing himself to a belief system and a political program, Hope prided himself on remaining aloof from religious and political causes. He saw himself as the uncommitted modern man who could not endorse the predigested ideologies of others.

In his critical writing and in his poetry Hope is a mocker of belief systems. This very mockery, however, is part of a commitment to the traditions of Western intellectual thought. Hope expressed his early traditionalism through satire but in the fifties he began a struggle to find a more positive kind of poetry which nevertheless could remain clear of easy and obvious ideological commitments. Hope is, in many ways, the poet most representative of the ideals of fifties Australia: he is suburban, politically conservative, educated, aware of older civilisations but also facing the implications of materialism and unbelief. It is Hope's kind of traditionalism rather than McAuley's passionate commitment which exemplifies the attitudes of the new generation of Australian professional men who came to prominence in the postwar years.

In 1951 Hope became professor of English Language and Literature at the Canberra University College (now the ANU) and for more than thirty years the title of professor has reinforced the view that he is an academic poet, looking towards the traditions of Europe and uninterested in Australian social life. The stereotyped associations of the 'professor' should not be taken too seriously in the case of Hope. Although he won a scholarship to Oxford, he failed to take out a degree and returned to Australia in the early thirties to face unemployment. After a time as a schoolteacher he joined the staff of Sydney Teachers' College and he was almost forty when he became a university academic at Melbourne University. Hope had to work hard to establish himself in the academic world, and his controversial early literary criticism owes a good deal to the need to make a name for himself.

During the thirties and forties Hope was better known as a reviewer and critic than a poet. He wrote reviews for the *Sydney Morning Herald*, wrote an issue of *Current Affairs Bulletin* (1956), gave book talks for the ABC and lectures for the Commonwealth Literary Fund. For a time, he was Anthony Inkwell on the ABC's children's program, 'The Argonauts'. He contributed articles to *Hermes* (1945) and *Melbourne University Magazine* (1955) as well as *Meanjin* and *Southerly*. Hope was a contributor to the first issues of *Southerly* and *Quadrant* and to the fifth issue of *Overland*. It is in this critical writing that Hope displays the attitudes behind his choices as a poet.[1]

Hope has claimed that his main interest as a literary reviewer was 'to raise the standard of reviewing' in Australia, particularly the reviewing of Australian books. He believed that often reviewers applied a special set of standards to Australian literature which gave a certain value to 'Australianness' and praised local products far beyond their deserts. This gave him the rationale for his own witty and controversial attacks on Australian literature. He was not, like the socialist realist writers or his friend McAuley, intent on developing literature as the means to display some essential truth about modern life. When he accepted the chair at Canberra University College Hope declared his intention to teach Australian literature courses. This was an innovation at the time and an apparently nationalistic one, but Hope's nationalism was very different from that of Vance Palmer or Clem Christesen. He did not want Australian literature to feed student nationalism nor to improve his students morally in any way. He taught Australian literature in order to increase the critical reading of Australian work and, therefore, provide a firmer base for writers themselves.

Hope's father was a Presbyterian minister, and the Presbyterian God of hellfire and remorse dominated Hope's childhood as it had dominated the youth of other Australian writers before him. Catherine Helen Spence, Joseph Furphy and Norman Lindsay were among those writers who found it necessary to cast off the bondage of Calvinism in maturity. In each case, Calvinism left a lasting influence on the writer's work. In Spence and Furphy this was a continuing interest in social problems; in Lindsay and Hope it appears as a conscious rebellion against social concern. As a young man Hope read Nietzsche and quite deliberately used the German philosopher to reject the inhibitions and doctrines of Calvinist Christianity. John Anderson, the philosopher at the University of Sydney whose teaching had spawned libertarian ideas, helped the process by demanding that all dogmas should be challenged. Sin was, after all, a human invention and, with discipline, it could be invalidated rather than avoided.

By the time of the Second World War Hope could be called an agnostic and a pacifist. He was old enough to remember World War I and to decide never to take part in any war himself—'not a practical resolve as I gradually came to see'.[2] At this point, McAuley clearly shared many of Hope's views on the world.

But when McAuley found religion Hope would not follow him. In letters to his friend, McAuley prayed for Hope's conversion, and Hope was curious about McAuley's changing enthusiasms; on the day of McAuley's Sydney baptism he sat in St Christopher's Co-Cathedral in Canberra thinking about his friend and his new faith. But after the struggle to expel Calvinism a conversion was out of the question. (It is, perhaps, more difficult for the son of a Presbyterian minister to accept Catholicism than for the son of a lapsed Catholic.)

For all his sympathy with McAuley, Hope came to regard his new religion as part of the inevitable pattern of McAuley's life. McAuley would seize a new enthusiasm, become totally absorbed in it, then begin a process of criticism which led him to reject it. Hope saw McAuley's activities in the late fifties, in particular his arguments with Cardinal Gilroy, as the beginning of a rejection of Catholicism.

A. D. Hope

McAuley's religious commitment meant an intellectual parting for the two poets. In 1960 Hope suggested that McAuley had initiated the break:

> We share the view that poetry is an independent literary form that doesn't tail off into prose, a suspicion of experimental modes, a conviction that good poetry is coherent. We are against extreme forms of dissociation—we were opposed to surrealistic poetry from the start. . . . We diverge mainly because of the outcome of Jim's conversion to Catholicism. He considers me in the agnostic line of poets.[3]

Even here, Hope resisted the label of 'agnostic'. He did not wish to be categorised with any particular program—the word 'agnostic', like 'pacifist' or 'nationalist', might imply attitudes to which he did not subscribe.

Like his resistance to nationalism, Hope's religious wariness was part of a wider suspicion of commitment to political and religious causes. In his book reviews and critical articles Hope saw commitment as a threat to literary values. His attack on David Martin's book of poems *From Life* deplored the rise of 'social purpose' literature and argued that literature should be judged by literary rather than social standards. He objected to any view of literature which saw it as utilitarian. However, he did not reject didacticism in literature and his recognition of the greatness of some didactic art forced him to consider the source of socialist realism. He concluded that, 'The didactic impulse is about as likely to be stimulated to acts of creative imagination by the arid doctrines of dialectical materialism as the maternal instinct is likely to be by marriage to a mechanical man'.[4] Behind the outrageous simile is Hope's conviction that socialist realism was a formula approach to art.

In an article entitled 'The Activists' he argued that a whole range of commitments, not simply Marxism, could destroy art. These included 'religious, educational, scientific, patriotic, or just vaguely progressive'. Once again Hope acknowledged that much of the great world literature did have such purpose, but he objected to the measuring of literature in terms of these purposes. Essentially, Hope was attacking the simple reflection, mimetic or, as he put it, the imitation theory of art which limits literature to the role of representing 'the truth about the world in which we live: to

---

99

inform us, and by informing to instruct and delight'. The limitations of such literary theories eventually came to be recognised by Marxists, but, at the time when Hope was writing, socialist realism did restrict itself to portraying a reflection of reality and his criticisms struck at the heart of the theory.[5]

The popularity of theories such as socialist realism during the postwar years in Australia influenced Hope's continuing commitment to poetry as a literary form. As a poet, Hope needed to defend his art against demands that it be representative or directly related to social reality, and the frequency of such demands during the forties and fifties strengthened Hope's determination to pursue the form most free of moral, social or political suggestion. In attacking those who demanded political commitment in art, Hope began to define his own views on the nature of poetry. In 'The Activists' Hope declared that 'what literature *is*, is not entirely what it is *about*' and he attempted to define 'what literature is' by reference to music: 'Primarily and essentially [literature] creates by means of its material something as completely *sui generis* as music creates. Nothing remotely resembling a Mozart concerto occurs in nature. The composer adds a new order of being to the existing orders of nature. And so does poetry.'[6] This comparison of poetry to music recurs in both Hope's critical writing and in his poetry. In choosing to write poetry Hope was seeking the most 'literary' form of literature, the genre which was most free of ideological associations.

Yet Hope also criticised modernism in poetry and he did not accept that literary experiment or personalism was a valid way to remove art from ideological commitments. Some observers might see modernism as the logical choice for a poet who was impatient with representational art; Hope saw it as a turning away from the intellect, a surrender to disorder. His critical rejection of 'activism' on the one hand, and modernism on the other, left him with a narrow range of choices as a poet.

In 'The Activists' he criticised cultural congresses or writers' conferences which discussed the role of literature in society. Nevertheless, Hope was one of the first literary figures to join Cultural Freedom and he became a member of *Quadrant*'s editorial advisory board. In 1971, he recalled his acceptance of the role of editorial adviser to *Quadrant* as follows:

> I believed, rightly or wrongly, that its model was the recently
> launched and highly successful English magazine *Encounter*. I was

sceptical about all this; though, as a conservative sort of chap myself, I was in sympathy with any organ of arts and letters which would not automatically lean to the left. I favoured an upright stance and walk myself, and still do. A man who leans much in any direction is unlikely to keep his balance.[7]

Hope's reference to 'any organ of arts and letters which would not automatically lean to the left' and his protestation of innocence of political motive appears disingenuous given his knowledge of James McAuley's 'leanings'. Like other liberal intellectuals Hope was not unduly concerned by McAuley's links with the DLP and Santamaria's National Civic Council; he believed his own independence could not be affected by McAuley's commitments. In the same article Hope commented that *Quadrant* seemed more political in 1971 than it had in 1957 and that the Vietnam war had contributed to the changed view. Hope sympathised with the student protests of the late sixties, not because of a radical change in his own politics but through a recognition that these protests were challenging one kind of dogma and from a belief that war should be resisted. Nevertheless, he tried to maintain his uncommitted stance by refusing to sign any of the protest petitions circulating at the time: 'My declaration was against war (full stop) not against any particular war.'[8] Despite his identification with the conservative forces in Australia, Hope's poem 'Inscription for a War', which reset the inscription at Thermopylae, became well known as a Vietnam protest poem and the anti-Vietnam anthology, *We took their Orders*, took its title from his poem.

If he wished to avoid political commitment why did Hope join Cultural Freedom? At the time, after his appearance before the Petrov Commission, Clem Christesen had become increasingly strident in *Meanjin*. The personal attack on his integrity had convinced him that Armageddon was at hand. Although Hope was present at two of the contacts which Nina Christesen had with Russian embassy officials in 1953, he apparently did not sympathise greatly with Christesen's public outrage in *Meanjin*. He was among those who found Christesen's nationalism narrow and inhibiting, and when McAuley approached him on behalf of *Quadrant* he was pleased with the possibility of a less nationalist literary journal. He was not alone in this view. Manning Clark was another member of *Quadrant*'s advisory board who was disillusioned with *Meanjin* at the time he joined.[9]

Quadrant welcomed Hope's views on the long poem and the

need for traditional form in poetry. It provided an outlet for opinions that would not suit Christesen's view of literature—though, as Lynne Strahan was noted, the appearance of otherwise politically innocent material such as Hope's poem 'The Kings' alongside *Quadrant*'s attacks on communism suggested a political position, possibly further to the right than Hope would have chosen.[10] In the fifties, Hope's confidence in his own political independence left him open to manipulation by ideologies. He freely admits to conservative views both in politics and in poetry, yet his conservatism was clearly liberal rather than extreme. McAuley, of course, found liberalism too weak and tolerant a philosophical position for the endangered modern world. Where James McAuley endorsed Lionel Trilling's view that the liberal imagination could not produce great art, Hope took up the challenge to create poetry from 'uncommitment'.

Recently, several critics have attacked Hope as the archetype of the academic poet who denies poetic freedom to a younger generation and maintains the narrow beliefs of a literary and political reactionary. John Docker and Andrew Taylor have attacked Hope for his portrayal of the artist as a Nietzschean hero who achieves power through the degradation of women. In his *Snow on the Saltbush* Geoffrey Dutton has characterised Hope as the destroyer of experimental literature in Australia, and of experimental writers themselves in the case of Michael Dransfield. Rodney Hall has quietly reduced the number of Hope poems in his *Collins Book of Australian Poetry* to five compared with John Manifold's nine and Hall's own nine. Clearly, some critics and younger poets see Hope as the champion of a rigid traditionalism which has stifled the development of Australian poetry.[11]

Yet the evidence of Hope's poetry is that he has rejected modernism because of his belief in the importance of the intellect and his perception of modernism as a new orthodoxy. Rather than a dogmatism of his own it is Hope's very determination not to fall victim to dogmas which has led him to denounce the idea of the poet creating from his subconscious mind. At the same time, he is relatively unperturbed by the accusation of sexism because he sees a new dogma in the feminism of the seventies and eighties.

Hope's rejection of commitment stems from a distrust of emotional solutions to human problems. Like McAuley, he saw the communist belief in the goodwill of the Soviet Union as an essentially sentimental attitude. But in Hope's view McAuley's commitment to Catholicism also implied a surrender of the intellect. In poetry, Hope resisted the notion that the emotions are the source of art. The intellect has always been the touchstone for his poetry and he scorns the techniques of modernism because they seem to place personal emotion above intellectual control.

This desire to avoid commitment to causes has led Hope into a commitment to challenge any irrational, comfortable or self-righteous viewpoint. He has continued to defend traditional form in poetry because rigid formal rules force the poet to rely on intellectual rather than emotional responses. Ironically, it is Hope's resistance to ideologies or causes which has made him the champion of traditional form.

Though Hope's choice of traditional form can be seen as a result of his convictions about the importance of the mind, it is also true that he believes that he has little 'lyric gift'. His experiments with automatic and 'stream of consciousness' writing convinced him that he could create poetry only from conscious intellectual effort; unlike Coleridge in Hope's poem 'Persons from Porlock', Hope himself has been bound by Porlock's limitations. So his decision to write in formal modes has been a matter of temperament as well as intellectual choice.

To describe Hope's poetry as formal, traditional and intellectual might suggest that it is merely an antiquarian oddity, an anachronism or even pastiche. However, any comparison of Hope's traditionalism with that of his eighteenth-century models, Pope and Swift, reveals the romantic and modern nature of Hope's attitudes. Pope and Swift believed in the fallen nature of humankind; Swift, in particular, was fighting a rearguard action against the new scientific materialism of his age. Hope, on the other hand, rejects God and religious order as a first premise and he accepts that science has revealed a knowable material universe. Hope's poetry must work within a universe which is not presided over by God and which relies on the human intellect for its knowledge. Where many romantic poets have turned away from science and reason in order to find a source of meaning within themselves Hope has tried to reconcile the scientific approach to the material world and that of the poet.

The formality and impersonalism in Hope's poetry gives it some of the scientist's discipline of objectivity. Hope forces himself to see the human race and the world as they are, no matter how disgusting or hopeless they might be. But the persona behind the formality also registers despair at this vision and it is this despair which puts Hope firmly within a romantic tradition. In this way, Hope's use of traditional form allows him to express a contemporary dilemma. He sets up a tension between formal control and romantic despair, between the rational, objective acceptance of the nature of the world and the emotional, subjective response to that world. Hope's poems are concerned with a contemporary crisis despite their references to the past in form and allusion, and the personality within the poetry is an 'uncommitted modern man' who must challenge easy solutions to his crisis.

The development of Hope's attitude to poetry was a gradual process. The witty satires of his youth gave way to a period of concern with formal art and to a later period of reflection and experiment. And, though Hope began writing with an acceptance of a scientific materialism which took the physical nature of the universe as its first premise, he also became interested in reaching an understanding beyond the physical through his poetry. In fact, Hope's preoccupation with the emptiness of the physical world and interest in the possibility of art as a means of reaching beyond it reflect the concerns of McAuley, Patrick White and numerous critics who saw Australian postwar society as devoid of any awareness beyond the concern for physical well-being. The philosophical materialistic attitude—that the universe was made only of matter and could be known and understood by examining the properties of matter—had links to the popular attitude known as materialism with its concern for money and the purchase of consumer comforts. For, without a non-material world and purpose, the human race could only seek physical comfort and the pleasures which consumer goods—many developed as a result of the success of science—could bring. In Australia, the denial of the non-material had a long history and it lay behind the political commitments of the left. In the absence of a spiritual world, the purpose of humanity was to improve physical conditions. Hope writes from within a society which acknowledges only the physical world and its limits; he is part of Australian postwar existence in ways that McAuley and White, with their eagerness for religious or spiritual comfort, could not be.

Hope's first book of poems, *The Wandering Islands* (1955), contains poems written as much as twenty years before. However, the poems, whether playful satires or cynical enquiries, insist on the emptiness and isolation of modern life. 'Observation Car',

—

A. D. Hope

'Easter Hymn', 'The Ascent into Hell' and 'The Wandering Islands'
announce the sentiments 'I am still on the train', 'There will be
no forgiveness', 'The Rescue will not take place'. In these early
poems, Hope quite deliberately removes the possibility of a loving
God and genuine human affection. He looks at mankind as simply
a complex and most powerful animal. The human body is not
individualised or valuable in itself; it is the skull of 'X-Ray Photograph' or the bones clothed in fat clothed in skin of 'The Return
from the Freudian Islands'.

As Leonie Kramer notes in her study of Hope, 'The End of a
Journey' indicates Hope's tough perception of modern life.[12]
Ulysses, observed with Hope's modern eyes, becomes a suburban
murderer rather than a hero communing with the gods. The
challenges and passions of ancient mythology have been reduced
by a vision informed by modern experience. Hope asks what, in
view of modern attitudes and understanding, has Ulysses achieved?
He is in the end only 'An old man sleeping with his housekeeper'.
Ulysses' tragedy becomes a tragedy of modern life, the reduction
of human status through lack of belief.

But in the title poem of the collection, 'The Wandering Islands',
Hope insists that honesty and intelligence demand such a reduction
of the human role. His islands are the uncommitted, unannexed,
non-national, irreligious, unsocial human beings. They are isolated,
without even the consolation of love, because they 'have never
treated with convenient lies' the nature of love. So the islands are
noble in their refusal to accept the doctrines which console others.
Such honesty, however, brings its own despair.

These early poems reveal Hope's lifelong interest in anthro-
pology, psychology and all sciences which explore the human
condition. He claims to be addicted to 'popular science', the
journalism intent on explaining scientific discoveries to the layman.
And his determination to see the world as it is, without consoling
philosophies, has some of the scientist's pose of objectivity. For
example, he has explained that when composing 'Imperial Adam'
he had in mind the idea of Adam as the king of beasts, the
creature destined to control the rest of creation. Thus, Adam in
the poem is no more than a beautiful and noble beast, waking to
find Eve, to embrace her like the animals and to watch dumbly
like them as she grows pregnant and produces Cain.[13]

As in 'The End of a Journey' Hope looks at the old myth with a
cynical modern intelligence. The problem of evil and the human

105

capacity for sin is not the subject of the poem though it is the whole basis of the biblical story. Hope's Adam and Eve are not responsible for Cain's murderous nature. They do not sin, but are caught up in the horrific implications of human nature. Human sexuality cannot be innocent like that of the 'clean beasts'; murder will be an inescapable feature of all human societies.

The conjunction of sex and murder at the end of 'Imperial Adam' sends readers back to find the moment of the Fall. Usually, they discover that Eve's sexuality causes it: 'sly as the snake she loosed her sinuous thighs'. A residue of Calvinism and its condemnation of women as tempters lies within the poem. But 'Imperial Adam' cannot be classified quite so simply. For the irreverent reference to God in the first stanza hints at the playfulness of the whole poem. Hope is led on by possibilities which the Adam and Eve story presents. He enjoys portraying Eve as a luscious fruit then elaborating the grotesque qualities of the newborn. He may not intend to suggest that sex is evil but he cannot resist ending the poem with a sensational flourish: 'And the first murderer lay upon the earth'.

The key to Hope's presentation of sexuality and the general human condition lies in his imagery. Especially in his early poetry Hope insists that men and women are beasts. He takes evolutionary theory as evidence not that men and women behave *like* beasts but that they *are* no more than the most highly developed animals. This depiction of the human as bestial is not intended to reveal the human fall from the high ideals of civilisation as it does in the satires of Pope or Swift but to assert that bestiality is the true nature of the human—as revealed by scientific evidence. By taking eighteenth-century satires as his models, Hope often appears to be satirising men and women for their animal behaviour when he is actually asserting that humans are no more than animals. In 'The Dinner', 'Massacre of the Innocents', 'Lot and his Daughters', 'Pasiphae' or 'The Young Girl at the Ball' Hope adopts images which Swift or Pope might have used for satire. Hope does not so much criticise humans for their animal natures as acknowledge their reduction in stature because of this.

Hope occasionally does use the human-as-animal figure in straightforward satires. In 'Toast for a Golden Age', for example, Hope has his fellow-creatures celebrate the achievements of 'a middle-aged, middle-brow male of the middle class' who is, after all, but

—

the pensive ape who invented civilization
And lived on his wits at the rest of the World's
expense.

But the generalised man in this poem is not so disgusting as the
particular woman in 'The Dinner' who becomes a carnivorous
animal before the speaker's eyes. In another satire, 'The Brides',
Hope avoids the use of the animal image altogether—the young
women being prepared for marriage are machines, motor cars.
'The Sportsfield' presents lovemaking as that most organised of
human recreations, the football game. Satires such as these are
directed at general modern follies, particularly the loss of 'natural'
or animal instincts, and they use non-animal imagery. It is the
poems without a clear satiric purpose which use predominantly
bestial images.

Hope's early poems criticise human nature in two ways. On the
one hand, he attacks 'Technocratic Man' for his loss of dignity, for
the small-minded, conformist, suburban limits of his life—'The
Kings', 'Sportsfield', 'The Brides', 'The Lingam and the Yoni',
'Conquistador'. On the other he insists that the human is no more
than a 'pensive ape' and emphasises the bestiality of human activities
and appetites. The second is the pose of Swift in *Gulliver's Travels*,
but Hope prefers to use this pose as an image, rather than an
exaggeration, of the human condition. As well he tries to avoid
moral codes by which to arraign bestial humanity. Swift's yahoo
figures gorging themselves on carrion, playing in their own excre-
ment, become, in some of Hope's poems, the true state of man
and woman.

The effect of such a habit of imagery is quite powerful. For it
creates the suggestion of the poetic 'persona' as the only fully
human creature on the face of the earth. The castaway on the
island, the man in the 'Observation Car' or in 'Ascent into Hell' is
alone observing the hideous, inhuman qualities of others. But the
man, if not hideous, is nevertheless detached in observation of
himself. He sees himself as the sum of his physical parts just as
much as the women of the poems. For the loathing of sex and the
obsession with it demean the 'persona' as much as women or the
rest of mankind. The central figure in the poetry is tragic, bereft
of heroic stature, living a life without challenge. He is more
clearly a man of postwar Western society than any other creation
of an Australian poet. This personality is alone, unbelieving, both

—
107

eager for sex and disgusted by it. He is the uncommitted modern man, the man who consoles himself by material pleasures and yet finds no lasting satisfaction and contentment.

Though this figure may be the victim of criticism in some of Hope's poems—the suburban man of 'Conquistador' or 'The Lingam and the Yoni'—he is also noble in witnessing the truth. He recognises the vanity and falsity of religious explanations, political systems or conventional moral codes; he stands apart from commitment. As the fifties progressed the poems show this figure to be more and more clearly the poet himself. Hope's poems of the late forties and fifties accept the scientific, reasoning account of human life which makes human behaviour part of physical processes, but they also register the bleakness of this scientific vision. They ask, 'What meaning can remain for individual life in such an ordered and unmysterious world?'

The early poems which experiment with grotesque imagery and the satiric portrayal of modern humanity may be seen as exercises necessary to Hope's eventual definition of his poetic task. In them he deliberately sweeps aside the consolations of charity, sexual love and the dignity of man's separation from the animals. This reduction of man to a creature of bestial habits is the first step to Hope's discovery of what is essentially human: the creative imagination, the desire for beauty and the willingness to make sacrifices for art.

'An Epistle from Holofernes' displays the growing seriousness of Hope's poetry in the period after the war. It is one of the few poems by Hope which wavers in its allegiance despite, or perhaps because of, being composed over nine years. Its failures give a fascinating insight into Hope's interests at the time. This poem, because it lacks the unity and certainty of direction of most of Hope's work, reveals a great deal about the various claims on the poet's attention. He begins with the sort of biblical myth which gave him so much room for play in 'Imperial Adam'. But the story of Judith and Holofernes is a more complex legend. Judith, without God and the faith of the Jews, is a murderess who uses her sexual beauty to tempt Holofernes to death. Hope emphasises the horror of Judith's act by dramatising Holofernes' threat of revenge from the grave.

This is further complicated by the poem's reference to a modern parallel:

—

A. D. Hope

In Judith you, in Holofernes I
Might know our legend.

But the parallels are not clear; the most significant element of the Judith story seems to be that faith in God gave Judith the strength to act against her nature—and against the accepted codes of female virtue and morality. Hope's lovers do not have such a faith and so cannot feel that certainty which allowed Judith to cut off Holofernes' head.

In the poem Hope moves on to consider the meaning of the myths for modern readers and declares that it is the 'poet's trade' to 'recreate the fables'. The very difficulty which he finds in retelling the story of Judith demonstrates the problems of the poet's task. For Hope, the myths must not be taken on their own terms but related to contemporary life. He must hold both the realities of everyday life and the possibilities of ancient meanings together: 'Vision that keeps the night and saves the day'. In this case, Judith's story with its reversals of morality and conjunction of sexual temptation and death seems to defy any modern retelling. Love is also invoked in this poem as one of the puzzles to be examined by the poet. Later poems such as 'Meditation on a Bone' (1956) and 'An Epistle: Edward Sackville to Venetia Digby' (1959) explore the links between love, particularly frustrated sexual passion, and creativity.

'An Epistle from Holofernes' marks the change from the satirical and playful pieces which gave Hope some notoriety in the forties. But this change was gradual, like the composition of the poem itself, and there are recurrent concerns in all the poetry. The poetic persona in Hope's satires was a general 'modern man' who observed the desperate emptiness of his fellows. In poems such as 'An Epistle from Holofernes' this persona becomes the poet attempting to salvage some explanation from the emptiness.

Several of Hope's most successful poems written during the late forties and fifties identify the poetic task: 'Pyramis or The House of Ascent' (1948), 'William Butler Yeats' (1948), 'Meditation on a Bone' (1956), 'Persons from Porlock' (1956), 'A Letter from Rome' (1958), 'Letter from the Line' (1959), 'An Epistle: Edward Sackville to Venetia Digby' (1959) and in the early sixties, 'Conversation with Calliope' (1962). In these poems, Hope searches for the meaning of poetry and art in general. His poetry begins in a

—

rejection of all ideological comforts, then turns back on itself to examine the possibility of poetry as a source of meaning for life.

'Pyramis or The House of Ascent' reflects on the building of the pyramids and the ruthless will which demanded that other men should die in order to create one fitting burial place, but it goes on to celebrate Blake, Milton and Swift for defying the emptiness beyond their own minds. Hope's pyramid is 'in the waste' just as in other poems he depicts modern life as empty of meaning. The poet must struggle to create art while knowing his own mortality, and even accepting the transience of his art. Hope does not suggest that poetry is a path to immortality but that it is a measure of human aspiration.

Some critics have seen Hope as a Nietzschean artist seeking, through his poetry, to reach a status beyond the possibilities of ordinary men and women. Certainly, the influence of Nietzsche on Hope cannot be denied. Hope celebrates the artistic achievements of the past and he finds some transcendent possibilities for poetry. However, in the poems he does not claim such transcendence for himself. In a poem such as 'Pyramis or the House of Ascent' or 'Meditation on a Bone' the risk of artistic failure is as great as the acknowledgement of the power of the art of the past. Hope recognises that his own poetry and passing may be as unimportant as the death of the bird in the poem of that name. He is writing within the uncertainties of the modern world.

In 'A Letter from Rome' Hope presents a comic version of himself, an ordinary tourist treading the well-worn tourist path. It is an account of the daytime reality, familiar to every modern traveller. But Hope declares other possibilities. This everyday poet locked in the world of museum tours and lectures also manages to experience at Nemi a strange primitive 'impulsion', such as Byron felt there:

> And under this impulsion from the place,
> I seemed constrained, before I came to drink,
> To pour some wine upon the water's face,
> Later, to strip and wade out from the brink.
> Was it a plea for chrism or for grace?
> An expiation? More than these, I think
> I was possessed, and what possessed me there
> Was Europe's oldest ritual of prayer.
> But prayer to whom, for what? The Intervention
> Did not reveal itself or what it meant.

A. D. Hope

The body simply prays without 'intention',
The mind by the bare force of its assent.
That 'higher, more extended comprehension',
Which Byron, writing after the event,
Felt necessary to explain brute fact,
Came by mere power of my consenting act.
Well, let it pass: I have no views about it;...

As usual, Hope has no views, takes no stand about this experience; it is simply 'some link of understanding' or 'intimations'. This is the function of the poet in the modern world: to take part in a 'ritual of prayer' without offering a more ordered and limiting explanation, such as James McAuley might have done through religion or Yeats through his spiral theories of time. Hope declares both romantic and classic intentions, both the individual's intuition of a higher force, and the public poet's recognition of his place among men.

Where in poems such as 'Toast for a Golden Age' Hope attacked the gross materialism and cultural emptiness of the contemporary world, in the later poems he found that, even amid the degradation of modern life, it was possible to feel the workings of a 'higher' force. 'Conversation with Calliope' makes the task of the poet in the modern world even plainer. The corruption of modern culture is inevitable and the poet must live with it. While he cannot achieve the great artistic peaks of the past he may become a toiler on the 'lower slopes' and his role is to 'celebrate and praise' and to create 'new modes of being'.

The earlier poems, with their rejections of the emotional supports which make modern life bearable, may be seen as necessary steps towards Hope's identification of the essential function of poetry. By discarding the possibility of sexual love, religious belief, political commitment, or even the 'civilised' nature of man, Hope narrowed his vision to the one capacity which defined humanity. This was the ability to create new 'orders of being' from existing material through visual arts, music or poetry. Music was Hope's favourite example of this capacity both in his critical essays and later in the poems 'Moschus Moschiferus' and 'Vivaldi, Bird and Angel'. This was the ability which he wished to develop himself, and his finest poems are both about this human capacity and an attempt to achieve it through perfection of form.

In 'Conversation with Calliope' Calliope explains that the creation of 'new modes of being' is analogous to the continuation of the evolution of humanity. The order which they create is beyond the immediate comprehension of men and women, or precise definition by them. Thus, Hope proposes complete freedom for the artist and a role in the progress of the human race. Calliope's analogy is the man who sees colour attempting to convince the colour-blind of its existence.

This search for 'new modes of being' places Hope firmly in a romantic poetic tradition. His lectures on Christopher Brennan, delivered in 1967, show that Hope saw his own affinity with the romantics and the romantic symbolists. Brennan's technique and language is so different from Hope's own that it is surprising to discover Hope's sympathy for Brennan. In the lectures, Hope argued that Brennan interprets Mallarmé's 'Nothingness which is the absolute' as a reaching beyond the human to the superhuman. [14]

To explain the superhuman Hope offers a series of analogies, many of which appear in his own poetry. The quest for the superhuman is like a dog having intuitions of a higher intelligence as expressed in a Mozart concerto; it is like a blind man attempting to understand colour. In the second lecture he explained that this transcendent world can be glimpsed only as an intelligent bird might comprehend a Mozart sonata. Brennan, according to Hope, is reaching for those new modes of being discussed in 'Conversation with Calliope'. Human comprehension of these modes of being is of the same order as the bird's understanding of human music in Hope's poem 'Vivaldi, Bird and Angel'.

The appearance of these ideas in 'Conversation with Calliope' in 1962, in 'Ode on the Death of Pius the Twelfth' in 1965, in 'On an Engraving by Casserius' in 1967 and in 'Vivaldi, Bird and Angel' in 1969 suggest that they are crucial to Hope's poetic thinking throughout the sixties, and, indeed, crucial to the creation of his finest poems. In the Brennan lectures, Hope gives an account of the rise of progressive humanism over the past two hundred years. He describes the new scientific attitudes of the eighteenth century which placed progress in the hands of humanity. However, this 'left man alone in a universe of dead matter and inanimate forces, able to do what he liked in theory, but sadly aware that no matter what he chose to do, he did not matter to anyone but himself. He was a meaningless atom in a completely indifferent universe'. [15]

This vision of the human predicament is apparent in all Hope's early poetry. It is the premise on which his poetry stands. Modern

—

life gives a totally physical and ultimately knowable universe to humankind but it also deprives us of heroic status and meaningful belief. Hope's lecture concludes that the poet must humanise the physical world by the use of the imagination and struggle to glimpse those new modes of being beyond present comprehension. Hope identifies himself with the romantic tradition which he calls a 'tradition of becoming' rather than being. For all his acceptance of the material world, he sees the poet's role as reaching for a knowledge beyond the bounds of the known world.

It is for this reason that Hope refers to a future where new intellectual truth will be discovered in 'On an Engraving by Casserius' or to a Spirit 'past our ken' which can see the triumph of death in 'Ode on the Death of Pius the Twelfth'. Hope does not claim, as James McAuley did, that there is a spiritual order pre-siding over human physical life. However, he does speculate about the existence of an order which can only be understood through the human imagination. The possibility of such an order gives back to poetry a central role in the progress of the human race because it gives the poet a parallel role to that of the scientist; just as the scientist pursues new truth about the material nature of the world, the poet pursues new imaginative truth which is at least as important as scientific truth. Hope followed the famous 'Two cultures' debate of the fifties in which C.P. Snow argued that science and the arts had moved irreconcilably apart; his own proposal for the role of the poet ended such divisions by asserting that the poet's use of language to seek truth was of the same order as the scientist's pursuit of physical truth. He honoured Snow in a comic argument along these lines in 'Poor Charley's Dream' in *A Late Picking* (1975). Poems such as 'An Epistle: Edward Sackville to Venetia Digby', 'Meditation on a Bone', 'The Planctus' sonnets or the 'Ode on the Death of Pius the Twelfth' may be read as Hope's demonstration of the way in which human poetic skills may reach a new order. In his attacks on activism Hope commented that literature has to be 'about something or it is only a gabble of words'. Hope's own poetry is often about the bleakness of the modern world and about the poet's role in such a bleak universe. However, when he moves beyond this struggle of definition and discovery Hope's poetry is clearly about personal emotion—about love and loss. The poet who seemed to dismiss the possibility of sexual love in early poems like 'The Wandering Islands' now proposed sexual love as a source of inspiration. In 'An Epistle:

—

113

Edward Sackville to Venetia Digby' Sackville declares that love is the 'music of the spheres' which has provided him with 'Fresh modes of being'. In 'The Planctus' sonnets the patterns of frustrated love are traced through historical and biblical example. These sonnets demonstrate the range of Hope's interests, learning and technique yet they are openly personal in emotion, so personal that Hope admitted at a reading in 1987 that he did not like to read them in public. Eloise and Abelard offer the historical situation which Hope considers from the point of view of a modern scholar and the poems elaborate a modern and personal situation. However, the sonnets do not succumb to love; like the love of Edward Sackville this love is already lost and ready to be disciplined into artistic form. Hope's modern lover in 'The Planctus', like the lovers in 'An Epistle from Holofernes', cannot place his love and loss within a belief system which will give it meaning. The very lack of belief makes the modern lover more alone and hopeless than Abelard or Abraham could be. In the epigraph to these sonnets, 'Paradise Saved (another version of the Fall)', Hope casts Adam as a man of reason, logic and justice who has refused the forbidden fruit and taken God's part in casting Eve out of the garden of Eden. Adam then discovers that the waste is Paradise, while he has chosen to live immortally as a prisoner of Eden.

As well as expressing the personal anguish of lost love the poem also sets up an opposition between rational judgement and human failing, between reason and emotion. The poet, like Adam, watches the pattern of human feeling from the wall of the Garden of reason, and the whole piece is set in the rigid structure of a sonnet. Hope, like Adam, has chosen reason and order but he watches enviously the emotion beyond the limits of order. As in many of Hope's poems, the formality and intellectual tightness of 'Paradise Saved' measures the loss of feeling so that both elements are held in tension.

It is this tension between the strict order of Hope's poetry and the desire for something beyond order which keeps his best work from becoming facile. When one encounters the range of learning and language skill in a series of sonnets such as 'The Planctus' it is difficult not to define Hope as an academic poet. Yet these poems are possibly Hope's most personal and self-exposing. The learning and the technical control are the means to look out at possibilities beyond themselves. In 'Paradise Saved' Hope seems to recognise the price which he has paid for resisting emotion. Some readers of his poetry find that Hope's formality and constant disguising of his own emotions render his poetry cold and inhumane. Perhaps there is a real fear of emotion behind Hope's evasion of personal feeling. Whatever the case may be, several of the later poems— poems which I believe to be his finest work—recognise that discipline has its losses.

Like 'The Planctus', 'Meditation on a Bone' and 'Sonnets to Baudelaire' also set up tensions between intellectual discipline and human passion, and provide further evidence for Hope's romanticism. Yet he is more widely known for pieces such as 'Imperial Adam' or 'The Double Looking Glass', both of which support the accusations of sexism. It would be pointless to deny that women are often portrayed as objects in Hope's poetry, but those who read him in order to find offence sometimes miss the real direction of the poems. Women are often objects in them simply because the world Hope confronts is utterly material and the reduction of women to things conveys this in a shocking way. In Hope's poetry every offence is calculated.

In *Australian Cultural Elites* John Docker cites 'The Double Looking Glass' as the principal evidence against Hope, but to read this poem without considering the implications of its title, or the way in which the reader is forced to share the voyeur's role with the elders, is to miss Hope's point. Certainly, Susannah's sexual fantasy is a male fantasy imposed on a woman's mind, but this kind of projection and reflection is the point of the poem. One cannot be sure where the sexual act is taking place—in Susannah's, the elders', the poet's or the reader's mind. In the same article, Docker concludes that 'Like James McAuley, Hope is against contraception, abortion, masturbation and, by implication, homo-sexuality', on the scant evidence of 'A Commination'.[16] Docker wants to provide Hope with a moral program, just as some younger poets want to see Hope as insisting that others follow his own poetic prescriptions. Moral, political or literary programs of this kind were precisely what Hope sought to resist. However, his resistance to commitment brought with it distinct limitations in the kind of poetry he could write.

It was unlikely that Hope could escape moral, political and poetic causes in a society where statements of opinion become doctrines and in a language whose every word seems to carry moral suggestion. Nevertheless, far from setting himself up as an anti-abortionist or poetic authoritarian Hope has tried to avoid

---

115

these kinds of commitments. His whole approach to poetry has been an attempt to see things without moral condemnation or emotional distortion, though this may have been at the cost of human passion. Hope's account of Western history in the nineteenth and twentieth centuries suggests that he sees the human intellect ultimately as the destroyer of all meaning and purpose in life. But he refuses to deny the intellect, and his poetry seeks some meaning and purpose through the intellect and the creative imagination.

Hope's pose as 'uncommitted modern man' disguises a complex attitude to society and poetry. In his writing a commitment to learn, accept and explore the nature of the universe emerges from a resistance to commitments which have faith and emotion at their core. This resistance demands a price which is clearly portrayed in Hope's poetry: the solitary figure on the island, or observing humanity from the wall above, suffers for his objectivity.

Because so much of Hope's poetry is cast in terms of myth or historical event it seems to have little direct relevance to the place and time in which it was written. In the fifties Hope scorned the 'pack-horse and the slip rail and the spur' nationalist poetry (though he has unveiled some country poems in the seventies and eighties). He felt no need to display Australianness. But this was partly a reaction to the strong nationalism around him in the postwar years. Hope resisted religion and, to a degree, politics because these were commitments which might destroy his power to see clearly. In the eighties, he is still prepared to mock the 'committed' as his satire on Manning Clark and Patrick White, 'Rough-riders in the chariot', shows.[17]

Hope's notion of the poet striving to create new 'modes of being' beyond ordinary human comprehension gave him a direction and inspiration for his poetry of the late fifties and early sixties. It took him beyond the limited role of the witty satirist and allowed him to find an optimism about human life despite the evidence of human failure. The kind of order Hope proposes is imaginative rather than 'metaphysical' or religious/spiritual: he states again and again that it is like the order created by music and his analogies are always based on knowable scientific phenomena. Similarly, Hope does not suggest that this is a moral order; 'Moschus Moschiferus', one of the most restrained and balanced of the sixties poems, rejoices in the amoral nature of music and the ironies of its celebratory and destructive power.

—

A. D. Hope

Whether or not Hope believed seriously in the idea of the poet contributing to human evolution through the discovery of new modes of being, it was an idea which led to impressive poetic achievements. Yet, at least up to the eighties, Hope has had few imitators in Australia and many poetic opponents. There is a toughness and discipline in Hope's poetry which repels readers who believe that poetry should be lyrical or emotional. His attempts to achieve an amorality often offend feminists in the eighties as they offended moralists in the forties and fifties. Although Hope is the most internationally recognised poet Australia has produced, relatively few critics have written about his work. His refusal to write poetry on Australian subjects may have meant that nationalist critics have overlooked him. As well, his poetry does not conform to the lyrical trend which has made the equally non-nationalist and formal poetry of James McAuley the subject of critical study.

Hope's influence on other poets is also difficult to detect. David Campbell read Hope's *The Cave and the Spring* in the sixties and became excited by Hope's theory that the poet could seek a part in human evolution. For Campbell, this relieved the poet from a belief in God or a religious supernatural order and gave poetry a place on the frontiers of human development. Other poets acknowledge the importance of Hope's support and friendship, in particular, Bruce Dawe, Gwen Harwood, Alan Gould and Mark O'Connor, and it is possible to see similarities in some of their work and the poetry of Hope. However, this does not amount to any clear influence on their work. In fact, Hope's desire to remain uncommitted may have prevented him from taking a position of influence on other writers.

Some younger Australian poets, particularly those such as John Tranter who have adopted a deliberate program of poetic iconoclasm, have denounced Hope's poetry as the epitome of dullness, conservatism and moribund tradition while some of his contemporaries have found his poetry pessimistic, materialistic or lacking in feeling. His reputation stands principally through the admiration of critics and readers who appreciate the intellectual strength and honesty in the poems.

In the context of Australian literature in the fifties and sixties Hope can be seen as representing a poetic equivalent to the burgeoning science of the postwar period. Hope accepted the scientist's orderly, logical approach to the universe, with its need

—

117

to recognise even unpalatable truths about human nature. His poetry reaffirms the patterns of Western logical thought which also lie behind the reasoning of the postwar scientist. Hope's poetry struggles to maintain, at least, the pose of objectivity which is also the pose of the scientist.

In seeking such objectivity Hope declared himself to be an 'uncommitted modern man' who denied the social, national, moral, political or religious commitments of his Australian contemporaries. This denial of commitment meant that Hope has not influenced Australian poetry and criticism as a poet and critic of his standing might have been expected to do. Without a nationalist, moral or social program Hope could not exert the kind of public authority which belonged to committed literary editors such as Clem Christesen or James McAuley.

Nevertheless, Hope's poetry offers a commitment of a different kind, to rational order, to mockery of belief systems, to acceptance of scientific findings about the physical nature of humanity, to recognition of human imperfection. These commitments came from a continual challenge to any views which might claim the force of dogma. In Hope's poetry, we find an attempt to resist the linking of literature and politics, or literature and morality, which were part of the prevailing literary attitudes of the postwar years. Hope scorned the political writing of the socialist realists equally with the moral literary reading of Leavis.

However, Hope's search for some positive role for the poet, as opposed to that of satirist and critic of belief systems, led him to adopt an equivalent role to that of the scientist. In Hope's poetry the rational logic and objectivity of the scientist are displayed, and he developed the idea of the poet seeking new 'modes of being' through the imagination on the basis of analogies with scientific discovery. In some ways, Hope's resistance to political, religious, moral or social commitments was also a withdrawal from the major political and social debates of his time and his poetry represents a deliberate intellectual and emotional distancing from them. On the other hand, this withdrawal can be seen as an appropriate and honest response to the demands of these debates.

The scientist was a hero of the technological advances in the postwar years and, in identifying with science, Hope allied himself to the apparently non-political call for progress. Hope's ideas of progress did not venture much beyond the notion of human evolution through the exercise of the poetic mind, yet the kind of poetry he wrote confirmed a belief in the human intellect and its power to improve the world. This belief in human intellect implied a complacent political view and was in keeping with Hope's declaration that he was a 'conservative sort of chap'.

Other poets were less confident about human intellectual powers, especially when exemplified by scientists, and Hope's attitudes contrasted vividly with those of Judith Wright, who gradually saw technology as an instrument of destruction, as they did with James McAuley who saw all kinds of evils in scientific materialism. Hope did, however, represent a confidence in the intellect which could be found among other Australian professionals in the fifties, and his pose of uncommitment may have been one which most reflects the prevalent attitudes among the Australian intelligentsia in the late fifties and sixties.

5

Douglas Stewart and the *Bulletin*

While James McAuley and A. D. Hope resisted nationalism because of its ideological associations, there remained an interpretation of Australian nationalism which was right-wing rather than radical. In the years after the war it was possible to be a committed nationalist and still reject socialism or a belief in egalitarianism. The experience of war had strengthened the Australian military pride which had first emerged in the First World War and though the Australian soldier might be noted for his larrikin attitude and individualism he was also ready to serve an authoritarian military system. After the Second World War, ex-servicemen whose loyalty to their nation could not be questioned often expressed conservative political views. The RSL version of nationalism was nationalism as surely as the version promoted by the communist socialist realist writers or the radical nationalists.

This conservative kind of nationalism could also claim a link with the nineties legend which sustained the radical nationalists. The magazine which claimed a major part in the nineties legend, the *Bulletin*, had limped on into the 1940s, still declaring 'Australia for the White Man' as its banner, still preserving the jokey, jolly view of the Australian bushman. If this was the true heritage of the egalitarian tradition it was a strange egalitarianism indeed. In the fifties the *Bulletin* cover bore the motto 'Entirely Australian' above a photograph of one of England's stately homes, 'The

Homeland Series from the House of Seppelt'. Inside its pages it gave advice on investment and politics, news on the Australian soldier in war or in the RSL, and jokes about the stupidity of Aborigines, Chinese and women.

Nationalism, in the *Bulletin* terms, meant white racial pride, a bond with Britain and the preservation of the Australian continent from possession by other races. The radical nationalist interpretation of Australian history was not the only interpretation. From the point of view of a postwar *Bulletin* nationalist, the age of squatting had been a pioneering struggle for wealth, the Eureka stockade was a revolt by free-enterprise capitalism, and the European war saw the values of the British Empire flourish anew in Australian manhood. Even the bushranger could be seen as an expression of an adventurous masculinity of a kind which, on the right side of the law, might show forth in military heroism.

Yet by the fifties the *Bulletin* had clearly had its day. If one gets a sense of *déjà vu* when reading the magazine over the ten years before it was bought by Australian Consolidated Press in 1960 it is undoubtedly because the staff adopted the practice of making up new issues from old files.[1] The cartoons, the stories from readers, even the political comment seem to have appeared before. The only change might be the occasional introduction of the television set as a source of laughter as the fifties came to a close. During the war, the *Bulletin*'s light-hearted nationalism had given it popularity, but by 1955 circulation was so low that the magazine failed to show a profit. In 1960 Australian Consolidated Press bought the magazine and merged it with the *Observer* to form the *Bulletin* as we know it today. One link with the nineties was gone.

The change in the *Bulletin* at the end of 1960 can be seen as a reflection of the change in political conservatism in Australia after the war. The inward-looking national pride had gone, to be replaced by the international, progress-oriented style of Australia's very own version of *Time* magazine. Where the old *Bulletin* defined Australia by reference to Britain, the new *Bulletin* looked to America as its guide. The new *Bulletin* catered to the new kind of Australian—the new 'ideal' man of the professional and commercial world who claimed no connection with the Bush. In his first editorial for the revamped *Bulletin* Donald Horne commented that Australia was 'now a country of revolutionary change' both socially and culturally.[2] The old backward-looking conservatism had become irrelevant.

As the old *Bulletin* stumbled towards collapse one tradition had been maintained with a degree of energy. Douglas Stewart became editor of the 'Red Page' in 1940 and his weekly comments on writing remained important in the Australian literary community right up to 1960. For the *Bulletin*'s weekly appearance made it a major vehicle for poetry, short stories and reviews in the forties and fifties. Stewart published most of the emerging poets of this period including Kenneth Mackenzie, John Blight, Rosemary Dobson, Francis Webb and Chris Wallace-Crabbe. With Ronald McCuaig, Stewart selected stories by Hal Porter, Brian James, R.S. Porteous, Gavin Casey and others for publication and praise.

Douglas Stewart read the work of most of his Australian contemporaries though he favoured the non-academic and the politically uncommitted writers. As literary editor he could offer advice and encouragement to writers, even of his own generation, such as David Campbell and Judith Wright. Campbell once commented on Stewart's role as editor: 'I appreciated Doug's conservative, well-informed criticism. We were lucky to have him on the *Bulletin* taking a middle line—not avant garde, not too staid.'[3]

Stewart's critical ideas were guided by his awareness of a general audience. His conservatism reflected his ideal of poetry for the people—an ideal shared by the left. He could not be 'avant garde' because, to Stewart, this meant support of obscurity, of poetry for poets. If he was 'not too staid', it was because he was interested in finding a poetic voice for his times. In 1949, Stewart wrote of Campbell's poetry:

> Because it shows what can be done by pure artistry with an Australian imagery springing naturally to the lips *Speak With the Sun* has an importance beyond its immediate attraction as a book: it points to the way along which not only David Campbell's poetry but Australian poetry as a whole will probably develop. It is a deepening of the ballad tradition into poetry; surely the natural and inevitable poetic speech of this continent...[4]

Stewart's interest in the bush ballads and Australian imagery was part of a belief that they would form the natural language of a poetry both accessible and serious. In an interview with John Thompson in 1965, he recalled that at school the balladists were the only poets liked by his fellows:

> from that I got a very distinct impression that school children perhaps in Australia should always be given Paterson and the balladists, because if that's all they can appreciate, well, they might as well at

least have that; and it wouldn't be a very long step from that to lead
them on to Judith Wright or David Campbell or somebody who's
rather close to the balladists today.[5]

Stewart was aware that poetry had lost a popular audience but he
was nevertheless determined to write poetry which might appeal
to popular tastes. He admired Paterson and C.J. Dennis, not so
much for their poetry, but for their ability to win audiences—
proof that ordinary, uneducated people could enjoy verse when it
dealt unpretentiously with their own interests.

Stewart's criticism for the *Bulletin* reflected his desire to appeal
to a general reader rather than a particularly educated audience.
He set out to entertain readers and might employ a Shean and
Gallagher dialogue, a letter to Shakespeare or an anecdote to
sweeten the bitter pill of literary discussion. Stewart scorned
pretentiousness; his pose is that of the non-academic reader, and
obscure prose and poetry are always dismissed. As a result his
reviews turn away from any intellectual issues. Stewart assumed
that his readers were not interested in critical discussion which
made intellectual demands upon them. He implied that a healthy
anti-intellectualism was appropriate to Australian readers and
critics.

Stewart's nationalism was in keeping with the journal for which
he worked. He did not reveal racial prejudice in his reviews, but
he kept clear of the depths of intellectual discussion which might
seem un-Australian, consistently dismissed modernist literature
and offered only what he saw as a 'Rabelaisian' attitude to sex. In
his poetry, Stewart avoided sexual subjects with a strange timidity
for a man who so often claimed love of the bawdy in literature and
the visual arts. Often Stewart allowed Norman Lindsay to express
his views on racial and sexual superiority on the Red Page or he
gave the column to M.H. Ellis for his attacks on the left.

It is difficult to see any immediate connection between Norman
Lindsay's paintings of aggressively naked women in classical or
mythological setting and Douglas Stewart's poetry of the Australian
landscape. But Stewart's admiration for Lindsay began before a
personal meeting, when as a youth in New Zealand he discovered
Redheap:

We hungered for revolution—anything that would help to destroy
adult authority and remove from us the icy prospects of having to work
for our living. There wasn't anything actually political in *Redheap*, but

it proclaimed the freedom of sex, it stood for the wildness and the mutinousness of youth, and the glorious Mr. Bandparts hurled Christianity and most of the established moralities of the world superbly out the window with his cocoa. It was our *Das Kapital* (and a great deal easier to read)...[6]

Stewart responded to Lindsay's call for a sexually free, more passionate life; it was an attitude which Buckley called 'vitalism' in his *Quadrant* article on Australian nationalism. The aside 'and a great deal easier to read' was typically Stewart. In poetry and criticism Stewart has one eye on his audience lest he lose its sympathy by being too 'intellectual'. Stewart faced the constant dilemma of a serious artist who wished to be popular.

Redheap proposed a strange sort of revolution. It was not a political change but merely 'the mutinousness of youth'. Stewart himself never wrote anything which proclaimed sexual freedom; but then, Lindsay's own sexual stand had elements of a Calvinist fear and condemnation of women as sexual tempters. Stewart met Lindsay when he began work for the *Bulletin* at the end of the thirties and their close friendship lasted until Lindsay's death in 1969. In the twenties, Lindsay had propounded his own version of Nietzsche in his *Creative Effort* (1920) and several writers, including his son Jack, were enthusiastic about its theory of the artist as a godlike figure free from the restraints on other men. *Creative Effort* also claimed white racial superiority and the artistic and intellectual superiority of the male sex. In 1923 Jack Lindsay with Norman, Hugh McCrae and Kenneth Slessor had established a short-lived journal, *Vision*, to act on Norman's theories and initiate a European cultural renaissance in Australia. Norman's paintings and the poems and short stories published in *Vision* avoided Australian realism. The writers took their subjects from myth or fantastic worlds of their own creation. Their efforts were directly opposed to the 'slip-rail and the spur' kind of Australian writing but, at the same time, they were isolationist in attitude. Australia was the centre of their world as surely as if they had written and painted of wattle and kookaburra. The group had little knowledge or interest in contemporary European art; Norman Lindsay, for example, had scorned the poetry of T.S. Eliot and regarded modern painting as infantile. To Norman Lindsay, Europe was the source of corruption in art and in life. Decadent Europe had wasted the lives of young Australians in its foolish war; Austra-

—

lian artists must rescue the best of European culture so that it might flourish in an uncorrupted environment.[7]

Though Lindsay came to reject *Creative Effort* in later life, it can be seen that certain features of his philosophy were enshrined in the old *Bulletin* where he worked as cartoonist for almost all of its twentieth-century life. Here they were clothed in the distinctive Australian features of the bushman or the returned serviceman. Douglas Stewart, coming to Sydney long after the demise of *Vision*, found its cultural renaissance ideas ridiculous but supported the notion of freedom from conventional morality and the role of the artist in expressing the intensity of life.

In the forties, he explained his admiration for Norman Lindsay: 'It is beyond question that the majority of Australian writers—and especially the poets—have accepted him from the beginning not only as an artist but as the fountain-head of Australian culture in our time'.[8] This was, at least, a highly questionable statement— Stewart had taken his own admiration as universal. He found that the reasons for this so-called acceptance lay not only in Lindsay's extraordinary personality but in the quality of his painting. He claimed that Lindsay's beautiful women achieved a spiritual per-fection; at his best, Lindsay painted goddesses, women so perfect and unattainable as to have a religious significance:

> To do this, to reveal the spirit shining white or glowing dark through the flesh of man and woman, is the supreme achievement in art. And it is, particularly, the task and the burden of the poet. All the arts, as far as I can see, have one great purpose: to reveal the existence of spirit. The art of the novelist, which is essentially an art of humour, reveals spirit chiefly by implication: the 'message' of the great humorists such as Fielding and Dickens (and, incidentally, of Norman Lindsay's comedies in paint) is that we might as well enjoy the comedy of life while we are living it, for it is *only a passing show*. The higher arts of poetry, painting and music bring the world of spirit to us by direct revelation.
>
> Sometimes poetry and painting talk to us in the language of pantheism: the art of Wordsworth and the art of a Hilder revealing the beauty of nature, showing that the earth itself is spirit or is visited by spirit. When a nature poet such as W.H. Davies brings us a tree that stands still in the moonlight 'with all his million leaves', time itself seems to stop still; we are in the presence of eternity. Sometimes the revelation is mystical, and we have the early religious painters that Powys wrote about or the poetry of a Blake or an Eliot: direct assertion of the existence of spirit.[9]

125

To an observer in the 1980s this judgement seems extraordinary. Lindsay's women, even when painted or etched with technical skill, have a monstrous quality about them. Far from representing the 'perfect woman' or an ideal of femininity they offer a challenge to the male observer; their lewd eyes suggest a destructive power or they pretend modesty as a device for sexual tantalisation. Humphrey McQueen has commented that these women were never intended to be women but sirens, only partly human in form, and points to the imaginative power which invented them.[10] But this does not answer the disquieting feeling that Lindsay, the *Bulletin* cartoonist, is unable to register humanity when he becomes Lindsay, the artist. A.D. Hope finds that Lindsay's women have a disturbing likeness to the Gibson girls, that they are essentially vulgar pin-ups.

Whatever one may think of Lindsay's women, the idea that they express 'spirit shining white or glowing dark through the flesh' remains odd. Stewart's judgement seems clouded by his personal relationship with Lindsay, and Stewart's poetry cannot be seen as any sort of poetic reflection of Lindsay's painting. His chosen 'pathway to the gods' would carefully avoid the female body. It was the safer path of Wordsworth, Hilder and Davies.

Vincent Buckley and, more recently, John Docker have seen a likeness between Lindsay's use of women in art and that of A.D. Hope in his poetry.[11] This, of course, forms part of Docker's attack on Hope. In his *Australian Cultural Elites* Docker does not give any attention to Stewart's poetry and attitudes and he seems to accept A.A. Phillips' view that Stewart is exceptional among the Lindsayites.[12] It is perhaps a moot point whether the artist who sees sexuality and woman as a means to transcendence does women a greater injustice than the artist who refuses to contemplate woman and sexuality at all.

Stewart, of course, belongs to the second group and so shares attitudes with the nationalist writers and his socialist realist contemporaries. If one applies a feminist critique to any of the political groupings of the fifties, the political differences tend to break down. And it must be made clear that in the fifties the Lindsayites suspected Hope because he did not seem to be reaching beyond the physical world.[13] Where Lindsay and Stewart tried to give mythological status to contemporary humanity, they saw Hope as reducing human status to the merely physical.

Norman Lindsay's philosophy of art offends the sensibilities

126

of many Australians today. His theories of race superiority, for
example, seem related to Hitler's justification for racial murder.
His campaign for sexual freedom, though supported by many as a
blow against wowserism in Australia, was related to his idea of the
male artist beyond the confinements of morality. Jack Lindsay
has recalled that, though he supported his father's attack on the
wowsers in the pen drawing *The Crucified Venus*, he could not
but see that it was his own mother on the cross and that Norman
had been one of her crucifiers in fact.[14] Sexual freedom in Norman's
terms was male sexual freedom. Norman Lindsay's influence
emerged in the fifties in the peculiar racism of Kenneth Mackenzie's
The Refuge, but Douglas Stewart made it part of an individual
approach to poetry.

To see life passionately was to see love and cruelty hand in
hand. The artist measured the extremes of human emotion and
need show no responsibility to society at large. Stewart brought
these notions to his own interpretation of the poet's role as the
man of feeling who spoke in the voice of ordinary men about the
world which they knew. Though he defended Hugh McCrae's
poetry of satyrs and nymphs at every opportunity and shared
Norman Lindsay's views on the basis of art, Stewart believed that
the poet must appeal to the tastes of his contemporaries.

Stewart expressed an opposition to modernism which was in
keeping with his attitude to life. In a long article, 'Escapes from
Art' (1942), he listed three major dangers to contemporary poetry.[15]
The first of these was the notion that an age of 'chaos and despair'
such as the war years could produce only poetry which was 'chaotic
and despairing'. He called the second danger 'Freudian Obscurity'
but this was simply the recourse to personalism, the poet's concentration on the state of his own mind. The third danger was the
'Leftist movement' which proposed 'a sentimental belief in the
immediate perfectibility of mankind by way of slaughtering the
middle classes'. Stewart, like Hope, admitted that many major
artistic works had been achieved by poets with political commitments, but these 'aesthetically convincing' poems had succeeded
despite their 'debatable' politics:

> The 'suspension of disbelief' always operating to make acceptable
> artistically works that might politically be unacceptable, there would
> be no difficulty in approving aesthetically of the verses or novels of the
> left if they were written with that 'delight', tragic or joyous, which, one

agrees with Matthew Arnold, is the ultimate test of excellence of a work of art.[16]

The purpose of art was 'to reveal the existence of the spirit'; the criterion of excellence was 'delight'. Stewart regarded the imperfectibility of man as a reason for rejoicing. Novelists should 'paint the human comedy', poets express the deeper meaning of an incongruous and fascinating experience.

Stewart's book reviews for the Red Page were consistent with this view. He preferred novels such as Eve Langley's *The Pea-pickers* or Lawson Glassop's *We Were Rats* for their gaiety and courage to more serious or political works. He enjoyed *Such is Life* by reading it as a human comedy rather than a political contemplation and he thought that *Rigby's Romance* had been destroyed by the re-introduction of Rigby's long speech on socialism.

Stewart's attitude to the role of art in society is evident in the work he produced in the forties and fifties. In the war years he wrote *Elegy for an Airman* (1940) and *Sonnets to the Unknown Soldier* (1941), and the verse plays *Ned Kelly* (1943) and *The Fire on the Snow* (1944). The series of poems *Glencöe* was published in 1947, in the years of recovery from war.[17]

Fire on the Snow dramatises man's continual challenge to nature. In this play Scott, the Antarctic explorer, leads his men into unnecessary and eventually pointless suffering which nevertheless shows a kind of human triumph. Scott tells Wilson:

A man must learn
To endure agony, to endure and endure again
Until agony itself is beaten out into joy.

This is Stewart's passionate life. The life of the individual achieves value by the intensity of that life.

Ned Kelly, too, contrasted the conventional, insipid lives of the bank clerk and the schoolteacher with the wild, adventurous existence chosen by Ned and his gang. Stewart's version of Ned Kelly's story takes little account of the social situation of Kelly, or any of the features which have made Kelly the hero of some socialists. Kelly is Stewart's hero because he has escaped the restrictions of a moral and social order; he has chosen to live, and inevitably die, passionately. Once again, adventure and death are romantic pursuits. Stewart adapts his vitalism to the spirit of the warrior.

Stewart claimed that *Shipwreck* was his response to the Japanese

advances in the Pacific and news of conditions in Changi prison.[18]
Like *Ned Kelly* and his other play *The Golden Lover*, *Shipwreck*
presents two orders of existence, the orderly, tedious life where
the limits of human possibility can never be tested in action, and
the adventurous and dangerous life where man's relationship to
the gods can be sought. The enclosed cruelty of the camp of the
survivors of the shipwrecked *Batavia* may bear some resemblance
to the sufferings at Changi prison, but Douglas Stewart's answer
to such suffering appears to be acceptance. Pelsart's final comment
takes cruelty as a price for action:

> I cannot pity you, prisoner; but sometimes, my friends,
> I am sorry for the race of man, trapped on this planet.
> A man alive must act, must think and do,
> And stand to a harsh judgement for what he does.
> Decision, action, judgement.

If one reads this in the context of the sufferings in Changi prison
or along the Burma railway it may seem glib and inhumane.

As comments on the realities of Australian life in the forties,
Stewart's plays are most comfortable with the notion of masculine
action and heroism. Ned Kelly, the romantic hero, might be seen
as an image of Australian heroism appropriate to a time when
young Australians were setting off, once again, to battle. Scott of
the Antarctic provides a further vision of heroism in the face of
physical pain and death. But it is a clean kind of heroism far from
the realities of death at the hands of war. We can read the plays as
Stewart's attempt to put realities into historical perspective for his
audience. So it is that unbearable miseries were inflicted by the
Batavia mutineers and suffered by Australian prisoners at Changi.
By versifying the events of the past, by presenting them in a form
which has dignity and grandeur, Stewart was performing one of
the tasks which he saw for the contemporary poet. He was providing a parallel for contemporary events which transformed them
into 'significant actions' and gave them stature.

Where a poet such as A.D. Hope could look to the heroic myths
as a mockery of contemporary human status, Stewart worked to
make new myths which gave a nobility to his contemporaries and
their struggles. So Ned Kelly, Captain Scott and Cornelius
demonstrated a courage which embraced death as the price of life.
In *Shipwreck*, however, Stewart's hero reached death by a path

—

of brutality. In conjunction with the real brutality of wartime imprisonment its solutions appear too easy.

John Manifold, the dedicated communist poet, shares a striking range of interests with Douglas Stewart. Like Stewart he admired 'Banjo' Paterson's verse and experimented with the ballad. Like Stewart, and Paterson before them both, he collected bush ballads and songs. Stewart edited two books of ballads with Nancy Keesing in the fifties—*Australian Bush Ballads* and *Old Bush Songs*, a revision of Paterson's original collection. Manifold published the study *Who Wrote the Ballads?* and *The Penguin Australian Song Book* anthology in the sixties.[19] When one encounters two poets with such a similarity of interests and poetic objectives living in a small literary community it is impossible not to wonder that they did not contact each other and, perhaps, offer some mutual support. Manifold and Stewart even had a mutual friend in David Campbell.

However, Manifold's communism made him an outcast during the fifties. Rodney Hall has claimed, with some force, that the literary establishment (and he specifically names the *Bulletin* and the Lindsayites, though not Stewart) found a Cambridge-educated communist beyond their range of interests.[20] In short, it appears that the political rigidities of the fifties made any recognition of Manifold's and Stewart's common interests an impossibility.

But the comparison between the two poets has further interest. While Stewart was writing *Ned Kelly* as a verse play, Manifold was producing *The Death of Ned Kelly and other ballads*. The bushranger is one of Manifold's favourite subjects but, true to his political vision, the bushranger, and Ned Kelly in particular, is a hero of revolution and social change. Manifold's ballad ends with the sentiment: 'It's a thousand like Ned Kelly who'll hoist the Flag of Stars'. Stewart's Ned Kelly is a hero of a different kind, a man with the courage to defy the conformist existence which binds ordinary men. This hero has no program for social reform.

In Manifold's most famous poem 'The Tomb of Lt John Learmonth, A.I.F.' Learmonth dies with a bushranger's courage crying 'They'll never capture me alive'. This poem expresses a proud nationalism without Manifold's usual reference to social morals—'There is no moral, that's the point of it', he writes. Once again, Manifold comes close to Stewart's attitude to nationalism. And, perhaps, Manifold's early admiration for one of Stewart's models,

Roy Campbell, provides a further link between the different political positions. Certainly, if Manifold's elegy is read alongside Stewart's 'Elegy for an Airman' Manifold, not Stewart, emerges as the poet of action and romantic death.

When Stewart writes a play such as *Fire on the Snow* which offers a romantic hero venturing out to suffer and eventually die, it is also possible to see some similarity with Patrick White's *Voss*, written ten years later. Stewart's Scott sets himself a task which necessitates suffering and death—we know from the beginning of the play that the outcome will be failure. And the force of the play comes from the poetry. Stewart contrasts the painful cold and the warmth of human aspiration, the infinite expanse of white snow and the transience of human life, the eerie beauty of the Antarctic landscape and the extremes of human suffering.

In *Voss* White chooses a similar subject—the explorer who fails physically but triumphs in will—and the desert, like Stewart's icy wastes, creates images of hallucinatory experience. *Voss* is much more a work of the imagination than *Fire on the Snow*; Leichhardt and Eyre are the inspiration for White's novel rather than references, while Stewart creates his poetry from Scott's journal. In a strange reversal of expectations White's novel is free to create archetypal figures while Stewart must work from the experiences of real men.

Stewart was one of the dingoes who began to howl when *Voss* appeared in 1957, and his review in the *Bulletin* demonstrates some of the real dilemmas created by Stewart's notions of the roles of poetry and prose. The heading of the review, 'The Big Boss Voss', must have angered White quite as much as its contents. But the contents, too, could not move beyond the obstacle of 'mysticism'. Stewart resorted to personal taste to explain his resistance to White's novel: 'This may be unkind, or uncultured; but none of my favourite novelists from Petronius to Fielding and Dickens ever bothers his readers with mysticism, or even by going in for too many exquisite subtleties of thought and feeling: they just paint the human comedy...' Stewart felt that mysticism was the proper preserve of poetry and it did not belong in the novel. He also criticised White, with some justice, for failing in the portrayal of ordinary reality.[21]

Certainly, there is more ordinary reality in *Fire on the Snow*, despite its form, than in *Voss*. Stewart claimed that the poet's role

—

was to express 'spirit', but his own writing implied that spirit might be no more than the human power to survive or die gloriously. When Stewart wrote about spirit he meant little more than the poet's ability to ennoble the actions of men (again it seems inappropriate to include women) to make them gods.

In 1947 he published *Glencöe*, a series of ballads and variations on the ballad form, which narrated the story of the massacre of the Macdonald clan. Once again, a kind of appropriateness can be found for the poems: the horrors of the Nazi concentration camps were being revealed to the world as Stewart wrote about the destruction of a Scottish clan. Stewart may not have consciously taken on the task of transforming the holocaust by putting it into the perspective of clan history and the set of poems may have been inspired simply by the aftermath of a devastating world war. Nevertheless, the poems show Stewart's conception of the role of the poet in his society: the brutality of Scots warfare can be made into a beautiful work of art. The lesson for postwar society is that the perspective of history and the detachment of art can make even the most painful human events into a mythology greater than the moment.

In *Glencöe* Stewart's convictions about the Scottish border ballad as the great popular form were put to the test. He demonstrated his own ability to vary the form , to provide both strong narrative and lyrical motif. The clansmen, with their code of honour and bravery, fit Stewart's notion of the hero, while their opponents show deception and petty greed. But Stewart's celebration of struggle and death moves inevitably to acceptance:

Oh, life is fierce and wild
And the heart of the earth is stone,
And the hand of a murdered child
Will not bear thinking on.
Sigh, wind in the pine,
Cover it over with snow;
But terrible things were done
Long, long ago.

Things which do 'not bear thinking on' must be covered over. In Stewart's hands atrocity becomes an essential element of life; his poetry is a means of accepting the imperfection of life, and even creating 'joy' from it.

Stewart's habitual response is to turn away from the implications of human suffering. According to Nancy Keesing he wrote the poem 'B Flat', which concentrates on man's quest for harmless knowledge, as his reaction to the declaration of war between India and Pakistan in 1965.[22] Throughout his poetic career Stewart asserted that man would triumph against man-made disasters ('B Flat'), death ('At Circular Quay') or even atomic warfare ('Rutherford'). In this way, much of Stewart's poetry can be seen as response to social and political events of his time, but Stewart's impulse is to ennoble these events in order to make them bearable and to escape from their implications.

It is easy to criticise Stewart for not being Patrick White, but his determination to remain accessible to 'ordinary' readers placed heavy limitations upon his poetry. This determination was admirable in itself; the loss of an audience for poetry is, after all, the most obvious feature of contemporary poetry publishing. Within Stewart's self-imposed limitations his achievements were notable. His *Sun Orchids* poems, in particular, explored new areas which led the way for other Australian nature poets. A number of the poets of the eighties pay homage to David Campbell as the poet who renewed the possibilities of Australian nature poetry, but Stewart was also exploring new possibilities and his movement to the lyric of small objects must be seen as innovative.

Most of Stewart's best poetry may be found in *Sun Orchids* published in 1952 and *The Birdsville Track* published in 1955. In his earlier nature poems, Stewart liked to develop imaginative fancies about the natural world. He might, for example, personify a native animal or create an amusing or threatening interpretation of nature by exaggerating one or other of its features. In these early poems, the poet dominates the subject by insisting on his own clearly distorted vision of reality.

In *Sun Orchids* Stewart avoids these fanciful poetic fictions. Instead, he chooses the small details of nature and concentrates on close observation and reflection. Here Stewart appears to find meaning from his observation of the natural world rather than imposing meaning upon it. By turning away from the heroism of man in action, Stewart approaches a humbler and, ironically, more ambitious task. Through the small elements of nature he contemplates the source of life itself.

Bearing in mind Stewart's view that the function of poetry is to reveal the existence of spirit, 'Nodding Greenhood', 'The Gully', 'A Robin', 'The Goldfish Pool', 'The Green Centipede' and 'Kindred' must be considered among the most important of the collection. These are the poems in which Stewart comes closest to the mystery. The 'globe of silence' in the greenhood orchid contains the source of life; the tiny flower is seen as the bearer of the same creative power which man has developed through his history and which has created as well the entire natural world. In observing the tiny features of the natural world Stewart seeks the essential beginning of life, the cause of all creation and therefore, the central meaning of all life.

But in 'The Gully' the mysterious source of life is also death's source, as the pink trigger-flower reaches out in the embrace of love to strike the bee. Life means hunger and, therefore, death. Elements of Norman Lindsay's philosophical attitude are beginning to appear. Love and cruelty are the primitive complements which make up natural life in the gully.

'The Green Centipede' finds universal meanings in the discovery of the stinging centipede under a cassia bush. Stewart implicates an underground source of life in this poem:

> Down where all rivers meet
> Deep under stony ground

which produces the yellow of the cassia flowers to light 'the whole universe' and, in the same way, the beautiful centipede which will sting on touch. Man appears, at first, to stand outside the poem; the poet seems a detached observer. But, of course, it is a human whose hand will be burnt by touching the cassia bush with the centipede beneath. Man sees the beauty and the danger, so that the suggestion of the mysterious underground source of life cannot be observation but a human need for explanation.

In 'The Goldfish Pool' the persona is obvious and important; for it is the watching human who turns the 'water-scorpion' into a devil and observes him threatening the pleasing pond full of 'suns and scaly moons'. Looking through 'the eye of God' the observer is unsure whether to rejoice or regret the nature of the universe. But, in keeping with Stewart's proclaimed love of life, he decides that 'all was well'.

Stewart's presentation of the human as the god of this small world is nowhere more apparent than in the poem 'To Lie on the Grass' where a human observer watches the ants and grasshoppers with amused detachment and then senses other eyes watching him from above. It is not an argument that there is a god and, if

God exists, Stewart suggests that he is 'indifferent and amused' by human struggle. Clearly, a human is at the centre of the *Sun Orchids* poems. It is a human who feels dejection or joy because of the colours of the bush or the bird. Stewart makes it clear that only a human can give moral roles to the insects who stalk each other in his goldfish pool. But this human is detached—he will not interfere with the natural world.

Stewart could have developed these observations into full-blown melodramas of struggle in the natural world but, by and large, he resists the temptation in *Sun Orchids*. The extraordinary achievement of the poems is the way in which Stewart disciplines his tendency to romantic fancy so that natural things appear both beautiful and evil as essential components of their own and all nature.

This apparent search for meaning is also evident in some of the poems published in *The Birdsville Track*. 'Mosquito Orchid', 'Bird's-eye', 'Everlasting' and 'The Snow-gum' contact the infinite by observation of the flower, animal or tree. When the orchid stings or the snake rears up to strike, the poet feels that the whole universe threatens him. 'Everlasting' takes the flower's mimickry of the sun as evidence 'That earth and heaven chime as one'; Stewart seems to make a decision that the universe is an ordered creation, such as man as God would create.

'The Snow-gum' is perhaps Stewart's most complete attempt to reveal spirit. For an instant the tree provides a perfect shadow on the snow, and tree and shadow become images of all natural and created beauty. It is as if the noon-light, the bitter cold which brings the snow and the tree, perfect in itself, have deliberately conspired to provide the perfection of the moment. Yet we are told no more: 'Something is done on the snow'. The universe has an order, its bitterness and cruelty produce passing moments of ecstatic beauty, but this does not lead to any discovery of the human role in the universe or the existence of God.

Instead, Stewart suggests that the image of an image is the closest we may come to understanding. He offers us the perfection of the shadow, the perfection of the tree which it reflects and the perfection of the poem as an image of both. Just as the shadow suggests some perfect order, so the poem reflects that order. In 'Brindabella' Stewart is even less specific about the universe's meaning. His 'I' is an observer of nature who listens but does not pretend to know the full meaning of what he hears. The song of the mountain in this poem is a song of 'being' not of purpose and Stewart, as poet, has no greater role than that of the magpie:

> Then it was, struck with wonder at this soliloquy,
> The magpie lifting his beak by the frozen fern
> Sent out one ray of a carol, softened and silvery,
> Strange through the trees as sunlight's pale return,
> Then cocked his black head and listened, hunched from the cold,
> Watching that white whisper fill his green world.[23]

In poems of this kind Stewart seems to be rediscovering John Shaw Neilson as the model for Australian poetry—the lyricist rather than the balladist. In the sixties and seventies James McAuley and Judith Wright could also be found writing nature lyrics which attempted to erase the ego of the poet and the poet's tendency to intellectualise. In particular, poems such as McAuley's 'Numbers and Makes' of *Surprises of the Sun* (1969) and the poems of *A World of its Own* (1977) and the poems of Wright's *Birds* (1962) seemed to follow Stewart's lead in creating lyrics which did not force interpretations onto the natural or social world.

Stewart developed from a kind of postwar 'Banjo' Paterson to a lyricist, and, in doing so, he sounded out a new direction for a range of other Australian poets. Stewart has been a popular poet in Australian schools because he has demonstrated that poetry can be accessible, entertaining and related to the familiar world. This has been his aim as a poet and it is no mean achievement. Yet, for all their skill, humour and buoyancy the poems can be unsatisfying because they concentrate so steadfastly on the non-human world or they move all human action onto the plane of mythology. Stewart's impersonalism is much greater than that of Hope or McAuley whose personalities ironically emerge in their poetry through the various subterfuges they employ to hide themselves. His critics, from Vincent Buckley in the fifties to Paul Kavanagh and Dennis Robinson in the eighties, have felt it necessary to remark on the limitations to Stewart's art.[24] Where Buckley found Stewart unable to separate the human from other levels of the natural world, Robinson has noted that Stewart's detachment prevents him from submitting fully to the powers of nature. Paul Kavanagh sees Stewart as consciously turning away from the full range of experience in order to concentrate only on the more noble aspects of human existence. Stewart deliberately limited his art to aspects of the universe which were manageable. The detach-

—

ment from nature and the interest in information about it, which Robinson discusses, seem part of an unwillingness to take risks with his own imagination. Nevertheless, many readers will agree with Paul Kavanagh that these limitations may be overlooked in the enjoyment of Stewart's intelligence, his technical command of his art and his optimism.

By the late fifties and sixties Stewart's desire to entertain and to tell stories led him to new subjects. 'The Silkworms' demonstrated that Stewart could write the kind of satire favoured by A.D. Hope, but characteristically Stewart looked down on conformist lives and chided them for unadventurousness, while Hope might look despairingly up from conformist existence. In *Rutherford* Stewart found that scientists were the adventurers of the modern age—whether the ridiculous Professor Piccard or Rutherford splitting the atom.

Progress, the cry of the fifties, was a fact which the *Bulletin* poet had to face. In 'Rutherford' he contemplated the destructive power of the atom and he saw clearly the way in which history had turned knowledge to evil purposes. Stewart's Rutherford consoles himself with the belief that 'not all men were savages', though we know that the scientists so trusted by Rutherford did offer their destructive skills to the 'conscience of the tribe'. Stewart clings to the good which accompanies evil as the source of optimism in a nuclear age. Perhaps his 'The Man from Adaminaby' gave a truer picture of Stewart's view of progress. This traveller (with some taste) rejects the new town and rides into the water to drink at the pub of old Adaminaby, flooded for the Snowy Mountains Scheme.

This flooding by progress was certainly the fate of Stewart's magazine, the old *Bulletin*. After its demise, Stewart concentrated on his work for Angus & Robertson, selecting and editing manuscripts. This is the third area in which Stewart influenced Australian writing in the period after the war. Like the *Bulletin*, Angus & Robertson was an institution without left political sympathies which was committed to nationalism, in that it was the largest and most established publisher of Australian literature. It was interested in selling books and so had a vested interest in writers who were accessible and likely to be popular.

Stewart's advice undoubtedly benefited the publishers in the forties and fifties and helped them acquire the copyrights of many Australian 'classics'. Stewart's favourite Australian contemporaries— Brian James, Kenneth Mackenzie, Judith Wright, Eve Langley

—

and Dal Stivens—were among those published by Angus & Robertson in the fifties. By the end of the sixties Angus & Robertson were able to produce a paperback Australian classic series which had some justification for the name: Miles Franklin, Frank Dalby Davison, Katherine Susannah Prichard and Marcus Clarke had been added to the Angus & Robertson stable.

So, while the communists and their sympathisers were attempting to retrieve the Australian tradition for a new generation, Stewart and the publishing firm for which he worked promoted a similar ideal. The Australasian Book Society tried to establish a supply of good Australian books for Australians to read, but it was Angus & Robertson, without a political program, which succeeded in doing this. Stewart's dislike of politics in literature did not prevent him from seeing the value of good writing by those on the left (though the more extreme, such as Judah Waten, might be excluded). The communist Australasian Book Society suffered not only a lack of subscribers by the end of the fifties, but a lack of good manuscripts as well. The narrowness of their definition of socialist realism prevented the Book Society committee from publishing a variety of writing though, like Angus & Robertson, they found that the traditional writers like Alan Marshall were the strongest sellers.[25] (The socialist realist bestsellers, Frank Hardy's *Power Without Glory* and Eric Lambert's *Twenty Thousand Thieves*, were published by British commercial publishers.)

Stewart, for all his dislike of socialist politics, knew an entertaining writer when he found one. With his help, Angus & Robertson were able to achieve some of the aims of the communist publishing society—to make the Australian realist tradition available to postwar Australians. Of course, Geoffrey Dutton claims that Angus & Robertson's Australian classics series was simply a response to the challenge of his own Sun books.[26] Be that as it may, the books were published and sold.

When Stewart wrote about the Australian tradition he emphasised the robustness and fun in the writing of Lawson and Furphy, Eve Langley or Brian James. And, for all the narrowness of his definitions of prose and poetry, he was able to see the value of 'outsiders' such as Ethel Anderson or Hal Porter. Literary history always perpetrates distortions of the truth. 'Brian James' (John Tierney) is one of several novelists who do not fit the broad groupings of this book, but Stewart's judgement of him must be vindicated by any reader of *The Advancement of Spencer Button*. It is a comic delight. Similarly, the controlled wit of Ethel Anderson's *At Parramata* stories will be rediscovered and enjoyed during the eighties. Stewart was perceptive enough to ensure that some of these stories would appear in the Angus & Robertson anthologies which he edited with Beatrice Davis.

Through Douglas Stewart's criticism, his poetry and his editorial work runs a common thread of optimism about Australian life. Stewart, certainly, had no intention of finding religious consolation in the 'crisis' of postwar life. Nor did he despair at the drudgery which would be the human experience in an industrial society. He could even contemplate the atomic age with equilibrium.

Stewart's conception of the poet's role demanded that he concentrate on the joyous elements of human existence. He could make heroic moments out of atrocity and find an order in the universe from contemplation of a daisy. Stewart always makes it clear that he knows that there is another path—a way of despair—but he chooses knowingly to turn away from it.

Although Stewart's ideology and his poetry were timid by the standards of younger poets, Wright and David Campbell have acknowledged his importance to them as patron and adviser. As well, his struggle to find an Australian subject and voice prepared the way for Les Murray's kind of popular, but anti-socialist, nationalism. Where James McAuley asserted that Australian poetry should be spiritual or religious, Douglas Stewart demonstrated that it could be nationalistic without being radical or socialist.

Stewart did not disguise his hatred of communism as an influence on writers, nor did he have any patience with the techniques of modernism or the exploration of the personal. His conviction that these were 'escapes from art' meant that he must pursue an art which was free from obvious political commitment, which was traditional in technique and kept away from personal subjects. As a result, Stewart's poetry looked at the moment in the perspective of eternity: consolation for the sufferings of Changi prison or the mass murders of the Second World War could be found by reference to the history of human suffering and triumph, and the small elements of nature could teach us to see good and evil as part of eternal patterns.

This resistance to political commitments was in many ways more attractive to readers, and other poets, than the more intellectual poetry of A.D. Hope, for Stewart maintained an anti-ideological stand without abandoning the traditions of the Australian nature poet. In fact, Stewart's revival first of the ballad, then the lyric tradition, led the way for other poets who were nationalist without sharing the left-wing politics of the socialist realists and radical nationalists. With the decline of ideological extremism in the sixties it has been Stewart's kind of relaxed, lyrical nature poetry which has continued to dominate Australian poetry.

6

The Writer and the Crisis: Judith Wright and David Campbell

While Douglas Stewart could accept the changes in Australian society—particularly technological progress—with an easy and often amused attitude and A.D. Hope believed that the poet might achieve, through the imagination, a parallel progress to that of the scientist, one poet saw the rapid growth of technology as a threat to the bases of human understanding. Judith Wright emerged as a poet during the crisis of war but she soon turned her attention from the external threat to Australian society to the threats to human values within it.

In 1952 Judith Wright published two essays, entitled 'The Writer and the Crisis', which considered the role of the writer in the 'modern crisis'.[1] This crisis was not the imminent threat of communism, nor the absence of belief which rendered contemporary society bleak and materialistic: Wright's crisis was a crisis of communication, in particular the failure of the language to meet the demands placed upon it.

The word, which had evolved from the human need to describe the visible world, was now called upon to elucidate the split atom on the one hand or the inner mysteries of human consciousness on the other. Physicists, mathematicians, poets and ordinary people were trying to use the same language to communicate their very different needs. Wright believed that the crisis had divided society

—
141

so that scientists could only communicate with scientists, poets with poets, and ordinary people listened to the words of each group with increasing bafflement and confusion. Without some massive release of creative energy to make the language anew it seemed that it might fail us completely.

The threat was not to one particular social group or another, but to humanity itself and the possibility of achieving human understanding. In such a crisis, the poet had clear responsibilities to retain the usefulness of the language as a means of communication and to renew it by creative means. Wright saw language as the expression of humanity, and the failure of the word damaged human consciousness in an essential way. The task of the poet in the postwar world was serious and crucially important.

Though Judith Wright has modified these views slightly over the past thirty years they remain a fair statement of the source of her dedication to poetry. Her concern for the state of humanity has made poetry an urgent task, and has led in recent years to an active part in social issues beyond poetry. But Judith Wright's poetry, her literary criticism and her historical writing may be linked with the more specific issues of conservation and Aboriginal land rights which have taken so much of her energies in the seventies and eighties. There is no division in Judith Wright's personal role as poet and her public role as spokesman on social issues. Indeed, in Australia she has become a public poet, the kind of poet who expresses the conscience of her society.

In the sense that she has directed her energies to specific social issues Judith Wright is the most political of the writers publishing in the forties, fifties and sixties. Yet, at a time of political extremism—the fifties—she was not seen as political at all. Where John Manifold and David Martin held up the banner of the socialist poet, and James McAuley the claims of anti-communism, Judith Wright remained a socially concerned poet standing apart from political parties. Certainly she was identified as a nationalist, but not as a radical nationalist. Her poetry was welcomed by *Meanjin* and *Quadrant* alike.

All of Wright's poetry can be read in terms of the challenge to language. She has been labelled simply as a landscape poet, one who has developed the nature lyric for postwar Australia. Yet even the concern with the landscape is part of Wright's desire to revitalise the language. In the foreword to her collection of essays *Because I Was Invited*, she writes that the source of life and language is 'the living earth from which we have separated ourselves, but of which we are part and in which we cannot help participating', and she states clearly 'There is a link between the decline of our inner and of our outer worlds'.[2] Her own poetry links the inner world of language and the outer world of nature. Indeed, it is through the outer world of the 'living earth' that she seeks ways to create for the inner world of human consciousness. If, in the past few years, Wright has been more concerned with the outer world than with poetry, this is because she believes that both ends of the chain— the natural world and the word which creates it in the human mind—are equally crucial. In the 1980s it may appear that the natural environment is more threatened than the human power to respond to it.

During the war years, however, when Judith Wright first gained attention as a poet, the importance of the human response seemed paramount. Wright shared some of Clem Christesen's sense that the threat to Australia demanded a taking stock of Australian culture. If Australians were to fight and die in defence of their society, the cultural achievements of that society needed examination. When Wright looked at Australian poetry she found that a sense of exile lingered. Australian writers, despite the achievements of rare poets such as John Shaw Neilson, looked at their land with European eyes and felt alienated from it. A.D. Hope's accusation that Australians were no more than 'secondhand Europeans' drew some support from Wright. But rather than accept this as unchangeable fact, Wright was determined to participate in forming a real relationship between Australians and their country.

She has been one of the few writers and critics to defend the Jindyworobak movement of the thirties and to give the Jindyworobak poets credit for addressing a serious problem—Australians' failure to understand and belong to their homeland. In her own poetry, Wright has selected those aspects of the Jindyworobak approach which seem useful for her different purposes. Not for her the absurd mix of Aboriginal words and pseudo-primitivism, but she has recognised the richness of Aboriginal culture and the importance of Aboriginal history in the history of the land we now occupy. As well, she has drawn attention to the real merits of Roland Robinson's and William Hart-Smith's poetry.[3]

Wright was a nationalist in the forties, at a time when war gave nationalism a new impetus. But her nationalism sought universal

—

meanings. She believed that by addressing the urgent tasks of a particular time and place it was possible to create work of universal significance, just as she believed that a poet courageous enough to be himself or herself would be the most human, and therefore, expressive of all humanity. When other nationalists refused to listen to the voices of 'internationalists' or 'Europeanists' Wright was willing to consider the various points of view. She rejected the polarities between nationalism and internationalism, or between the bush and the city, or even the political polarities of radical nationalist and conservative, because she believed that these polarities could be reconciled in poetry.

The evidence of Wright's early poems suggests that when she argued that poetry should renew the language she meant that poetry should draw out the links between the actual, physical world and the life of the human imagination. In particular, she was concerned that Australians, when they looked at the physical world in which they lived, saw only trees or plains or bush and did not invest this physical world with meaning.

Many of the poems of her first book, *The Moving Image* (1946), concerned themselves with the history of Australia: with the life of the Aborigines, with white settlement and its struggle, with particular archetypal characters of the white past. In these poems, language was the means by which the failures and tragedies of the past became part of the human consciousness of the present. These were history poems which were not concerned with the large moments of history but with specific places in the present and the past they invoked. Thus, 'Nigger's Leap, New England' begins with a close observation of the sun going down and night engulfing a particular place in the New England ranges where an Aborigine leapt to death. Wright demands that we recognise the place of the Aborigines in the land: 'Did we not know their blood channelled our rivers, and the black dust our crops ate was their dust?' and she stresses the unities between the Aborigines, the landscape and the white present: 'And there they lie that were ourselves writ strange'.

In *The Moving Image* the language is often biblical, as if Wright is asserting that the European past, and its language, can be applied to the alien past of Australia. 'Bora Ring' makes explicit the links between the history of the land, made human by Aboriginal ritual and experience, and the history of the European imagination expressed in the biblical story of Cain and Abel. The

poem, like the corroborees of the Aborigines, is attempting to link
the Australian landscape of the present with a continuing human
consciousness. As well, of course, this poem refers to the contemporary threat of invasion and suggests that white Australians may
have less right to defend the land than the defeated Aborigines.

Throughout *The Moving Image* Wright can be found observing
the landscape, towns and people of contemporary Australia and
seeking the meaning of the history behind them—'South of My
Days', 'Bullocky', 'The Hawthorn Hedge', 'Remittance Man',
'Country Town' and so on. In each case, she finds some correspondence between the European attitude to the past and a present
which includes an Australian past. So the remittance man is a
figure from an English and Christian inheritance—'the scapegoat'—
as well as a familiar figure of the Australian past, the bullocky calls
up images of Moses and the old woman's hawthorn hedge is a sign
both of the European notions of order and the tangled wilderness
of Australia.

Though her language is never obscure, many of these poems are
written in an elevated style which suggests that Wright is creating
a new set of sacred writings for postwar Australia. These writings
have elements of Aboriginal chants as well as their obvious debts
to the psalms and the language of English public pronouncement:

Remember Thunderbolt, buried under the air-raid trenches.
Remember the bearded men singing of exile.
Remember the shepherds under their strange stars?

('Country Town')

Wright often addresses her white Australian audience directly or
includes the whole of her society when considering time and its
passing by the use of 'we'. At times, she breaks into secular
prayers on behalf of her fellow countrymen: 'O vine, grow close
upon that bone and hold it with your rooted hand.' Her poetic
role is public and communal.

Here, Wright's linking of the physical world of Australia with
white human consciousness comes through a naming of the physical world and exploring its past. This 'naming' places the Australian
landscape within the contexts of a European heritage while insisting on its non-European reality. Her means of fending off the
crisis was to claim the physical world by adapting the ritual and
public language of Europe to it. Though *The Moving Image* established Wright's reputation as a nationalist and wartime poet her

next book, *Woman to Man* (1949), showed that her achievement was not simply the result of the pressures of wartime threat. Once again, Wright sought unities between the exterior physical life and the interior life of the mind. The title poem demonstrated her belief that human life and nature were one by taking as its subject the conception and birth of a child. This poem refused to allow readers to look at the natural world as something outside themselves. Where Douglas Stewart might contemplate the source of life in a flower, Judith Wright had the courage to recognise its presence within the human body.

This can be seen as a natural progression from Wright's concern with the earth and the human relationship to it. In 'Woman to Man' the lovers are alienated not from the land, but from the child they have created and who will be dependent upon them. The poem proclaims a fear of nature's mysteries at the same time that it preserves a reverence for such mysteries. The unborn child is related to time, that inexorable reaper of *The Moving Image* poems. But even when time brings creation Wright finds it difficult to be consoled. 'Woman to Man' and the similar poems which accompanied it may now seem strained and rather impersonal treatments of personal subjects, but this cannot diminish the boldness of the poems and their confrontation of the human place in the natural world. In general, though, the most successful poems in the second book were those which presented a concrete image and followed the implications of this image. 'The Twins' and 'The Mirror at the Fun Fair' developed observed moments into considerations of human loneliness. 'The Cycads' allowed the living paradox of the ancient plant to lead back to the beginnings of human existence. 'The Killer' told the story of an encounter with a snake and transformed that encounter into a comment on human destructiveness. Here, most clearly, Wright was making an inner human consciousness from outer experience.

The war had passed but the crisis remained. Human life still needed to be reconciled to the rest of the natural world—in 'Spring after War' the human heart found it difficult to find peace even in the peaceful landscape. But by observing and meditating on Australian life Wright attempted to achieve such peace.

Twenty-five years after the war, Judith Wright wrote her interpretation of what the war meant to Australian poetry. In 'Australian Poetry after Pearl Harbour' she argued that the presence of educated and curious Americans in Australia during the war had given Australian poets a new self-confidence. The old feeling that an Australian poet could only be a poor imitation of an English poet had gone; those poets brought up on the standard works of English romantic symbolism suddenly saw further options.[4]

Whether or not this is true for Australian poets in general—and Wright lists the work of McAuley, Hope, Campbell, Webb, Dobson and others as evidence—it provides some insight into the way Wright felt about her own poetry. She was full of confidence that what an Australian poet had to say was as important as what an English or American poet might say. In her opinion, no over-seas writer after Yeats, Pound and Eliot stood out as so 'great' that all other poets should humble themselves in submission. Wright was not claiming to be a 'great' poet herself but she found during the war years that there was no need to apologise for being Australian. Australian poets were not at the forefront of technical experiment, but that was no reason for Australian poets to cease writing: 'New things come out of new experiences and Australia's experience has not been all that new. We have been insular, we have been isolated, we have been ill-educated, and we still are; we are not a thinking but an acting race, and even the impact of the Pacific War did not make us wince and think things over.'[5] So Wright accepted that her writing would reflect the limitations of Australia. Her poetry had to achieve any universal meaning by grappling with the particular. Her nationalism was not a banner like that of the socialist realists but she would not reject it for the mirage of 'internationalism'.

One of the curious aspects of Judith Wright's career is the way in which the poetry of her first two books has remained her most widely known and admired. She has commented herself on the effects of the limited romantic symbolist poetry teaching of her childhood, but Wright's own poetry (at least in the early books) has come to represent Australian poetry to two generations of Australian schoolchildren. It is Wright's version of wartime and postwar nationalism which has shown the way for younger writers. Wright herself has become angry at the role her poetry has been forced to play in this promotion of nationalism and, in 1986, she announced that she had withdrawn 'Bullocky' from all future anthologies because 'it is being blown up into a kind of justification of the whole invasion of Australia'.[6]

By the fifties Wright was already beginning to doubt the importance of the new nationalism. It had come to have a shallow and even commercial aspect. Wright was aware, too, that nationalism had become the preserve of radical writers whose attitude depended on an analysis of society which reduced it to material elements; both consumer capitalism and Marxist materialism saw society in terms of the physical world alone. In her introduction to her discussion of Australian poetry *Preoccupations in Australian Poetry* (1965), Wright expressed some sympathy for the 'Australian ethos' and its concern for the equality of all human beings.[7] But she commented that the ethos could be used for shallow purposes; even in the fifties she could see the beginnings of the 'ocker image'. In Wright's opinion, the radical nationalist interpretation of Australia, optimistic and humane though it might be, led to sentimental assessments of human nature and, worse, dismissed qualities which were essential to human understanding.

So Wright, who had seemed to be a nationalist in her first books of poetry, saw that nationalism had its own dishonesties. The task which she set herself in *The Moving Image* and *Woman to Man*, of relating Australians to their own environment, no longer seemed sufficient. And Wright's comments since the sixties suggest that she was expanding her range and her perception of the crisis. It was no longer simply a matter of linking Australians with the Australian environment; it was also a matter of linking human individuals with their own emotions. Wright lived in the same bleak world which preoccupied A.D. Hope, and she saw the 'creating word' as the means of reconciling aspects of that world. Where Hope stripped modern life to a fundamental emptiness then sought intimations of higher understanding through his art, Wright recognised a physical unity in all matter and sought out the links between the human mind and the physical world. When Hope wrote about 'humanising' the world by means of art he seemed to share something of Wright's attitude, but Hope's humanising comes through the artist's creative powers, while Wright has seen the artist as linking the real physical world with the world of the mind.

For Wright the postwar crisis could not be accepted as an inevitable result of human destructive powers, nor could she console herself with Douglas Stewart's notion in 'Rutherford' that there are always good men as well as evil. The threats to human life and to humanity itself were only too clearly manifest.

Foremost among the threats of the fifties was the atomic bomb and the possibility of the total destruction of the earth and all

—

humanity. As Shirley Walker has explained in her study of Judith Wright, this was not only a direct physical threat: the structure of the atom was part of that physical unity which Wright recognised in all matter, so the manipulation of that structure for atomic weapons attacked the very basics of Wright's philosophical vision.[8] Wright became increasingly concerned with evil and the awesome duality in physical and human nature.

The threat of atomic destruction hangs over Wright's fifties books, *The Gateway* (1953) and *The Two Fires* (1955). Several poems from *The Gateway* can be read as pursuing the nationalist aims of *The Moving Image* and *Woman to Man*, and these poems continue the task of coming to terms with the Australian landscape and history, of overcoming the alienation of Australian people from their land. 'Train Journey', 'Eroded Hills' and 'Old House' follow the line developed in 'Bullocky' and 'South of My Days'.

But *The Gateway* also offered a new kind of poem which made no reference to the landscape or the familiar world. In 'Transformations', 'Eden', 'The Traveller and the Angel' and other poems Wright began to create fables about the nature of human struggle. 'Legend' made an Australian fairytale out of the need for endurance, experience and confidence in creation. Wright still saw time as a destructive force, but the poems of *The Gateway* celebrated the creation which emerged from such destruction. This was Wright's means of understanding the duality in nature.

When Wright contemplated the perfection of nature in 'Birds' or 'Lion' she was led to consider both the imperfection of humanity and the creative struggle of love which resulted from such imperfection. In confronting the imperfectibility of human nature and human life Wright declared herself to be apart from the radical nationalists or utopians. But she did not celebrate imperfectibility in the way which Douglas Stewart preferred. Stewart admired Wright's poetry from its first appearance, but he lamented the 'certain lack of joy, spontaneity and simplicity; and, in consequence, an impression of seriousness and, sometimes, strain' in Wright's poetry.[9] For Wright, unlike Stewart, human imperfectibility was a problem which threatened life itself; in her first three books, the threat was too urgent for Stewart's kind of levity.

Some critics were disappointed with Wright's two books of the fifties. *The Moving Image* and *Woman to Man* had been so forceful and new that they expected Wright to continue presenting striking new work or, at least, to produce further nationalist contemplations of the land. Some saw her as a war poet who may have lost her subject with the coming of peace. Harry Heseltine, however, has argued that *The Gateway* and *The Two Fires* represent Wright's struggle to find new perspectives. He sees 'The Traveller and the Angel' as, partly, a fable of Wright's own career: the first encounters with the angel have left the poet, like the traveller, exhausted and looking for new directions. Rodney Hall, too, prefers to read Wright's poetic development as a search which had reached a new stage by the 1950s.[10]

The threat of the atomic bomb which inspired 'Two Songs for the World's End' in *The Gateway*, also fed the despair of 'The Precipice' in *The Two Fires*, but this book of poetry shows that Wright was not tied to the emotional 'female' concerns with which she identified in *Woman to Man*. In *The Two Fires* Wright made her first steps towards satire with the two poems, 'The Wattle Tree' '...And Mr Ferritt'. More impressively, 'Request to a Year' proclaimed the need for the artist to achieve detachment. This poem told its story with simplicity and directness yet it used the female predicament to great effect. Wright's great-great-grandmother, with eight children, was an artist without time for art. In Wright's poem she watches 'with the artist's isolating eye' as her son is catapulted towards almost certain death. Wright's request for a similar sense of perspective suggests that she is also aware of the dangers of emotional exaggeration. Like Hope, Wright seems to reject the use of art for propaganda purposes. She offers detachment and perspective as the key to artistic vision. But Wright has always been deeply engaged with the problems of the 'crisis' period in which she lives. Where Hope takes 'uncommitment' as a guide for intellectual detachment, Wright's sense of urgency and imminent threat makes such detachment difficult to achieve and in the poems written after the mid-fifties Wright increasingly adopts an ironic voice to control her convictions. The aesthetic example of 'A Request to a Year' is no easy goal in her case.

In the late forties Judith Wright had begun research for a fictionalised biography of her grandmother, *The Generations of Men*. This research obviously gave new subjects for Wright's poetry, though she could not find a publisher for the biography until 1959. She believes that this was because no publisher saw a market for Australian history—another sign of the lack of self-understanding which bedevilled Australian life. A people who denied themselves a history had no choice but to feel alien and rootless.

—

Judith Wright and David Campbell

One of the signs of the slow process of Australian understanding is Wright's need to revise *The Generations of Men* as *The Cry for the Dead* thirty years later. *The Generations of Men* had been a first step towards understanding, but Wright's discoveries (and those of other historians) in the intervening years forced her to recognise an earlier history of Australia and the price for pastoral expansion paid by the Aborigines and by the land itself.[11] Wright's interest in history forms part of her poetic role in reconciling the human with the natural world. In her view, postwar Australians were doubly alienated by their ignorance of their own history on the Australian continent. To Australians the land was simply there; no relationship between white settlers and continent had been established. Wright's task was to link the human sense of identity with the land, and history was as important as the direct linking of language and land through poetry.

In *The Two Fires*, the poem 'At Cooloola' brought together the various strands of Wright's interests, in poetry and in life. The history of her family, the driving out and murder of the Aborigines, the present Australian environment and the difficulty of finding a true appreciation of it were linked with the need for 'love' rather than 'arrogant guilt'. Her searching in the poems of the forties and the early fifties confirmed her belief that understanding Australia and its history was necessary to conquer the fears expressed in *The Moving Image* and *Woman to Man*.

'At Cooloola', with its blue crane wearing the colour of the lake, also made clear allusion to John Shaw Neilson's poetry. During the fifties Wright had come to admire Neilson's poetry and that of Charles Harpur. These poets seemed to offer a way of being nationalist without taking on a narrow political position or a phony jingoism. But both poets had been neglected, just as Australian history had been neglected. There was no reliable, let alone complete, edition of Harpur's poetry until the sixties, and a complete edition has only recently been published by Elizabeth Perkins. John Shaw Neilson's poetry still awaits a persistent editor. Wright's interest in these poets led her to write the 'Australian Writers and their Work' study of Harpur in 1963 and to edit the 'Australian Poets' selection of Neilson's poetry published in the same year.[12]

Wright saw Harpur and Neilson as models for her own approach to poetry. Her introduction to *Preoccupations in Australian Poetry* identified two literary attitudes to Australia: the 'literature of exile'

—

151

and the 'literature of hope'. She showed clearly that she understood the nationalist debate, with the position of the 'Europeanists'
expressed by McAuley and that of the 'nationalists' by Russel
Ward, A.A. Phillips and others. But Wright believed that neither
view recognised the full nature of the Australian dilemma. She
understood the sense of rootlessness portrayed by Henry Handel
Richardson, Christina Stead, and Martin Boyd. She read Patrick
White's *Voss* as an attempt by the exiled European to achieve
reconciliation with the alien land. Wright accepted the 'literature
of exile' view that European migration to Australia was a process
of loss. It seemed to her an essential part of understanding the
Australian present.[13]

On the other hand, Wright found that beneath the sentimentality
and forced optimism of the radical nationalist position lay values
which might lead to a reconciliation with the land. The belief in
the equality of humanity behind the shallow mateship deserved
expression in deeper and more considered ways. Her essential
objection to the 'literature of exile' was its exclusive concern with
the past and with loss; her objection to the radical nationalist
literature was that it looked only to the future and rejected those
elements of the past which did not give cause for optimism.
Preoccupations in Australian Poetry called for a recognition of
both elements in the Australian heritage—not the dismissal of
Boyd, White, Richardson and Brennan as 'cultural cringers' nor
the dismissal of Furphy, Lawson, O'Dowd and Eleanor Dark as
utopian dreamers.

For this reason, Charles Harpur appealed particularly to Wright.
Harpur could be placed with the radicals because of his commitment to the making of a new land of human freedom and equality.
At the same time, his admiration for Wordsworth and Milton
proclaimed his links with English tradition. Furthermore, Harpur
was the first poet to take on the task of recreating the Australian
landscape. He had begun to name the outer world of the environment for the inner world of the Australian mind.

John Shaw Neilson offered an even more impressive model for
the kind of poetry Wright wished to create herself. For Neilson
absorbed the traditions of his Celtic forebears without strain while
approaching the natural world of Australia with apparent unself-
consciousness. The circumstances of Neilson's life and sympathies
would seem to place him with the 'radical nationalists', but Neilson's
suspicion of rational systems and celebration of the intuitive crea-

tive impulse precluded simple political commitment. Neilson's poetry proclaims his concern for humane values and even a clear pacifism but, like Wright, he saw exaggerated nationalism as 'rare old Humbug' ('The Sundowner').

With these two poets as models Wright was able to trace a path between the two vocal (and political) literary extremes of the postwar years. These poets were nationalists who did not reject their European heritage and who had strong political beliefs without submitting to an imposed political vision; Harpur and Neilson gave her new inspiration and contributed to the more relaxed poetry of her later books. *Birds* (1962) was written for her daughter Meredith and shows that, like Neilson, Wright valued the humbler tasks of poetry. The poems of this book observed the various kinds of Australian bird and developed such observations into a familiarity with the peculiarities and delights of each. Wright was prepared to be whimsical but she was also concerned to know each bird, not to find alien elements or threat in the natural world.

'Extinct Birds' paid loving homage to Charles Harpur who had observed and described 'the birds of his time's forest' only to be forgotten by generations of later Australians. *Birds* is Wright's taking up of Harpur's lost task of recording the details of Australian nature so that they may become part of the heritage of the transplanted Australian.

By 1962, however, Wright's concern with the landscape had led her to a public platform. She helped form and became the president of the Queensland Wildlife Preservation Society. She has described this as the beginning of 'her education in the problems of being a conservationist' though all her writing reveals her fundamental concern with these issues.[14] Wright now saw the immediate postwar years not as a time of nationalist self-confidence but as a period when white society's destruction of the land gained new vigour. Those visionary schemes which filled Australians with pride in the fifties—the Snowy Mountains Scheme, the new cities, industries and buildings—now appeared as a more powerful and systematic destruction of the fragile Australian environment. The more Wright researched the details of Australian history, the more she discovered white history to be a process of destruction in the name of progress. When she looked into the particular features of Australian bird and plant life she found that many species were extinct or endangered. For some, the task of naming the environment and creating it anew in the human consciousness had come too late.

The writer who had remained so free from political labels in the forties and fifties was a political lobbyist through the sixties. In 1973, the Whitlam government placed her on a committee of inquiry into conservation and she continues to speak publicly on conservation issues and on the associated problems of Aboriginal land rights. It may be these public experiences which have influenced Wright's movement towards satire and comic verse in her later books, though the signs of this skill are present in *The Two Fires* collection of 1955. *Five Senses* (1963) may be read as continuing the task of naming and understanding, but *The Other Half* (1966) offered a sharper and wittier poet than the well-known nature lyricist of the Australian schoolroom. 'To Another Housewife' enjoyed the ironies of the change from squeamish girl to the killer and cook of domestic life. 'Eve to Her Daughters' gave wry advice about the logic of female submission and its likely end. And the detachment Wright admired in 'Request to a Year' surfaced in 'The Typists in the Phoenix Building'. Wright's concern about humane values could display itself in a variety of styles and voices, not only the nature lyric or the philosophic argument.

Wright continues to publish poetry, but there is a recurring note of disillusionment about poetry throughout her prose writing. When Jim Davidson interviewed her for *Meanjin* in 1982, she commented on the difficulties of publication for the contemporary poet and her reluctance to publish in book form. When Davidson asked her about the current state of poetry she spoke immediately of the misuse of poetry and the failure of people to understand their own emotions:

> When you've taken your physical analysis so far, then you ought to be able to turn around and take a look at your emotional life instead. But nobody very much even knows what's going on inside them, most of the time. Look at how crazy everybody is! It's manic, it's mad, it's insane! Look at Britain—look where you like, actually, the same thing's happening—we're utterly taken over by our feelings at any moment. It's murderous. There's no analysis, no knowledge of what's going on inside you, so you're prey to the worst demons. It's really bad. Unless we can stop and do something about that I see no hope for the world at all.[15]

The crisis of language which Wright perceived in the fifties—the failure of the language to reconcile inner and outer worlds—has

become the crisis of the eighties: the gap between human knowledge of material existence and understanding of inner human
emotion. Poetry stands at the centre of both crises and Wright's
poetry has tackled the challenges of both. Her notion of the poet's
role is to keep men and women in touch with themselves and the
world beyond their bodies. Wright's ideal poet must not shy away
from human emotion.

In the eighties, however, Wright does not hold the same faith
in poetry as the source of human emotional knowledge that she
had in the fifties. She believes that much contemporary poetry is
written and read mainly to escape from self-knowledge. And she
thinks that the way in which poetry is taught in schools, and
particularly in universities, destroys the power of the words.
Though Wright is an historian and critic as well as a poet, she has
been careful to avoid what she sees as an 'academic' approach to
literature. She has criticised the way in which the teaching of
literature in schools and universities has become little more than
the unravelling of intellectual puzzles. Wright believes that
students are encouraged to turn away from 'self recognition' to
more mechanistic ways of reading. It is not so much a rejection of
academic elitism (which Stewart was so anxious to avoid) but a
concern that academic methods destroy the personal, intangible
and humane qualities of literature.

Wright has always been a traditional poet in the sense that she
believes that poetry is the preserver and renewing source of
humane values. The nineteenth-century idea of the poet as priest
and prophet lingers in her role as spokesman for the emotional
lives of her people; it is a kind of bardic role. Her insistence on
poetry as a source of humane values leads her to reject techniques
which mimick mechanised effects, such as concrete poetry. This
also underpins her refusal to experiment with the obscurities of
the subconscious or any 'specialisation' of art which limits its
communication.

All of Judith Wright's poetry is accessible, whether it be written
in the forties or the eighties. Yet she has also been willing to try a
range of formal styles. Her experiments with free verse and even
stream of consciousness demonstrate how these 'modernist' techniques can be part of a poetic view which is committed to preserving the humane. Shirley Walker comments that the poem
'Habitat' from *Alive* (1973) uses experimental elements to reiterate
the themes of change, time, duality and creation which appear in
Wright's earliest work.[16] But the poem is spare and disciplined at

the same time that it is personal and apparently 'modernist'. It is an impressive display of that detachment which Wright sought in art.

This decision to experiment came after the change in Australian poetic fashion of the late sixties, but it does not indicate a change in poetic 'sides'. By this time, Wright's hold on her poetic purpose was so firm that mere formal change could not shake it. In her most recent book of poems, *Phantom Dwelling* (1985), she comments wryly on old age and the demands of rhyme: her style now is 'few words and with no rhetoric'.[17] Her stand has been anti-mechanistic, not anti-experiment.

In his *Essays in Poetry: mainly Australian* (1957), Vincent Buckley considered the possibility that Douglas Stewart was patronising 'a new *Bulletin* school' with Wright and David Campbell as its leading poets. He argued that this was not a new coming to terms with the landscape but merely a more sophisticated and pessimistic return to the themes of poetry forty years earlier. He attacked the landscape writers for their lack of real thought about the Australian environment, and particularly for their lack of interest in the human: 'From the standpoint of the *Bulletin* outback, human beings are in exactly the same order of reality—and, be it stressed, the same order of doom—as the gibber-plains, the mulga, soil erosion, crows, dead sheep and withered mountains.'[18] Buckley's view was not totally without foundation especially where the 'Birdsville Track' poetry of Stewart was concerned or the early poetry of Wright, with its constant fear of the future. But it was wide of the mark with regard to Judith Wright's source of inspiration; the human has always been her central concern though she sees the state of the human as vitally connected to the human understanding of nature.

Stewart, Wright and Campbell shared some attitudes to poetry and many subjects for poetry, but they did not form a school in the way Buckley suggested. Of the three poets, David Campbell has emerged as the most influential with regard to the younger poets who came to maturity in the sixties. Philip Mead and Alan Gould have paid tribute to Campbell's work in celebrating the mind as the creator, and Thomas Shapcott (accepting Buckley's notion of a *Bulletin* school) states categorically that he was the best of these poets.[19]

Born in the same year as Wright (1915) Campbell also gained

initial recognition for his war poetry. He had a similar background to Wright: his family had been squatters for several generations and he was university-educated. Like Wright he had a sense of harmony with the Australian countryside which came from living and working on the land.

Campbell produced relatively few poems in the fifties and sixties; it was not until the seventies that he was able to devote substantial time to the life of a poet. He himself grouped together the poems from 'Harry Pearce' (*Speak with the Sun* 1949) to 'Droving' (*Poems* 1963). So the three books of poetry *Speak with the Sun*, *The Miracle of Mullion Hill* (1956) and *Poems* can be seen as having a common direction. He has remarked in an interview: 'at that point I had to either stop writing or start writing about something else, and at that stage I really started shooting out in all directions.' And Campbell admitted that the Vietnam war forced him to reconsider his poetic direction.[20]

Campbell was as literary in his approach to poetry as Stewart and Wright, but he was not so enclosed by nineteenth-century romantic ideals. He was not influenced as Stewart was by the Lindsayite notions of the artist as superior being or the 'passionate' nature of existence. Humour and cruelty appear in Campbell's poetry but they do not preclude compassion.

Despite the range of Campbell's work since the sixties, he has become known for his poetry of the fifties, just as Judith Wright is best known for her forties poems and Douglas Stewart for the *Sun Orchids* and *The Birdsville Track* poems. He describes the characters of the countryside as Judith Wright had done. But these are not 'realistic' or closely observed like Wright's individual old men and women. Instead, Campbell creates them to his own literary purposes. Thus, Harry Pearce is a mirage, the timeless stockman. The Trapper, Kelly and others are figures equally suited to a Lawson story or Yeats' ballads of the Irish countryside. Campbell creates both a poetic persona of the farmer firmly established in the Australian present and a series of literary images which have a timelessness extending back far beyond the years of Australian settlement.

The poems can be read within Australian contexts. 'Harry Pearce' can be seen in the Australian 'tall story' tradition, as can 'Jack Spring' or 'Kelly and the Crow'. Several poems are quite consciously Australian: the reference in 'Soldier's Song' to Falkiner's sheep, in

—

157

'Conroy's Gap' to Darby Munro as well as the wattle, crows, magpie, kelpie, deliberately assert an Australian culture as well as landscape.

Furthermore, the Australian references are also literary. Campbell shows a firm hold on the traditions of the nineties which his poems of droving, shearers, barmaids, and the battlers of 'Soldier Settlers'. This excited Douglas Stewart about Campbell's work; he seemed to be using the popular traditions of Lawson and Paterson with new vigour and appropriateness. But at the same time that Campbell's early poetry touches essentially Australian points of reference it also touches with equal sureness the whole tradition of English poetry and European culture. Thus, the Australian stockman going through 'Windy Gap' immediately recalls the opening line of Yeats' 'Running to Paradise'—'As I came over Windy Gap'—but the poem which follows sets a peculiarly Australian scenario with hawk threatening and magpie singing to the sheep. Yet something of Yeats' original poem remains in the celebration of the freedom of the wind and the changeability of nature.

Other poems make direct reference to Shakespeare or Marlowe, or see the Australian countryside with a European pastoral attitude. Some of these poems make fun of the difference between European literary poses and the traditional figures of Australian literature. For example, 'Come Live with Me' takes the shearer and his girl instead of shepherd and shepherdess and, while keeping Paterson and 'The Banks of the Condamine' in mind, turns the poem to the incongruities of Australian rural life:

'Since time's a shearer, where's the sin
In kissing in the super-bin?'

It is amusing to see shearers and barmaids as the shepherds and shepherdesses of some lost pastoral age, yet Campbell maintains that the fancy has some validity. The care of sheep in a rural setting goes on; seasons change as they always have done; love continues to stir the imagination to idyllic visions.

Technocratic man makes no appearance in Campbell's songs of life. In fact, Campbell later told an interviewer that he felt an 'outsider' when he returned to Australia and to farming after the war, and he speculated that his return to poetry was an attempt to overcome this feeling of alienation.[21] If this is so, Campbell may be compared to Patrick White and Martin Boyd, two novelists

158

who also found themselves out of place when they returned to postwar Australia and wrote with new energy in order to come to terms with this feeling. However, rather than examine or criticise the paradoxes in Australian society Campbell set about absorbing the Australian pastoral life into his own imagination. Campbell's fifties poems do not lament the failure of natural instinct as in A.D. Hope's 'The Death of a Bird' but celebrate the miracle of continuing creativity as in 'Who Points the Swallow'. And the man who speaks in the poetry is at the centre of this creativity. The swallow's instinct in 'Who Points the Swallow' is the same quality as the love which binds human beings to each other. In 'Words and Lovers' the 'coupling of words and lovers' remains the salvation of humanity who must otherwise bear the anguish of thought and feeling without form to express it.

'Cocky's Calendar' insists that the poet who is both farmer and a more general image of human kind is the source of meaning for the changing states of nature. In 'Hawk and Hill' he observes the world and praises his own capacities of intelligence and sense:

> O all the coloured world I see
> And walk upon, are made by me.

The continuity of life is made meaningful through the creative powers of man. So, as the activities and environment of the year change, the poet sowing wheat, mustering cattle or sheep reflects on the extremes of nature and delights in its response as the seasons change.

Unlike Douglas Stewart, in the countryside David Campbell is no stranger ready to recoil with fear at each of nature's cruelties. Crows threaten the lambs, drought may ruin the oat crop, but the man at the centre of the poem is in command. He works with nature and finds reassurance in its recurring patterns—for though individuals die and minor details of the farmer's life change, the robins appear every winter all over the world, the wattle blooms each spring, drawing the young couples to them. In 'Song for a Wren' the mischances of human life are compared with those of a wren and the farmer must laugh at his own miseries, just as Burns could pity the mouse in his field.

This age-old wisdom seems totally isolated from the Australia of the postwar cities. Campbell's insistence on the eternal and universal patterns of agricultural life seem a deliberate turning away from the threats and failures which are apparent in Judith

Wright's poetry or the commitments of James McAuley. His poems of the forties and fifties emphasise the peaceful, natural and creative role of man. Even 'Conroy's Gap', 'Soldier's Song' and 'Men in Green' assert the perennial, courageous and creative aspects of humanity. Campbell looks out on a different world from that of A.D. Hope who fears the loss of cultural understanding, or James McAuley who could become so excited about totalitarianism. And, in his belief in a human place within the natural world, he is at odds with Stewart and Wright. For Stewart cannot but imagine the natural world in opposition to man, and Judith Wright feared human destruction of nature and humanity itself. In good times and bad Campbell's characters of the fifties are in harmony with nature.

In recalling David Campbell's experiences during the Second World War, Robin Gollan has suggested that Campbell buried his war memories in the fifties.[22] This determination to forget the horrors of war is not uncommon among returning servicemen, and, in a sense, was the pattern for a whole generation of Australians who experienced the Second World War. The fifties was a period when Australians devoted themselves to family life and the pursuit of peace. The shifts and strategies of the Cold War, including participation in the Korean War, were part of a fear of further major conflict. It was not until the Vietnam war and the protests against it that Campbell's memories of war seemed to force themselves on his imagination and the poems of *The Branch of Dodona* (1970) such as 'My Lai', 'Hotel Marine' or 'Operation Moonprobe' reveal a violent disturbance of the imagination which was so in control in *Speak with the Sun* (1949).

After the Second World War, Campbell's poetry was as traditional as his lifestyle, but by turning to older lyric traditions than those sought by Wright or Stewart he brought a new vitality to traditional nature poetry. Campbell expressed his preferences for poems 'with the economy and completeness of a theorem' and it is the spareness of his writing which makes it immediately more forceful than the early work of Wright or Stewart.[23]

Where Wright in an early poem such as 'Bullocky' is concerned to place the bullocky in a historical context which has meaning for postwar Australia, Campbell could take a similar subject in 'Harry Pearce' and place his own imagination at the centre of it:

I sat beside the red stock route
And chewed a blade of bitter grass

And saw in mirage on the plain
A bullock wagon pass.
Old Harry Pearce was with his team.
'The flies are bad,' I said to him.

The poem is more relaxed than Wright's 'Bullocky' and the 'I' is not distant from the old bullocky but shares his habit (chewing 'bitter grass') and language ('The flies are bad'). Where Wright rounds off her poem with an incantation ('O vine, grow close upon that bone') Campbell lightly shrugs off the implication of his mirage:

And he may drive his cattle still
When Time with us has had his will.

If Wright was inclined, at least in her early poems, to hammer home her point in the last stanza and to use an elevated, slightly self-conscious language to draw attention to its seriousness, Campbell preferred understatement and he risked being dismissed as simple. Nevertheless, Wright had clear public and educational purposes in her poetry while Campbell's poetry seemed to be an exploration of the creative process.

In a poem such as 'Song for the Cattle' Campbell allowed his 'persona' to ramble idly through a series of rural fantasies. This was not the dreaded dissociative technique or personalism promoted by modernism but it was a liberation from the patterned logic which dominated Australian poetry in the fifties. 'Song for the Cattle' celebrates a relaxed straying of the imagination which is placed within a clear context—a song which a farmer might make up for his animals.

When Stewart or Leonie Kramer wrote about Campbell's 'natural' language they were referring to the apparent simplicity of these early poems. Campbell did not write in the vernacular of a younger poet such as Bruce Dawe but his language was closer to everyday speech than many of his contemporaries and his occasional bursts of direct speech in a poem do not interrupt the unity of language in the poem. When younger poets, such as Thomas Shapcott or Alan Gould, prefer Campbell's work to that of Wright it may be because of this relaxed kind of language and also because, without indulging in personalism, Campbell was interested in the way in which dreams and imaginative associations were formed.

In interviews Campbell referred to poetry as a gift. Most of his poems have sprung into his mind as a single line or an idea, so

—

that he described the initial spark of creativity as a kind of 'cheating'. The source of poetry for Campbell was spontaneous and mysterious and a number of his poems celebrated this source as being part of all the creative aspects of the universe. Campbell was fascinated by the way in which the physical world was created anew in the mind: 'at times I had the sense of riding around my own world of the imagination, my own creation'.[24]

In the early sixties Campbell seemed to become more theoretical about this creative unity in the world. About this time, Roderick Shaw asked Campbell to define art and Campbell referred to James Joyce's theory on art as expressed in *Portrait of the Artist as a Young Man*: 'beauty or art has three qualities, one is wholeness, that is the whole canvas making something that is significant, then harmony, which are parts of the whole and which harmonise with one another, and that could be completely dead unless you have the third thing which is radiance'. Campbell recognised the importance of these three elements in his own poetry. He had become friendly with A.D. Hope, and read his essays on poetry, *The Cave and the Spring*, with enthusiasm. In his discussion with Shaw, Campbell talked about the notion of thought causing evolution, an idea close to Hope's idea of the poet creating new 'modes of being' and so contributing to human evolution. For Campbell this was important because it 'does away with God and makes evolution terribly exciting'. Campbell saw this as a way for the poet to be part of a physical world which was not dead matter but constantly renewing itself.[25]

Both Leonie Kramer and R.F. Brissenden have argued the significance of Campbell's interest in scientific theory for his later work.[26] In the last years of his life Campbell's readings in physical science were systematic to the extent of a return to formal university study. But Brissenden has noted that Campbell's interest in cosmic harmony can be found in his earliest work. Campbell's discovery of a clear theoretical and philosophical basis for his work seems to have come after years of writing poetry. However, this gradual clarification of a theory of art undoubtedly gave Campbell the confidence to explore new poetic styles in the sixties and seventies.

During these years he began to read and mix with younger poets and to experiment with free verse and more adventurous (and, sometimes, more obscure) thought association. Like Wright, Campbell felt that he had conquered traditional form and could confidently break the patterns of the past. Many of Campbell's

admirers value his poetry of the fifties and sixties more highly than
the work in his later books, but it is the poetry published after the
mid-sixties which reveals Campbell as a poet of range and courage.
Campbell made a clear contribution to Australian postwar poetry
by showing new ways to work the old rural themes, by applying a
'natural' Australian language to traditional forms and giving a new
energy to patterns which were familiar. Part of this energy came
from Campbell's interest in the intuitive and creative possibilities
of the human mind; even an early ballad-inspired poem such as
'Song for the Cattle' offered imaginative dreaming as its centre.
Obviously, this interest was not confined to celebrations of country
life, and the late sixties found Campbell translating other poets,
reworking Greek myths, interpreting paintings and re-examining
his family history.

Just as the death of Judith Wright's husband may be seen as an
influence on her later work, or personal crises may be marked in
A.D. Hope's poetry, Campbell's separation from his first wife and,
finally, his sufferings from cancer influenced his change to a more
personal and reflective poetry in later life. But, for all three poets,
poetry was not a 'self-expressive' art and never merely a therapy
for personal experience. It had a crucial role in preserving and
exploring humanity.

The way in which writers perceive their 'commitment', their
obligation as writers to their society, is as much a matter of those
various, indefinable influences of personality and experience as
well as of wider social, cultural and political forces. Wright's open
concern with a 'crisis' in society clearly binds her poetry to the
historical situation in which she found herself. Her writing shows
her awareness of the various arguments about culture in Australia
since the war. Campbell was more reticent about social and political
matters and the close connection between his life as a farmer and
his poetry made him seem even more isolated from such matters
in the fifties. Yet Campbell's poetry also follows a broader pattern
of a renewal of traditional form in the fifties to more experimental
and personal work in the late sixties and seventies. Like Wright,
Campbell found that he could approach political subjects late in
life without that fear of lapsing into propaganda which bedevilled
writers in the early fifties. Late poems such as 'Portents over
Coffee', 'Wether Country', 'Bellbirds' and the 'Red Bridge' series
about paintings raised urgent questions about the state of the
world, the abuse of nature and the relationship between human

creative powers and human cruelty. In the context of the Vietnam War and an escalated stripping of Australia's environmental resources these issues became political and associated with political 'sides'. However, such issues may be seen as fundamental concerns of poets who saw themselves as preserving and celebrating human creativity, and who sought out the connections between the human powers of imagination and the natural world.

Campbell and Wright were among those Australian poets who did not accept the options of political commitment or withdrawal to 'spiritual' or purely aesthetic concerns. They also rejected the idea that poetry should express self. In the early postwar years they could pursue the poet's time-honoured concern with peace and nature without being forced into political camps. Changes in Australian society over the fifties and sixties meant that such broad concerns came to have political support and political opponents. Where Judith Wright's fear about the destructive powers of humanity might seem appropriately 'poetic' in the early fifties, by the seventies the evidence that technological progress had deva-stated nature was too great for even politicians to ignore. Similarly, the Vietnam War gave a stark reality to the forces opposing Campbell's creative interests. For him (unlike James McAuley) the renewed evidence of human cruelty rather than communist against anti-communist was the undeniable feature of the war, and so his poetic interests brought him close to politics.

Wright and Campbell saw poetry as the preserver of the humane and they began their careers as formal traditionalists. Like most of their Australian contemporaries they rejected modernism in the fifties principally because, as Wright put it, modernism seemed either introverted or mechanistic. Wright, in particular, struggled to avoid an art which was concerned only with political interests on the one hand or only with the self on the other. By the late sixties, however, these poets understood their artistic role so clearly that they had the confidence to experiment with a range of techniques. Their individual engagements with the problems of poetry in contemporary society led them to develop theories which could sustain poetic creation through changes in poetic fashions.

Both Wright and Campbell, with Stewart, are sometimes re-garded affectionately as the poets who revived the Australian landscape as a subject for poetry after the Second World War. Their role was to make us 'feel at home' in an alien natural world. Such a classification of the poets reduces their achievements considerably and fails to account for the sophisticated understanding of art and society evident in their poetry and prose. Wright and Campbell have never been simple nature poets turning, with romantic fitness, to the country as the source of poetic feeling; their concern with nature encompasses the human place in a physical universe at a time when both are under threat.

7

A New Kind of Novel: the Work of Patrick White

In the postwar years Australian poets struggled to reconcile what they saw as the bleak realities of a technological and materialistic age with the human imagination. Some of them believed that this was the proper role for poetry, while the novel should examine more specific problems of the social world. For this reason, writers such as Judith Wright or James McAuley chose to write poetry as the genre central to the problems of their times. Poetry seemed most able to renew the language and to explore areas of life submerged under the pressure of science and materialism.

It was a surprise, then, to find that the writer who most clearly addressed all the current debates about Australian literature was a novelist, Patrick White. White had begun his career as a poet and thought of himself as a dramatist in the late thirties and forties. But various influences, including his return to Australia from Europe after the war, led him to choose the novel as his main artistic form. At the time of his return, White had no intention of continuing his career as a writer. In any case, there was little chance that his plays would be produced in Australia, though he might have joined Hope, Wright and Campbell as a poet. Instead, he chose to write novels; this choice was a response to his observation of Australian social life and his anger at the values evident in that life.

The Work of Patrick White

White became a novelist because he was interested in the social world which had become the preserve of the novel. But, he was also dissatisfied with the prevailing socialist realist limitation of the novel to a straightforward depiction of external social life. He shared with the poets a concern to find values beyond the traffic of day-to-day life, and a concern for the possibilities of language as a means of exploring that life. But White, even more than Judith Wright, felt an urgent need to connect this exploration with the society around him. Like Wright, White was a social teacher and the novel gave him the means to address contemporary Australians about their own lives.

In turning the concerns of the poets into the material for his novels, Patrick White opened up new possibilities for the Australian novel. White's early novels demonstrated that the language and imagery of the poets could enrich the storytelling of the novelist and that the novel need not shrink from examining the place of spiritual belief in human behaviour. In doing so, White developed techniques which, although seen by his early critics as modernist, became widely accepted and mimicked by Australian writers in the sixties and seventies.

White arrived in Australia when the call for a national literature which renewed the nineties tradition was at its peak. In *Meanjin* and *Southerly* critics were lamenting the failure of Australian prose writers to make the bush tradition anew. They cried out for a novelist who could make the democratic humanist concerns of the past relevant to postwar life in the cities. They wanted the Great Australian Novel of the Great Australian Cities to signify Australia's growth to maturity as a civilised, industrial nation.

Certainly, there was no shortage of writers willing to attempt the task. The socialist realists addressed nationalism, life in the cities and the socialist elements of the Lawson tradition. There were writers such as Kylie Tennant who produced entertaining studies of country and city life. Popular writers such as Jon Cleary and John O'Grady gave cheerful, if superficial, expression to modern Australian society. Frank Hardy offered *Power Without Glory*, rather inaccurately, as the 'first Australian novel of the city'. But no writer satisfied the need for a 'great' novel which confronted contemporary Australian life, gave meaning to Australianness and yet concerned itself with important, universal issues. There had been several contestants, of course, such as Joseph Furphy's *Such is Life* or Henry Handel Richardson's *The Fortunes*

—

of Richard Mahony but Furphy, honoured by being unread, belonged to a rural past and Richardson's novel did not fit the democratic tradition.

The search for the Great Australian Novel has become one of the enduring quests of Australian literary life—a kind of literary quest for the Holy Grail. Like the Great American Novel, this elusive goal has emerged from a sense of cultural colonialism and a corresponding need to establish a national cultural place in the world. For Australia this need was revived by critics after the war, when the nation's security had been shaken for the first time and the old links with Britain were being challenged. But it came at a time when the great three-volume novel which offered the whole sweep of a nation's life had had its day.

Nevertheless, Patrick White has done his best to give Australians the novel they wanted. In 1973 he was awarded the Nobel prize for literature, thus claiming the attention of the whole world for Australia. As an appropriate reward, in 1986 an opera of his novel *Voss* was produced—opera still being accepted in Australia as the ultimate art form. However, to place White's work within nineteenth-century perspectives of great literature and culture is to do him a disservice. No other writer in postwar Australia was quite so aware of the place and time in which he was writing. White even had a few amused comments to make on the quest for the Great Australian Novel. In his *The Vivisector* (1970) he created a jackeroo who was writing it. The jackeroo's main problem was that he hadn't experienced enough and if he wrote it all out of his head 'it wouldn't be real'.[1] Here White is enjoying a sideswipe at the idea that realism must be the guide to the novelist.

White's early novels address all the arguments about literature current at the time they were written. *The Tree of Man* (1955) and *Voss* (1957) examined the national tradition while refusing to accept the socialist realist version of nationalism. *The Aunt's Story* (1948) used various techniques, including modernist techniques, while examining a real world in crisis. All three novels sought out some understanding of the world beyond the material by means of the physical world. As well, *The Tree of Man* and *Riders in the Chariot* (1961) examined the values of modern Australian city life.[2]

Patrick White's early novels changed Australian novel-writing and opened up a range of possibilities for other Australian writers, while his later novels show the confidence and skill of an artist

—

168

prepared to look honestly at his own state. *The Vivisector* and *The Eye of the Storm* (1973) may be his most impressive achievements but it is the novels of the late forties and the fifties, *The Aunt's Story*, *The Tree of Man* and *Voss*, which caused the most debate and reconsideration of the novelist's task in Australia. White has sometimes been depicted as an elite artist, isolated from his society and concerned only with aesthetic values. But his life and his response to society reveal a different artistic approach altogether.

White grew up in Australia according to the established pattern for wealthy squatters' sons. John Manifold, David Campbell and Geoffrey Dutton had similar educations, though White's asthma barred him from the more robust activities, such as football. As well, White's parents sent him to an English public school so he missed the camaraderie of Geelong Grammar or the King's School. He went to Cambridge University a few years before Manifold and Campbell and was not part of a colonial group enjoying exile. Before the war White had decided that America, Britain and Europe would be all the homeland he needed, but the war forced him to reconsider.

As White has explained, his decision to return to Australia after the Second World War came from a sense that to remain in England would be fatal to his art. If Australians have come to see that White has enriched their culture then it is interesting that White returned to Australia in search of that obscure 'inspiration' which might benefit his art. White thought England to be 'an actual and spiritual graveyard' after the war. He found writing difficult and he feared that he might become 'that most sterile of beings, a London intellectual'.[3]

One of the most interesting factors in White's decision to return was his reading of Eve Langley's novel *The Peapickers*. In *Flaws in the Glass* he writes:

> I read *The Peapickers* and was filled with a longing for Australia, a country I saw through a childhood glow. Its people had tended to reject the Pom during the years spent there between school and university. But I could still grow drunk on visions of its landscape.[4]

The Peapickers, so praised by Douglas Stewart for its robust fun, is a novel which celebrates the innocence and cheerfulness of Australian life. It is not difficult to imagine a demobilised RAF officer in London seizing upon it as a reminder of carefree childhood.

White returned to Australia filled with nostalgia for a land as uncorrupted as childhood itself. The final part of *The Aunt's Story* was written on the ship which brought White to Australia for a visit in 1946. The novel, for all its criticisms of Australian superficiality, shows a real affection for Australian vitality. White leads his aunt through the trials and delights of Australian childhood to the chaos of prewar Europe, then brings her to a simpler place—in the novel it is rural America—for her final insight.

This progress follows White's own life up to the time when he was writing the novel. Theodora Goodman's childhood and family life rely very much on White's own experience, and the central section of the novel, as White clearly states in *Flaws in the Glass*, is drawn from his own experience of the war. It is the final section of the novel which suggests some of White's hopes for his return to Australia. Theodora flees from the European madness of the Hotel du Midi to the mid-West of America, a land of distances and simplicity. The setting for the ending of the novel, with its cornfields and framehouses, is specifically American, but White leaves Theodora in the hands of the kind of people he was to choose for the subject of his next book set in Australia, *The Tree of Man*.

When White returned to Australia his first response was to settle as a small and unambitious farmer at Castle Hill. It seems that he was, in fact, pursuing the same kind of peace which he gave his character, Theodora, at the end of *The Aunt's Story*. The novel traces a search for order amid the social and mental disorder of Europe in the thirties. Theodora embraces the lives of other people and suffers, through them, the misery of a civilisation on the brink of chaos. From all her fragmented experience Theodora eventually achieves a sense of unity in the world. But, for White personally, this kind of unity may have been more an aspiration than an achievement at the time.

Critical studies of *The Aunt's Story* quite rightly concentrate on White's handling of the themes of isolation, the interplay of illusion and reality in the novel, and Theodora's courageous quest for understanding through her experiences and her own mental life. But White also comments quite clearly on the state of the world. The concern with White as an artist should not blind us to his very real social concerns even in his early novels. While it is undeniable that *The Aunt's Story* takes the difficulty of human communication as a premise and major concern, White also suggests that this is associated with the false values and chaotic politics of the twentieth-century world.

—

The novel's concern is with the individual, but the individual has reached a point of crisis because of the state of civilisation. In the 'Jardin Exotique' section of the novel particularly, White presents the loss of purpose and honesty as an affliction of the times. All of the residents at the Hotel du Midi are expatriate, exiled by the peculiar diseases of Europe in the twentieth century. Nazism in Germany, communism in Russia, the purposeless capitalism of America and the effete posturings of England are represented in the state of the occupants of the Hotel du Midi. They are forced to rely on physical objects as signs of their own existence. Thus, the Bloch sisters endlessly catalogue their possessions, Madame Rapallo establishes herself by a complicated system of props and fights General Sokolnikov for the nautilus. Dishonesty, self-delusion and materialism support the shaky existences of the hotel's inhabitants, and these characters reflect the hollowness and dishonesty of all Europe.

It is this particular world—the world of prewar Europe—which rejects the honesty and perception of Theodora and which embraces madness rather than Theodora's perception of true reality. When Theodora's life becomes fragmented into the lives of others she is also enduring a vision of an actual world, of an historical Europe where all values have been distorted. This is quite obvious, but literary discussion can easily ignore historical influences, especially when confronted with White's great concern with the limitations of the novel as a form of communication. *The Aunt's Story* is deeply concerned with the collapse of European civilisation, not simply the fate of the individual.

White's modernism in this novel—principally in the central part—came from his concern about disorder. No realistic account of thirties life could convey the relationship between the disordered material world and the disordered interior life as *The Aunt's Story* does. In Australia in the forties, modernist techniques were seen as a commitment to disorder and even a celebration of it. White uses these techniques to seek order and in *The Aunt's Story* he is constantly drawing attention to the relationship between the physical world and the human consciousness. Far from seeking an abandonment of order, he struggles to achieve it by using physical objects to reflect human states.

When White attempted for himself the resolution which he gave Theodora he did not find simple peace in an uncorrupted country. Instead he confronted a monstrous society devoted to material possessions and material pleasure. His explanation of his emergence from the quiet of Castle Hill to publish another novel has now become quite famous. If White's outrage at the state of Australian society seems more exaggerated than that of other social observers, it must be because of the disappointment of his hopes and because of his appreciation of the meaning of the war and its atrocities. His gift for comic extravagance shines through this passage from 'The Prodigal Son':

> In all directions stretched the Great Australian Emptiness in which the mind is the least of possessions, in which the rich man is the important man, in which the schoolmaster and the journalist rule what intellectual roost there is, in which beautiful youths and girls stare at life through blind blue eyes, in which human teeth fall like autumn leaves, the buttocks of cars grow hourly glassier, food means cake and steak, muscles prevail, and the march of material ugliness does not raise a quiver from the average nerves.[5]

This criticism of Australia must by now be familiar to readers. It takes up a theme sounded by many of the new 'professionals' in Australia and to be developed at greater length by Robin Boyd in his *The Australian Ugliness* (1960). It can also be found in A.D. Hope's early satires and comic poems or in James McAuley's tirades for *Quadrant*. It was a criticism which placed White with those who found Australian life so concerned with the physical world that there was no place for spiritual values, for art or creativity. Of course, this ranged socialist writers against White, for they were concerned with the 'average' Australian—the 'typical'—and they believed that human salvation must be achieved through the material world. Also they did not fail to notice that White had inherited a wealth which put him above the common battle for a livelihood.

White was a social critic who wanted to observe and comment on the realities of Australian life. For this reason he declared himself to be a teacher helping to 'people a barely inhabited country with a race possessed of understanding'. This was an accepted role for the novelist in Australia; Dymphna Cusack, Frank Hardy or Vance Palmer might also see themselves as social teachers. But the kind of understanding which White wanted to communicate was more complex than Cusack's or Hardy's humane or political messages. It was an understanding which White himself was attempting to gain through writing the novel and it was akin to the perceptions which David Campbell or Judith Wright sought

172

through poetry. White was trying to find links between the increasingly debased and ugly physical world and the state of the human mind. At the same time he wanted to examine the way these relationships affected social behaviour. Material objects, things, dominate White's writing as they might be expected to dominate the work of a symbolist poet. But these things are reference points for human states, and White takes his analysis further than the poets by relating his perceptions back to visible human behaviour. White's concerns, especially in *The Tree of Man*, *Voss* and *Riders in the Chariot*, were social and moral, as well as aesthetic and spiritual.

As some socialist realist writers came to realise, White's response to Australia, *The Tree of Man*, took many of the socialist realist guidelines on their own terms. The novel examined the lives of two ordinary Australians—Stan and Amy Parker—acting out that general whole which might be termed 'typical' of their class. It also paid open tribute to the national tradition; Stan and Amy share the isolation and physical trials of Lawson's and Furphy's poor selectors. Furthermore, the novel had a sense of the individual's place in history. The European war takes up only thirty pages of the 480-page novel, the depression is merely suggested and the city quietly spreads out to engulf the piece of land that is Parkers', but social change does form a background to the novel and White makes time and its passing a major preoccupation.

Socialist realists might also have been impressed by White's refusal to use adventure or external crisis as a major source of interest in the novel. Just as Lawson's finest short stories avoided elaborate plotting and false excitement, White kept to his stated aim—to confront the boredom of the ordinary. No other Australian novelist was prepared to take on this task at the time. The socialist realists tended to find an historical crisis—the depression or the war—in order to heighten the challenges of ordinary existence. Social writers such as Ruth Park or Kylie Tennant sought out the extreme cases of poverty and hardship. Even Dorothy Hewett admits that the Alexandria textile mill of *Bobbin Up* was the worst of its kind. The socialist realist writers, in particular, believed that the working-class struggle would be sufficient inspiration but, as White observed, the working-class Australians of the fifties had more complex problems than poverty. It is impossible to deny that some poverty existed in Australia in the fifties, but for most Australians, including the working class, it was a time of relative plenty. Those who had suffered in the depression knew that the tide had turned. When White diagnosed material ugliness as the problem he was more aware of the contemporary world than many socialist realists. (Though *Bobbin Up* identified the tawdry consolations for workers under capitalism.)

The Tree of Man, then, could be called a socialist realist novel in some respects—and it was called so by the communist writer Mona Brand in 1963.[6] But White's technique formed a major obstacle to acceptance by socialists. His dissatisfaction with the 'dreary, dun-coloured offspring of journalistic realism' was a red rag to the red bulls on the left. The simple view that all technical experiment meant 'art for art's sake' led some to read *The Tree of Man* as evidence of the worst kind of artistic elitism.

If the left saw White as an elitist, the right attacked him for mangling the language or for a spurious mysticism. Alan Lawson has tried to correct the view that *The Tree of Man* and *Voss* were condemned on sight by most Australian critics.[7] He is right when he points to the sympathetic and considered judgements which appeared in journals such as *Southerly*. But in the fifties, just as today, the most influential book reviews are those which appear in the newspapers. These reviews give the first response to a novel and they are the most widely read. A.D. Hope's 'verbal sludge' review of *The Tree of Man* appeared in the *Sydney Morning Herald* and Hope's status and wit meant that it was found to be more important than, say, Harold Oliver's more considered article in *Southerly* several months later. With Kylie Tennant and Douglas Stewart adding their voices White had some justification for feeling persecuted.

But the technical 'innovations' of *The Tree of Man* all followed from White's preoccupation with finding the 'extraordinary in the ordinary'. The decision to concentrate on characters who could not articulate their own understanding of the world meant that White needed to suggest this understanding. He did so by developing a language which moved from the speech patterns of inarticulate people to a poetry of the universe and by making apparently trivial moments significant. In *The Tree of Man* White is an intrusive narrator totally in control of his characters and their possibilities. From time to time he delivers homely truths directly to us: 'Great truths are only half-grasped this side of sleep' or 'There are times when you know nothing, and times when you know all'. The didactic nature of the novel is as obvious as in any novel by Frank Hardy or Judah Waten.

The Work of Patrick White

Patrick White's solution to the problem of ordinariness was to find a universal significance for Stan and Amy Parker so that their daily experiences take on mythical proportions. White has explained that he was reading the Bible in the period before writing and the language, particularly of the first part of the novel, suggests Genesis. The wedding of the symbolic and the social fails from time to time when White overloads the trivial with significance. At other times though, White manages to choose experiences which are immediately accessible as suggestive of deeper knowledge, for example Stan Parker's response to the lightning before a storm or Amy Parker's pleasure in a walk through a paddock after rain.

But in forming his novel so clearly to a pattern White robbed his characters of human individuality. Stan and Amy Parker are not only simple and uneducated people, they also lack vitality. Where the socialist realist writers insisted too much on the active and progressive nature of the ordinary people, White makes them incorrigibly passive. The Parkers lack humour and character because such qualities would interfere with the symbolic roles which they are forced to play. No ordinary people in the world are quite as ordinary as the Parkers.

It is possible to appreciate Patrick White's exploration of spiritual possibilities through the physical world and to admire his ability to address universal problems through the most unpromising characters and still turn with distaste from the final scenes of the novel. Stan's death is so stage-managed, with his chair placed at the centre of a mandala and a passing evangelist to raise the question of God, that only the most submissive reader will not protest. Far from being a subtle artist, at this point White delivers the lesson with sledgehammer blows.

Could any reader of *The Tree of Man* miss the fact that White saw himself as the teacher of a materialist people? Addressing a godless society, White pointed to the ways in which life might be made meaningful. In *The Tree of Man* the spiritual world is not an 'other' world presided over by God, his angels and saints, as it is in the poetry of James McAuley, but an understanding which may be reached through a proper appreciation of the world of the senses. Through silent contact with nature, through a receptiveness to painting, music and drama, through observation of other people and even on occasions through religious rites, White's characters perceive the mysteries.

Nothing could be further from Douglas Stewart's notion of the novel as a celebration of character. But *The Tree of Man* belonged irrevocably to its place and time. White had made the Australian tradition anew and, in doing so, had offered a critique of the tradition—for Australian life with its peacefulness and boredom must look to the creation of a culture which provided some meaning beyond material comfort. The glib criticism of Australian society offered by commentators in various Australian 'way of life' books had, in *The Tree of Man*, become a creative contribution to that culture.

By turning away from a study of character White was able to trace the patterns of nature and the physical world in relation to his archetypal Australians. But this also made him appear less humane because he seemed to deny the creative powers of ordinary human beings. White's creative energy is the human creativity of *The Tree of Man* just as David Campbell is the creator of his own imaginative world. When Amy or Stan Parker look at a cabbage or a piece of coloured glass they see only the connections which White allows them to see. The characters participate in White's vision but, at times, they appear to be only objects—like the coloured glass—entirely dependent on the artist who creates them.

As well as pursuing the relationship between the physical world and the life of the spirit, White had clear social opinions to declare. In *The Tree of Man* he makes no effort to hide his contempt for the city and its values. The Parkers' son, Ray, finds a natural environment for his criminal behaviour there; Thelma Parker pursues her social dishonesties among a wealthier class of city dwellers. But Thelma, rather than Ray, draws White's greatest contempt: 'There is such nastiness in the evolution of the synthetic soul', says White. Thelma is the character who most embodies the values of Australians in the fifties as White described them: she is conventional, insipid, dishonest and single-mindedly in pursuit of material security.

Thelma indicates one of the continuing difficulties in White's view of society in his earlier novels. His wit finds rich material in the trivial concerns of characters such as Thelma, but his scorn for superficiality and materialism easily becomes contempt for the ordinary members of humanity who display them. In *The Tree of Man* White suggests that the ordinary people who may find some meaning in their existence form an exclusive group themselves— the artists, saints, madmen and innocent souls such as Amy and

176

Stan. White proposes a spiritual vision for the elect and damnation for the rest of us. And the revelation in *Flaws in the Glass* that Thelma Parker is a version of White himself softens but does not counter this view.

This mixture of cruelty and passionate concern for humanity is a feature of most of White's writing. If White had chosen to write poetry he might have been able to avoid his regular attacks on people for all kinds of trivial failings. As a novelist he must look more clearly at social behaviour than a poet need do. White is so observant and so easily irritated by petty vulgarities that he sometimes appears misanthropic. At the same time, these very qualities can bring him to masterful social satire and they create a productive tension between the writer's ideals and his practices.

If *The Tree of Man* expressed White's disappointment with the peace and simplicity of his life in Australia, his next novel, *Voss*, went back to the European tradition which he had fled. *Voss* has sent many readers in pursuit of information about the explorer, Ludwig Leichhardt, who seems to be the model for White's hero; the latest biography of Leichhardt, Elsie May Webster's *Whirlwinds in the Plain*, was written as a result of curiosity about *Voss*. Yet the most obvious model for such a hero was the man who wreaked the havoc which had destroyed Europe only ten years before the novel was written. In *Flaws in the Glass* White points to Hitler as a major source of his inspiration: 'The real Voss, as opposed to the actual Leichhardt, was a creature of the Egyptian desert, conceived by the perverse side of my nature at a time when all our lives were dominated by that greater German megalomaniac'.[8]

In *The Tree of Man* White presented the achetypal settler, in *Voss* the wanderer. But more than this, *The Tree of Man* confronted the Australian tradition and its inadequacies, while *Voss* re-examined the European tradition which White had rejected at the end of the war. The democratic interpretation of Australian history elevated the role of the small settlers in making Australia. White turned to the more heroic and elitist explorer tradition in *Voss*.

Perhaps it is not strange that Hitler and his atrocities did not impress Australians so much as the Japanese and the deprivations of Changi. That other novelist who returned to Australia at the end of the war, Martin Boyd, believed that Australians simply could not understand the nature of the crimes against the Jews.

Certainly, in his view the militarism and racism which had finally been revealed as the grossest evil survived in Australia. White, like Boyd, had experienced some of the European war and he felt the need to come to terms with its meaning for European civilisation.[9]

It was Hitler's war which forced White to leave Europe, just as it forced thousands of other migrants to settle in Australia. And the fact that Hitler's gas chambers were the culmination of a proud civilisation must lead thinking observers to question that civilisation and its values. It might almost have been predicted that a writer nurtured in European traditions, well read in German literature and forced to participate in the war against the Germans would want to examine the civilisation and its hero figure.

Voss places that European figure within an Australian setting. White contrasts the mediocrity and timidity of Australian life with the courage and cruelty of the European hero. In the early pages of *Voss* White offers a vision of Australia close to that of A.D. Hope in his poem 'Australia'. Voss' comments on the timidity of the settlers huddling around the coast of Australia recall Hope's:

> second-hand Europeans pullulate
> Timidly on the edge of alien shores.

Voss ventures into the deserts which Hope suggested may have more to teach than 'civilisation'. White suggests, though, that only a man of German arrogance, a man willing to challenge conventional morality, can discover anything. There has been a great deal of discussion of White's notion of God in the novel—particularly the portrayal of Voss as a Nietzschean hero 'beyond good and evil'. In fact, White seems to be examining the failures of that hero figure. Voss claims at the beginning of the novel that he is his own god:

> But I do believe, you must realize. Even though I worship with pride. Ah, the humility, the humility! This is what I find so particularly loathsome. My God, besides, is above humility. 'Ah', she said. 'Now I understand'. It was clear. She saw him standing in the glare of his own brilliant desert. Of course, He was Himself indestructible.[10]

When Voss criticises humility his scorn is for the failure of courage implied in the belief in God as protector and the safety of a Christian afterlife. Clearly, White has little sympathy for this kind of conventional religion. But Voss has his counterpart in

Laura, also an unbeliever, who manages the difficult translation of love of God into love of man. The important element of the understanding given to Laura at the height of her illness is the human attempt to know his or her own relationship to God:

> How important it is to understand the three stages. Of God into man. Man. And man returning into God...When man is truly humbled, when he has learnt that he is not God, then he is nearest to becoming so. In the end, he may ascend.[11]

Ann McCulloch has suggested that *Voss* demonstrates a true understanding of Nietzsche's philosophy: that the overman (or superman) does not replace God but learns that God can only be found by denying His existence.[12] Certainly, it is Voss' attempt to set himself up as God which results in his humiliation and death. But it also brings a kind of apotheosis—the blacks claim that Voss' spirit remains in the country.

If we read *Voss* as an examination of the European romantic hero who dares to defy both conformist morality and the fearful God who demands such morality, then we must note White's very careful modification of that hero. In Laura, Voss meets a loving humanity and through her his cruelty and arrogance are subdued. At the end of the novel Judd, the materialist of the expedition, tells us:

> Voss? No. He was never God, though he liked to think that he was. Sometimes, when he forgot, he was a man.... He was more than a man.... He was a Christian, such as I understand it.[13]

Voss is not a Christian in the conventional sense but in acquiring human love to match his spiritual courage. In *Voss*, then, the Hitler figure has been brought to salvation. Defiance of God and conventions of God ends, not in an inhuman rampage but in humility and the return to human love.

But human love is not easily attained in White's early novels. The novelist himself finds it difficult to love the extroverted vulgarity of Australian life. Even in *Voss* White comments on the stultifying Australian mediocrity and empty materialism. Once again, White hammers home his lesson in the final chapter. Here, the surviving truth-seekers gather around Laura Trevelyan while she instructs them in the importance of seeking 'true knowledge'. Their discussion speculates on the future of Australian society, and the musician Topp comments:

If we do not come to grief on our mediocrity as a people, if we are not locked for ever in our own bodies. Then, too, there is the possibility that our hates and our carnivorous habits will unite in a logical conclusion: we may destroy one another.

Willie Pringle, 'who, it transpired, had become a genius', answers him:

The grey of mediocrity, the blue of frustration. . . . Topp has dared to raise a subject that has often occupied my mind: our inherent mediocrity as a people. I am confident that the mediocrity of which he speaks is not a final and irrevocable state; rather it is a creative source of endless variety and subtlety. The blowfly on its bed of offal is but a variation of the rainbow. Common forms are continually breaking into brilliant shapes. If we will explore them.[14]

When Ludlow asks when the 'country with a future' will become the land of the present, Laura answers 'now'. She prophesies that Voss' legend will be written down and the novel itself, is, of course, the record of this legend. So, in the end, the novel is offered as an attempt to overcome the ordinary limits of life through art.

Such a schematic account of *Voss* cannot convey the extraordinary energy with which White invests the physical world with human meaning. The landscape encountered by the explorers has little basis in reality but it is as imaginatively conceived as Spenser's *Fairy Queen*. The strength of the novel does not come from the rather commonplace social analysis of Australian life but from the way in which White links 'things'—'the rocks and sticks of words'—with human states. In short, White demonstrates the power to remake the physical world in the mind which he sees as the salvation from destructive mediocrity.

White has expressed his anger that *Voss* has been read as a 'costume romance', a novel about Australian history with no relevance to the contemporary world.[15] But it is very difficult to read the novel in such a way when it is directed so explicitly to a postwar society, the kind of society described so often by social critics of fifties Australia. White's characters utter his own despair at Australian complacency; it is not a criticism appropriate for a nineteenth-century pioneering community but for a comfortable modern society.

The three novels which created White's reputation can be seen as examining the conflicting attractions of Australian and Euro-

—

180

pean life. *The Aunt's Story* observes Europe on the point of self-destruction. *The Tree of Man* tackles the awesome boredom of Australian life. And *Voss* tries to retrieve from the great European civilisation some of the elements which might make Australian life meaningful.

If *Voss* sent readers back to the lives of the explorers that, in itself, could not conflict with White's desire to give Australians an understanding of themselves. The discovery of the nation's history might be part of that cultural awareness White hoped to stimulate, though he suggested music and painting as obvious sources of understanding. Like *The Tree of Man*, *Voss* did not baulk at underlining the lesson at the end. The novel's success as art rests, like its predecessor, on White's painstaking care in turning over each moment for its poetic possibilities. Most readers accept Laura Trevelyan's obvious spelling out of the message at the end simply because they have endured the wonder of Voss' struggles in the desert.

White manages human love more comfortably in an historical setting. In *Voss* White not only makes Voss' love for Laura central, he is also more gentle with the lesser members of humanity. White certainly attacks the Bonners, Lt Radclyffe, the Pringles and the other members of Sydney society for their timidity and concern for comfort, but these attacks lack the acid of the comments on Thelma in *The Tree of Man*. Belle Bonner, in particular, might have been presented as an insipid coquette like Fanny Goodman of *The Aunt's Story*, but instead is allowed a childlike innocence and a beauty which reflects the natural world rather than the shallow values of society.

This observation might also be made about White's other historical novel, *A Fringe of Leaves* (1976), which surprised reviewers by its sympathetic treatment of even its most conformist characters. There White also asserted that 'God is love', not a 'Lord God of hosts'. But the historical setting in both *Voss* and *A Fringe of Leaves* deprived White of the real source of his animus—the daily trivia of Australian contemporary life. White reserves his most trenchant wit for the things closest to him, so Thelma Parker suffers while Belle Bonner, locked away in the nineteenth century, does not.

No novel expresses White's anger at contemporary Australian society more clearly than *Riders in the Chariot*, published in 1961. Sarsaparilla and the adjacent suburb of Barranugli reflect the ugliness of expanding Sydney. There people live in uniform boxes (hot water, no sewerage) complacently admiring their own possessions. Among the vulgar inhabitants of Sarsaparilla walk White's elect group of visionaries: Miss Hare the eccentric, Himmelfarb the Jew, Mrs Godbold the saint and Alf Dubbo the artist. These people are despised and mistreated by their neighbours simply because they are different. Australian society, White suggests, is not only conformist and materialist but actively evil in casting out nonconformists.

In *Riders in the Chariot* this evil culminates in the outrageous crucifixion of Himmelfarb by a group of drunken workers. White portrays the Australian worker of Sydney's western suburbs as the perpetrator of ugliness and brutality, not, as a more sympathetic observer might put it, the victim of ignorance and the temptations of consumerism. When White tells Himmelfarb's story he is once again attempting to explain the meaning of the Second World War to Australians who were largely untouched by it. Recent studies of Australian responses to Jewish immigrants indicate that Australians did confuse German and Jew during the war years. Many postwar immigrants tell stories of misunderstandings and deliberate cruelties by Australians. But crucifixion on Good Friday? This does not even give the Australian worker credit for his famous indifference to religion.

Yet the characters which reveal White at his most intemperate are suburban women—Mrs Jolley and Mrs Flack. White created these two harridans with a gusto which makes them strangely attractive. They are close sisters to Barry Humphries' Edna Everage who had made her first appearance on stage a few years before the novel's publication. Here is Mrs Jolley in full stride:

'It was a letter from Mrs Apps,' Mrs Jolley pursued. 'That is Merle, the eldest. Merle has a particular weakness for her mum, perhaps because she was delicate as a kiddy. But struck lucky later on. With a hubby who denies her nothing—within reason, of course, and the demands of his career. Mr Apps—his long service will soon be due—is an executive official at the Customs. I will not say well-thought-of. Indispensable is nearer the mark. So it is not uncommon for Merle to hobnob with the high-ups of the Service, and entertain them to a buffy at her home. *Croaky de poison.* Chipperlarters. All that. With perhaps a substantial dish of, say, *Chicken à la King.* I never believe in blowing my own horn, but Merle does things that lovely. Yes. Her buffy has been written up, not once, but several times.'[16]

White clearly enjoys each of Mrs Jolley's entrances in the book. Her conversation ranges so energetically over the clichés and trivia of suburban existence. Mrs Jolley is a 'Mother' who makes domesticity into a kind of religion. She is awful but she is also a rich source of comedy. In casting her as a villainness White is denying his own appetite for comic extravagance, an appetite which he later allowed full rein in *The Eye of the Storm* and *The Twyborn Affair*.

The issues of *Riders in the Chariot*, however, are no laughing matter. White's 'riders' are all trying to reach a deeper understanding of their own existence, through instinct, knowledge, charity or creativity. In this novel White's contempt for what he sees as ordinary people denies them any hope of salvation at all.

Two essential approaches to the world are in conflict in these novels. One may be called a secular humanism which sees all humans as equal and concerns itself with the material well-being of all people. The other is a spirituality which demands sacrifice and action, and which recognises struggle as necessary to understanding. In Christian terms they are the injunction to 'love one's neighbour' and 'to love God'. Patrick White has himself called the two forces the 'nostalgia of permanence' and 'the fiend of motion'.[17] White knows the attractions of both approaches but he feels himself to be exiled from the secular humanist community. On the other hand he finds the discovery of a spiritual world to be no easy matter and his strong sense of values leads him towards charity and humanism. White sets up a dialogue between the two positions in his early novels and he cannot be classified as committed to either camp.

White sees Australian life as fundamentally drugged by its humanism. The democratic view assesses human life only by material comfort and possessions and cuts down the 'tall poppies' who dare to challenge the mediocrity of the norm. The European tradition, on the other hand, admires the courage and honesty of the outsider who may sacrifice comfort for solitary achievement. White recognises that this tradition is crueller than Australian passivity and in *Voss* he suggested that a reconciliation of the two might be possible. In *Riders in the Chariot*, however, by a savage distortion the democratic tradition is presented as cruel, and the representative of the European world, Himmelfarb, is not the daring wanderer but the universal victim, the Jew. White's anger at the daily vulgarity of the society around him has pushed him into the elitist camp.

Yet there is a further complication in those nasty suburbanites of *Riders in the Chariot*. Look how White describes Mrs Jolley and Mrs Flack dissecting the world:

> As tea and contentment increased understanding of each other, as well as confidence in their own powers, it was only to be expected that two ladies of discretion and taste should produce their knives and try them for sharpness on weaker mortals. Seated above the world on springs and petty point they could lift the lids and look right into the boxes in which moiled other men, crack open craniums as if they had been boiled eggs, read letters before they had been written, scent secrets that would become a source of fear to those concerned. Eventually the ladies would begin. Their methods would be steel, though their antiphon was always bronze.[18]

This might be a description of White's own methods when dealing with them. Somehow White has reached a fury which turns back on himself. The author does not quite go so far as to identify his own art with that of the suburban matrons, but the destructive element in his art is clearly apparent.

In his later novels, and *The Vivisector* in particular, White recognises that his kind of art is destructive as well as creative. Both Hurtle Duffield in *The Vivisector* and Elizabeth Hunter in *The Eye of the Storm* use other people in the course of their quest for enlightenment. But they also reward those people by offering a focus for their existences and a sense of a greater purpose.

After *Riders in the Chariot* White never again attacked Australian life quite so immoderately. His later novels turn to the role of the artist and the nature of his inspiration. The daily aspects of Australian life no longer seem to raise White's anger to the same pitch and he softens his portrayal of 'ordinary' people so that a sense of the absurd leavens the novels. In the first part of *The Twyborn Affair* (1979), a version of Mrs Jolley appears as Joan Golson—the Australian in Europe—and she is unequivocally the source of comedy rather than satire.

This change, or mellowing, of White's attitude to Australian life may be attributed to his gradual resolution of the problems which he confronted in the fifties. The development of his interests as a novelist from that first desperate concern to shake Australians into consciousness to a growing desire to examine the dilemmas of the artist may be seen as a natural progression. However, it is also appropriate that White's scorn for Australian materialism was at its

—

peak in the fifties and began to diminish with the sixties. For this was also the case with other writers and social observers. By the sixties A.D. Hope had almost abandoned satire for more subtle considerations of art and its meaning, and after *Captain Quiros* James McAuley found himself less inclined to harangue Australian society through his poetry. The world had changed on the left, too. After 1956, writers began to leave the Communist Party and by the early sixties Cold War alignments had faded.

The life-and-death issues of the fifties were blowing away like puffs of smoke. Modernism no longer implied decadence and the descent into chaos. Nationalism did not require a commitment to realistic accounts of working-class struggle and above all, 'commit-ment' was disappearing as the vital issue for writers. It was possible for an individual to achieve a sense of cosmic harmony without recourse to conventional religion or a rejection of humane con-cerns. An appreciation of the spiritual need not preclude apprecia-tion of the material world. White's novels played their part in reconciling these various positions.

Stranger than these literary discoveries was the gradual accept-ance in Australia that beauty was the province of the political left rather than the right. In the course of the sixties, the Australian Labor Party, which had been associated with the material demands of unions, with rough-spoken workers and 'basic' needs, began to support educational reform, subsidies to the arts and conservation of Australia's natural and manmade heritage. As time passed Menzies had lost his pre-eminence as the urbane and sophisticated patron of the arts. After his retirement in 1966 and the end of Arthur Calwell's leadership of the Labor party in 1967 the new Labor Party leader, Gough Whitlam, became the political figure who most represented civilised values.

Numerous small incidents and large influences, such as the emergence of a new generation of educated Australians who were politicised by the Vietnam War, helped create this change. The significant element here is the way White's attacks on the vulgar workers and suburbanites of *Riders in the Chariot* may have been read as an attack on the political left in 1961. Ten years later, the left itself was trying to make suburban life more beautiful, anxious to protect the cultural rights of migrants and even putting 'green bans' on ugly building developments. Far from crucifying the cultured migrant on the nearest jacaranda tree, the left political activists were now anxious to learn any lessons he had to teach.

—

The gradual changes in the political and social outlook of Australians from the fifties to the sixties can be read through Patrick White's novels of the period. If he taught Australians that there was more to life than material prosperity, then Australians were only too anxious to learn.

In 1963, White moved from the farm at Castle Hill to a house in Sydney at Centennial Park. His dream of country quiet had ended and his interest in the range of social life is reflected in all the novels written after 1963. White's move to the city forced him to take a greater interest in political activities and by 1972, the recluse of Castle Hill emerged from his house in Martin Road, Centennial Park, to take part in a demonstration against the building of a sports complex near the Park. White has been a public political figure ever since. He joined a group of prominent republicans to express his outrage at the dismissal of Gough Whitlam in 1975 and has been active in the movement for nuclear disarmament in recent years.

So, in the space of ten years, the writer who had attacked Australian working-class values so vehemently in *Riders in the Chariot* found himself standing on the same platform as trade unionists and Labor politicians. White's essential view of humanity had not changed—in *Flaws in the Glass* he still reviles the joggers in the park as devotees of the body rather than the soul—but he had discovered that his concern for matters of the heart and mind was shared by a growing number of people. White may not have taught the 'race', as he put it, this new understanding but his novels focused an attitude already present in Australia. Certainly, by the mid-sixties White's attitude to suburbia might be found in commentaries by architects, dramatists, artists and other writers. Robin Boyd, George Johnston, Barry Humphries, Charmian Clift, Hal Porter and later Thea Astley can all be found offering the sort of criticism of Australian society which White made in the fifties and Hope had written in the forties.

White's particular contribution, though, was the passion which he brought to his observations of Australian life. In his novels we sense the struggle of an individual coming to terms with his own frailties as well as with the social changes which history has forced him to experience. There is a heartfelt distaste in all White's novels for the vulgarities of the flesh—the sweat, the dry patches on the skin, the pimples, the black hairs on male hands or the upper lips of women, the mischances of mastication and excretion.

—

His sense of the beautiful means that every fall from perfection, even those necessary to life, causes him disgust. In *Flaws in the Glass* he tells how he once turned away from his sister because he saw a flea emerge through the beautiful white lace on her dress. At the same time, this revulsion for the flesh sets up a tension in the novels as White struggles—just as Voss does—to achieve human love.

Yet these struggles are not simply the difficulties of an outsider— the 'colonial' in England, the Pom in Australia, the homosexual and artist—they also consider the whole range of social change in the world which the outsider confronts. Because the Australian ethos is based on the Christian command to 'love one's neighbour as oneself' without the corresponding injunction to 'love God', White's personal difficulty in loving his fellows gives a cutting edge to his critique of the Australian tradition.

On the other hand, loving God is no easy matter in a world where the notion of an all-powerful, caring God has been dismissed and the attempt to elevate the human to godlike status has ended in the atrocity of the Second World War. White confronts the limitations of both philosophies even as he examines his personal failings. Though the notion of democracy and egalitarianism may be attractive in theory, White rejects it instinctively as asking too much of him personally while asking too little of the mass of humankind. Human love is a saving achievement in the novels, but White never suggests that it is an easy achievement. In the later novels, in particular, he insists that the artist honestly taking up the challenge to move beyond the bounds of democratic love may, in fact, benefit the ordinary people unable to move beyond those bounds. In this way, something of a reconciliation between the two worlds may be achieved.

White laid to rest a number of the prejudices which had bedevilled Australian writing. He demonstrated that any renewal of the national tradition must face up to the history of the world since 1900 and discard the sentimental myths of a distant past. *The Tree of Man* showed that a novelist could share Lawson's concerns without succumbing to the simplest narrative techniques. Indeed, in the sixties Lawson was re-examined and found to have a greater interest in the internal life than his imitators had believed.

By using modernist techniques within very ordered narrative structures White claimed those techniques for novelists who had no wish to wander into the chaos of the self. White was as impersonal a writer as Hope, McAuley, Stewart or Campbell and his technical experiments did not venture into that obsession with the self which writers of both left and right political persuasions feared. White sought order rather than the indulgence in despair which critics as diverse as Douglas Stewart and Stephen Murray-Smith believed would flow from too much technical innovation. Like Wright, White demonstrated that a writer could care passionately about social issues without commitment to the rigid ideologies of Cold War politics. Though White might appear elitist in his social views, his writing actually served to free the Australian novel—and poetry—for writers with more radical intentions.

White most deserves his Nobel prize and all the acclaim Australians can give him for the sheer ambition and breadth of his writing. He might have chosen David Campbell's path, seeking out a cosmic order through the material world and distilling his understanding in small poems. Instead he expressed such an understanding in novels of epic proportions which were bound to bring critical wrath on his head for their breaking of accepted literary rules. His sense of the urgent need to teach Australians meant that he took the risk of offending and alienating them. White, more than any other Australian writer of his time, pushed Australian literature forward to a more varied and lively future.

8

Drama, Old and New

The arguments about nationalism and its meaning, about secular humanism versus romantic spiritualism and the fluctuating political positions with which they were associated, about modernist art versus a realist tradition may seem, at first, to have little effect on Australian drama in the years after the Second World War. For the standard view of the drama registers the professional production of Ray Lawler's *Summer of the Seventeenth Doll* at the end of 1955 as the birth of postwar Australian drama. This date, so late in the period under review, suggests that Australian drama may have avoided the disputes and commitments of the early fifties, and may foreshadow the freer attitudes of the late sixties.

However, such a view of Australian drama adopts a very rigid definition of what drama means. *Summer of the Seventeenth Doll* was the first professional production of an Australian play in post-war Australia, but it was by no means the first production of an Australian play, nor was it the first professional production of Australian dramatic material as opposed to a conventionally structured play. In Australia, before the production of the *Doll*, there were socialist realist dramatists writing for the New Theatre, professional writers producing material for radio performance, and others who wrote occasional material for the university and commercial revues which were popular in the period. By and large,

—

the socialist realist dramatists developed a theatre which was naturalist and demonstrated the same kind of concerns evident in the socialist realist novel. Radio plays, such as Douglas Stewart's *Fire on the Snow*, might explore forms less dependent on representations of reality while revue sketches made little attempt at formal structure or character development.

Unfortunately, it is difficult to obtain texts for much of the material performed in Australia before 1956, partly because an Australian drama was not recognised until the production of *Summer of the Seventeenth Doll*. In this chapter, I will concentrate on a discussion of the *Doll* as a comment on the nationalism of the early fifties and on the sketches of Barry Humphries as an accessible representative of the revue tradition in Australia. In this way, I want to suggest that the Australian theatre of the late fifties shows some awareness of the changing values in Australia and a degree of impatience with the promotion of nationalism current in the early fifties. I also will put forward the tentative view that Humphries' kind of theatre was more important to the dramatists of the late sixties and seventies than Lawler's more formal play and, by reference to these dramatists, I will explore the changing political allegiances in Humphries' work.

There are a number of ironies about the fifties production of the *Doll*. The first is that this acclaimed play was produced within a year of television's belated arrival in Australia. Television meant a change in the demand for theatre entertainment. By providing the kind of mass popular entertainment which had been the province of the theatre and, later, films, television caused a reappraisal of drama. Some observers feared that television might end professional Australian drama before it had properly begun, but this has not proved to be the case. However, the coming of television marked the end of the nationalist dream of an indigenous theatre with its own distinctive traditions. It meant that Australians would know and learn even more about the popular culture of Britain and America and that Australian society must take its place among the group of wealthy urbanised nations who would consume and imitate the international entertainment culture offered principally by the USA. How ironic, then, that a play acclaimed as the beginnings of a nationalist drama should appear in the same year that television ended the last possibility of such a drama.

A second irony lies in the fact that the production of the *Doll* was professional only because the Elizabethan Theatre Trust funded it. The Trust had been formed in 1954 to raise funds for the Australian performing arts and it had the support of many bureaucrats, businessmen and politicians who believed that the performing arts were essential to a civilised modern nation. In its early years, the Trust distributed funds to ballet and orchestral concerts, but it was hard-pressed to find an Australian play worthy of its help. When the Trust wished to celebrate its emergence as a drama patron it was forced to fund a season of Terence Rattigan's *The Sleeping Prince* by an English touring company. James McAuley wrote a verse prologue for the first performance and, despite the Trust's hopes for Australian drama, the occasion might have been seen as a triumph for the promoters of an international rather than an Australian culture.

The Association for Cultural Freedom had no official part to play in the operations of the Elizabethan Theatre Trust, but Cultural Freedom members were also Trust members. In 1955 Sir John Latham, the president of Cultural Freedom, was also president of the Elizabethan Theatre Trust, and when Cultural Freedom members suggested that the Trust support a production of Arthur Koestler's *Darkness at Noon* by Doris Fitton's Independent Theatre Sir John might be forgiven for failing to see any conflict of interest. Cultural Freedom, after all, was an organisation dedicated to the protection of freedom in the arts; the Elizabethan Theatre Trust was the promoter of the performing arts. Koestler's *Darkness at Noon* was a play which fulfilled both purposes. In the theatre, as in other aspects of cultural life, the 'professionals' or 'the new breed of Australians' were evident, ready to patronise art which offered 'civilised values' and the prestige of cultural achievement. So it was the view of art as icing on the capitalist cake which promoted the success of the *Doll*, the national 'breakthrough'.

Furthermore, these ironies resound in the play itself, which sets up an image of the nationalist Australian only to probe the weaknesses of that image. The play calls on realist traditions but expands them into melodrama; rather than remaining the simple adaptation of the traditional, naturalist, three-act play to Australian experience that it has sometimes been called, the play uses these dramatic elements only to dismiss them as inadequate for the contemporary world.

The *Doll* did not lead to a continuing professional Australian drama. Richard Beynon's *The Shifting Heart* (1957) and Alan Seymour's *The One Day of the Year* (1960) were the only successes in its wake, and it appears that the necessary communal support for theatre was lacking until the late sixties. At the same time, Beynon and Seymour stuck firmly to the naturalist 'kitchen sink' drama and failed to take Lawler's hint that this drama belonged to the past.

Most discussion of the *Doll*, particularly in Leslie Rees' histories of Australian drama, emphasises the importance of institutional support for theatre. Rees gives an account of the attempts to establish a national theatre company and the belief that such a company would provide a firm base for Australian drama. Yet other elements besides the institutional base of a theatre company need to be considered.[1]

One of the major influences on Australian drama has been the emergence of talented Australian performers. Even without a national professional theatre company or a national school of drama, Australia in the postwar years produced a relatively large number of gifted actors. While drama may be seen as 'high' art, created by a writer and produced by a professional company, it is also an entertainment dependent on the skills of the artists who give it life. Looking at the reasons for a drama to come into being— particularly in the context of the fifties—we might consider whether an audience created a demand for Australian drama, whether politicians and other powerful members of the community believed an Australian drama would benefit Australian society, whether Australian writers needed to see their work performed, and also whether Australian actors needed Australian plays in order to give full outlet to their talents.

Of all these factors, the audience demand for Australian drama is the most difficult to assess; little can be claimed beyond the fact that audiences did respond to good Australian plays when they were produced. The attitudes of the promoters of institutional drama have been fairly fully documented, while writers in the early fifties wrote plays only when some possibility of production was in sight, as in the case of the socialist realist playwrights. However, the importance of actors and actors who became writers has often been overlooked. In Australia, the tradition of the actor who, desperate for a decent part, turns to playwriting has remained strong. From Oscar Asche creating *Chu Chin Chow* to display his own talents to Barry Humphries writing his own Edna Everage scripts to Bob Ellis and Michael Boddy collaborating on *The*

—

Legend of King O'Malley, the actor's need for new material has
been a major factor in the creation of Australian plays.

To consider the question of distinctive Australian qualities for a
moment, it is possible to argue that Australian speech and acting
styles make Australian acting the most clearly distinctive of all
Australian arts. Australian actors are generally more energetic,
more daring, more exuberant than their British counterparts and
they do not share the reverence for a text which British actors,
trained for Shakespeare, usually exhibit. This is not to suggest that
Australian actors are in any way better than the actors of other
nations, but to suggest that they are different. It is even possible
to argue that the extroverted nature of Australian performers may
have influenced the direction of Australian drama after the war.
For the fashion for naturalism on stage demanded a restrained
kind of acting, more British than Australian, and there is a tendency
for naturalistic plays to become melodramas on the Australian
stage. On the other hand, the kind of dramatic modernism which
informed Australian plays of the late sixties gave greater scope for
high-spirited acting. Acting styles may have been at least as important as the discovery of Ionesco, Beckett and Brecht in the
development of a freer kind of drama in Australia.

Ruth Cracknell has written a vivid account of the opportunities
for Australian actors in the forties and early fifties. She explains
that, at the time, most actors earned a meagre living by performing
radio scripts—often in endless soap operas. To restore their sense
of stage acting they would perform for 'amateur' theatres such
as Doris Fitton's Independent Theatre or May Hollinworth's
Metropolitan Theatre in Sydney. In every capital city of Australia
amateur theatre groups like these produced drama which was
'professional' in every sense but in the payment of performers and
technicians.[2]

As well, there were Australian writers turning out the radio
plays and serials which gave employment to the actors. Because
much of this playwriting was ephemeral it has been lost to us as
evidence of a drama tradition. Other writing for the stage, such as
the revue sketch, is often overlooked in the search for the starting
point for more serious and structured drama. In fact, in the case of
Australian drama it may be argued that although a national theatre
was expected to emerge in the form of the naturalistic three-act
play, various social and cultural conditions meant that it took quite

different forms. Lawler's play was hailed as the breakthrough because it met all the expectations of the formal Australian play. But perhaps the revues performed by the Phillip Street Theatre in the fifties gave the real moment of recognition to Australian audiences. Cracknell describes the Phillip Street Theatre in just those terms: audiences flocked to it because Australians were 'eager to look at themselves at last'.[3] In these revues, the writers, the actors and the audience came together to understand and enjoy. The Phillip Street revues may not exist as scripts for academic examination, but their influence was so strong that Australians still quote from them and sketches from them turn up in remodelled form in television revues and amateur shows.

Several stage traditions besides the 'serious' drama have contributed to the current Australian drama. Though nationalist writers such as Vance Palmer, Louis Esson or Katherine Susannah Prichard might have hoped to provide Australians with recognisable and novel images of themselves, Australian audiences before the film revolution preferred the rowdy music-hall entertainment. Australians will still leave their television sets for a night of old-style music-hall, or a theatre restaurant with a simple musical show—in Canberra, the local repertory society struggles to find audiences for its 'serious' plays, while its annual music-hall show is sold out for months in advance.

It is well to remember that British drama in the twentieth century fought its way out of the music-halls. For all intents and purposes, English drama had ceased to exist as a creative art form for much of the nineteenth century. The music-hall with its mixture of songs, dance and comedy sketches took the place of the drama. It was the extraordinary emergence of a national theatre in Ireland which helped to revive English drama—and, incidentally, as David Walker has shown, fed the hopes of Louis Esson and Vance Palmer that a similar national theatre might struggle into existence in Australia.[4]

Beyond the music-hall or the musical revue, the circus also offered its popular traditions of clowning, physical bravado and spectacle. All three elements remain part of contemporary Australian theatre. One can even point to the sideshow accompaniment to every Australian agricultural show as adding to the mix—the freak shows and the tawdry glitter of exotic dancers. Jim Sharman, the producer and director, can point to his family's boxing troupe tents as a worthy background for a serious Australian dramatic

194

artist. Before the fifties Australians may never have seen a play which presented Australian life on stage. But they may have seen comedy sketches which poked fun at their lives, such as Roy Rene's famous 'Mo' McCackie, and by the forties they would certainly have heard radio serials such as Gwen Meredith's *The Lawsons* which dramatised ordinary Australian life for mass entertainment.

There were serious single plays performed on radio as well as the popular serials, and Douglas Stewart's *Fire on the Snow* was acclaimed for its power and understanding of the dramatic form. But the call for a national drama was a call for the representation of Australian experience and Australian problems. The long-running radio soap opera or the radio quiz shows, such as those compered by Jack Davey, might represent the distinctive Australian way more clearly than Stewart's verse drama.

In drama, as in fiction writing, the Communist Party of Australia gave encouragement to nationalists. From the thirties the New Theatre League performed serious Australian plays as well as overseas plays with a social message. In the forties and fifties the New Theatres in Sydney and Melbourne performed plays by Frank Hardy, Dymphna Cusack, Oriel Gray, Mona Brand and other communist or nationalist writers. Just as the socialist realist writers' groups encouraged writers in a socialist and nationalist tradition, so the New Theatre groups gave them a venue for the performance of plays. Once again, it should be realised that the theatres did not exist only for the writers: they were an important focus for the energies of young communist supporters and a public platform for a socialist message. Some communists of the forties remember the New Theatre productions as the pivot of their social (as well as socialist) lives; the ideology did not seem so important as the communal sense and excitement of the theatre. In the same way, some communists later claimed to join the Party for the jazz concerts organised by the Eureka Youth league. Certainly, these people are likely to look back on their communist days with a nostalgia for carefree youth, perhaps, to counter the vision of a grim Stalinism. But there are always some people (at least in Australia) who join a political party for the parties.

By the end of the forties, the Party began to interfere in some of the activities of the New Theatre League and, with their comrades in the Realist Writers' groups, the dramatists and performers often found that ideological problems loomed larger than artistic ones.

But, on the whole, the New Theatres managed to avoid the implications of Stalinism. They remained responsive to their audiences and concerned to entertain as well as instruct.[5]

This is the context in which James McAuley's piano-playing and song-writing for the New Theatre's forties revue *I'd Rather Be Left* can be seen. The New Theatre's shows were fun and the ideological elements were so well disguised that the 'red' label has never stuck fast to their productions. It is interesting to note, though, that the New Theatre League's most successful production was not a drama in the 'high' art tradition but *Reedy River*, a musical entertainment which strung together a series of Australian folk songs with some 'typical' Australian dialogue. *Reedy River* was in the tradition of the music-hall and the revue; audiences sang along with the enthusiastic performers on stage. So, even from a socialist point of view, the national theatre tradition could call on the popular traditions of the music-hall.

Other theatrical elements were present in the years before the landmark production of *Summer of the Seventeenth Doll*. Just as young people were attracted to the New Theatre productions no matter how pale their socialism, so university students continued to produce both 'classical' drama and high-spirited revues. At Melbourne University the Union Theatre produced annual revues and established strong acting and writing traditions. This theatre, in particular, can claim to have a major part in both aspects of Australian stage entertainment. It was the original producer of the *Doll*, and it was the venue for Barry Humphries' first revue performance in *Call Me Madman* in 1952.

Writing for the stage in Australia was not dependent on the creation of a national professional theatrical company or patronage from organisations such as the Elizabethan Theatre Trust. The bursts of dramatic writing since the war have usually been linked to the enthusiasms of actors and acting groups, such as the Union Theatre, the Phillip Street Theatre, the New Theatre League and later the National Institute for Dramatic Art and the Australian Performing Group.

Ray Lawler's play did not come from a nationalist tradition and it did not establish one for the drama. One of the reasons for this is the fact that the music-hall and revue tradition was more important in Australia than the tradition of the naturalist three-act play. When a contemporary playwright, such as Jack Hibberd, dismisses the *Doll* as the representative of a so-called nationalist

Drama, Old and New

tradition and claims an international modernism as the influence on his own work he fails to see that elements of a 'modernist' drama were strong in Australia before the production of the *Doll*. The national elements, particularly in acting styles, may have been more modernist than he supposes.[6]

By considering Lawler's play alongside Barry Humphries' fifties scripts it is possible to see some of the changes in attitude to nationalism and art portrayed in both traditional drama and the less formal revue theatre.[7] In the fifties, Lawler and Humphries worked together as actors and as writers, but Lawler's choice of a formal play for the *Doll* has assured his place in any discussion of Australian drama. Humphries has most often been seen as a comedian in the music-hall tradition, and the identification of his dramatic monologues with his own performance of them has limited the perception of him as a writer. But Humphries offers an accessible example of the kind of writing which would have been seen at the Phillip Street Theatre and university revues of the time. In his work, rather than Lawler's play, the elements which became important to modernist writers in the late sixties can be seen.

Furthermore, both Lawler and Humphries were examining what it meant to be an Australian in the postwar world. They, like Patrick White, found the 'national' character narrow, uneducated, intolerant, but they presented their criticisms to an applauding Australian public. It is likely that, even in apparent satire, they expressed or articulated the opinions of their audiences—at least during the late fifties. Both writers left Australia in the sixties and their later work has little apparent contact with current Australian attitudes.

Lawler's play is less obviously critical of the Australian tradition simply because it uses some of the socialist realist ideas of the left. Lawler dramatised the Australian male hero as a canecutter, once young and energetic, now middle-aged and caught in his own childish version of manhood. Because of her unwillingness to accept adulthood, the city woman who waited each year for the canecutter to return kept this image of manhood as a shrine. The parallels were clear: Lawler believed that the distinctive Australian character had had its day and the time had come for city Australians to face reality.

In many ways, *Summer of the Seventeenth Doll* was a summary, as well as a rejection, of the past. The play was set in the city while depending on the bush myths. It is Olive, the city girl, who

197

develops a belief in the heroic lifestyle of the canecutters and embroiders this with language and detail which lifts her own drab life. So, too, urban Australians for generations had looked to the bush myth and its language to gain their own identity as Australians. The old battle between the city and the country was made into a marriage of sorts which depended on city ignorance and country willingness to collude in dishonesty.

Furthermore, the romantic strand in the Australian bush tradition was given its full force by allowing a woman to be the believer in the dream. Olive's love for Roo is a love based on the placing of his life within the romantic tradition of 'The Man from Snowy River', the bronzed Anzac or Douglas Stewart's version of Ned Kelly. But almost all the previous accounts of the romantic Australian were fundamentally masculine. The call to leave a dull routine and seek manly adventures (become a bushranger, go to war, take risks with life) was here seen as part of the vicarious experience of women who had no choice but to endure city boredom. The woman who must stay at home rather than go with the shearers ('The Banks of the Condamine') or join the bushrangers (*Robbery Under Arms*) was clearly closer to the experiences of urban Australians of the fifties. Olive, not Barney or Roo, represented the national crisis.

As Joy Hooton has demonstrated, Lawler's return to the *Doll* in the seventies to make a trilogy has seriously altered the values offered in the original play.[8] Lawler is much more distant from his characters: they are now quaint figures of an Australian past and the two new plays take liberties with them. With a seventies perspective, Lawler is much harsher in his judgements of the characters in the play and the *Doll* trilogy offers a fundamentally puritanical message: young girls ought to settle down to marriage and a family or in old age they'll be pathetic hags. The seventies version takes the view of the wise adult judging the naughty children, but this wisdom has been earned by Australian society in the intervening years; the *Doll* of the fifties presented something identifiably close to Australians for consideration. In the fifties, Lawler's discovery that a barmaid and a pair of canecutters were worthy of serious treatment on stage was a new and revealing insight. Olive's dreams of the canecutters coming down from the North 'like eagles' for the lay-off were part of the Australian dream, the bronzed Anzac image. Lawler's perception that these dreams were essentially empty, childish and blind to reality reflected on the whole national self-image. Nowadays, the trilogy seems to refer to one kind of Australian at a given place and time.

Lawler's fifties criticism of Australian values may easily be linked with Patrick White's condemnation of the national myths or the criticisms soon to emerge from Barry Humphries or Robin Boyd. But Lawler's characters command sympathy in a way that White's Mrs Jolley or Humphries' Edna Everage cannot. Lawler's people have embraced a national myth wholeheartedly, have acted the part of wandering bush hero and his patient, admiring maid, only to be cheated by their human mortality. The larrikin humour and irresponsibility of Barney, Roo and Olive may still be found among Australians, but those watching the play in the fifties were asked to recognise the limitations of such a national stereotype. The innocence which made it possible for Olive to see her commitment to the lay-off as noble could no longer exist in Australia. Self-knowledge, like Olive's forced recognition of Roo's physical decline, destroys such simple notions.

Barry Humphries' revue sketches were less gentle in their rejection of Australian nationalism, and they questioned the values of suburban life too. Humphries also saw that the Australian lifestyle was no longer a 'masculine' life according to the old national stereotype. The suburbs where returning soldiers were settling to raise their families had become the domain of women. Australian life could no longer disguise itself in the masculine fantasy of pioneering challenge or wild colonial adventures; the kind of life pursued by most Australians was peaceful and settled. Lawler's play offered this pattern as more mature than the adolescent pursuit of good times and wild days—with kewpie dolls rather than real children as the final result.

Humphries, however, had moved on to look at the monstrosities of the suburban dream. In 1956, the same year that Lawler's play was gaining its success, Edna Everage appeared on stage at the Union Theatre, Melbourne, for the first time as the 'Olympic Hostess'. This little sketch was firmly within the tradition of university revue in Australia. Edna might have taken her turn on stage as a simple satire of Australian ignorance and then disappeared forever. But Humphries had tapped a source of comedy which relied on the small, familiar details of suburban life. If Lawler's play formed a ritual act of disposing with the past, Edna offered the realities of a present which was also due for reassessment.

In 'Olympic Hostess' Edna revealed the intimacies of life in her

—

suburban household in the course of applying to billet an athlete. The sleeping arrangements of the household, Edna's pride in her dull children, her close relationship with her own mother and, above all, her suspicion of any 'foreign' aspects of foreigners were displayed for recognition and laughter. Edna, for all her ignorance and small-mindedness, represented the Australian ideal of 'niceness' which Patrick White found so despicable. It was nice to have a visiting Olympian to stay but only if the Olympian also observed the rules of niceness'.

The original Edna was only one of Barry Humphries' revue characters, and Humphries believed at first that the patterns of her speech meant that she could only be appreciated by Australians. He had already created Sandy Stone to represent the male experience of suburban Australia. In 'Days of the Week' Sandy detailed the utter dullness of social life in Gallipoli Crescent, Glen Iris. The Australian male of myth and legend was reduced to slide nights with the neighbours, Saturday shopping and football and the 'occasional odd glass' of beer at the RSL. Humphries claims to have invented Sandy Stone after meeting a tough-looking old Australian on Bondi beach. This man spoke in a high-pitched and timid voice which appealed to Humphries as the antithesis of the man's physical appearance.[9]

Sandy Stone may be seen as a representation of what Roo from the *Doll* might have become if he had abandoned canecutting for marriage after the war. Sandy's wife, Beryl, like Olive in Lawler's *Doll*, is obviously a more forceful character than her husband. Through Sandy Stone Humphries stated quite clearly that the male hero of the Australian tradition was, in the realities of the fifties, a subdued creature devoted to the rituals of the suburbs. He continued to act out the Australian patterns of masculinity—going to the football on Saturday afternoon or the RSL on Sunday night—but he needed the comfort of a thermos full of Milo or Beryl's cut lunch.

Edna Everage and Sandy Stone might have remained simply two characters in a music-hall comedian's repertoire. But Humphries invested them with a curious sympathy and, particularly in the case of Edna Everage, he was able to develop further aspects of each character. In the late eighties Sandy seems rather dated, but he still functions as a kind of hymn to past innocence. Edna, on the other hand, has proved adaptable to life beyond fifties suburbia and Humphries has turned her into a triumphant self-parody. Humphries himself has expressed surprise at this change in Edna. He has commented that he invented Edna to represent 'everything provincial and narrow about my homeland which I detested, but which I've gradually come to love as I love Edna herself'.[10] Where Sandy Stone was timid and debilitated, Edna was full of vitality. This mixture of the attractive and the repulsive has made her a source of fascination for audiences for thirty years.

If one compares Edna with other literary versions of her type— Patrick White's Mrs Jolley of *Riders in the Chariot* or Elizabeth Harrower's Lilian of *The Long Prospect*—Humphries' warmer attitude to this kind of character is apparent even in her earliest versions. In White's version Mrs Jolley's vitality threatens the very existence of more sensitive creatures such as Miss Hare. Her enthusiasm for banality and trivial materialism almost swamps the more spiritual concerns of White's 'riders'. Harrower's character holds power over a child, though her emotional bullying is at least more interesting than the dull family life which Emily must endure when she returns to her parents.[11]

Clearly, Humphries was not alone in fearing and hating the matriarch who he saw as the mistress of suburban Australian life. But Edna did not exist simply to tear apart the banalities of modern Australian life; her primary function was to make people laugh, and she is a slighter creature than White's Mrs Jolley. As well, Humphries appears to enjoy her vulgarity quite as much as he condemns it.

The ambivalence of Humphries' attitude to Edna is not only the source of her longevity; it also has made it difficult to determine his political stance. Was he a snob, deriding the attitudes of the common people? Or was he delivering some well-earned criticism? It is easy to see that in the fifties Humphries belonged to the group of artists who were rejecting the philistine and provincial attitudes common in Australia. But, in so far as these attitudes were seen to be embodied in 'ordinary Australians' or even the working class, the attack on suburban narrowness has also been seen as an attack on the left's sacred figure, the 'working man' (Humphries was probably wise to attack through a woman, as such women had never managed to gain a respected place in the mythology of the old left). In 1959 Stephen Murray-Smith praised Humphries' work and described it as an attack on the petit-bourgeois philistinism in Australia; Murray-Smith even went so far as to suggest that Humphries should expand his range to include 'working-class and upper middle-class philistines' among his victims.[12] But later critics have been less comfortable with Humphries' work. Since the seventies, he has more often been described as a reactionary, out of sympathy with the broadening of Australian attitudes and willing to attack any target regardless of the powerlessness of the victim.[13]

Humphries is proud of his early interest in Dada art and saw his early stage appearances as part of this tradition. In his opinion, the Melbourne Dada group who produced *Call me Madman* 'represent the only anarchic "social comment" on any Australian stage at that period'.[14] There was, after all, plenty of social comment from the left about the difficulties faced by working people, about trade union battles and continuing injustice to the Aborigines. But Humphries recognised that material deprivation was not a major problem for most Australians—even for ordinary Australians in the fifties. There were other kinds of deprivations and, without going so far as White in addressing the 'spiritual', Humphries attacked suburban taste. To be deprived of beauty, to be denied a meaningful past, to be told to conform to a dull and challengeless lifestyle, these were constrictions on freedom as surely as poverty.

As an artist Humphries drew on the banalities of the world he knew. The old belief that Australians could not create important art because nothing important had ever happened to them was being turned on its head. It was precisely this Australian lack of experience and understanding which was the source of Humphries' art. Patrick White may have written about 'the blowfly on its bed of offal' as the source of beauty, but Barry Humphries is the artist who chose the comedian's patter as the means as well as the basis of creation.

That Humphries should turn up in 1975 on the editorial board of Cultural Freedom's journal *Quadrant*, at about the same time that Patrick White was finding sympathies with the emerging left, may be the cause of some confusion. Humphries was, after all, alert to the narrowness and provinciality of Australia quite early in his career. His interest in Dada art and in the grotesque may be seen as a reaching out towards modernism. Humphries did not create Ern Malley—though Vivian Smith has pointed out how close Ethel Malley is to Edna Everage.[15] Instead, Humphries' ridicule was for those elements in Australian society which would crush Ern.

The early Humphries might have sympathised with Max Harris,

—

beaten by Australian narrow-mindedness in his eagerness for something beyond it. Certainly, James McAuley's kind of artistic conservatism would seem anathema to Humphries. Once again, we must confront the larrikin nature of Australian conservatism. McAuley's and Harold Stewart's attack on innovation was delivered with the anarchic zest expected of radicals. Humphries in his writing and in his stage performances outrages good taste as if he would overturn the social order. His choice of characters, however, tends to set this order firmly into place.

Here, too, we must notice the changes in Australian society and Australian conservatism after the fifties. Lance Boyle and Sir Les Patterson are creations of the seventies, inspired by the Whitlam years and the rise of the faithful left to prominence. Humphries attacks the notion that ignorant and vulgar people can summon up culture at will. In the fifties he might have attacked the Menzies approach to the arts, which offered meaner patronage on a similar basis. Then, however, he was inspired more by the patterns of suburban Australian life than by political figures prominent in the community. In the seventies and eighties even Edna has become a superstar rather than a suburban woman.

When he performs to an eighties audience, Humphries no longer seems to be satirising Australian vulgarity but revelling in it. He plays to the vulgar tastes of his audiences and seems to have more in common with the English music-hall comedians or the pantomine dame than an Australian satirist. Humphries' art has depended so much on the tastelessness of Australian suburbia that he has developed a vested interest in preserving it.

However, his work in the late fifties and early sixties was part of a growing criticism of the values of postwar Australian suburbia— evident in the writing of Robin Boyd, George Johnston, Patrick White and others. As the Cold War tensions between socialist/ nationalist and conservative began to break down there was an increasing interest in the nature of urban Australian society on the part of intellectuals, and Humphries gave a public focus to this interest.

The kind of entertainment offered by Humphries had clear influences on the drama which formed part of the new radical tradition in the late sixties. The so-called 'new wave' of Australian drama of the late sixties sprang, like Humphries, from the tradition of university revue. In Sydney, the old need for actors to have roles to play led to the experiments of the Jane Street Theatre connected with the National Institute of Dramatic Art. In Melbourne, La Mama and, later, the Pram Factory gave actors and writers the chance to collaborate on new work. Most of the writers were originally students from Melbourne University.

It is almost impossible not to see the connections between the kind of revue produced by university students in the fifties and sixties, or by professional companies such as the Phillip Street Theatre, and the plays which emerged from the pens of Jack Hibberd, Bob Ellis, David Williamson and others in the late sixties. This was not simply a spontaneous cultural awakening, it was a new drama based on the traditions of writing sketches for revues.

Hibberd, in particular, may be seen as the successor to Humphries. His first play, *White With Wire Wheels* (1967), tapped the (soon to be dated) language of a group of young Australian men, in a manner similar to Humphries' 1964 pieces 'Sydney Surfer: The Old Pacific Sea' and 'Melbourne Skier: Snow Complications'. His most critically acclaimed work, *A Stretch of the Imagination*, is a dramatic monologue by Monk O'Neill, a character archetype of the Australian tradition. His most popular play, *Dimboola*, recreates the vulgarities of Australian wedding customs; Humphries, too, sent up the Australian wedding through his 1968 creation, 'Rex Lear'.[16]

In all his plays Hibberd has made open reference to the music-hall and revue traditions which Humphries also has claimed as his forebears. Hibberd's humour plays with Australian language and enjoys the vulgarity of Australian speech, much as Humphries does. The important difference lies in the way in which Hibberd employs these techniques; Hibberd is a social critic who is much more conscious of the implications of 'popular' art. He belongs with the anti-Vietnam protesters, the new radicals of the late sixties. Though he does celebrate the language and vitality of the 'ordinary' Australian, his comic characters represent a clear criticism of values and a call for a reassessment of them. At the time when Humphries was preparing to launch his attack on the left through Les Patterson and Lance Boyle, Hibberd's characters attacked some of the complacent ideals of conservative Australia. In his introduction to the 1973 edition of *A Stretch of the Imagination* Hibberd grumbled about charges that he had plagiarised from Beckett. Rejecting the term 'plagiarism' for a play so original as this, it would seem more relevant to recall that Barry Humphries was an actor in the first production of *Waiting for Godot* in Australia. Humphries absorbed Beckett in his dramatic monologues. The revue tradition, Humphries' style of entertainment and a fair influence from Lawson's 'The Bush Undertaker' give more substantial predecessors for the play than Beckett alone.

Hibberd's attitude to Humphries, and Lawler, makes the relationship between the writers even more interesting. In 1977, Hibberd declared that, 'As a dramatist, the *Doll* has never affected me one iota', and a year later he complained about its melodramatic excesses. He rejected any links between his own writing and what he saw as a national tradition represented by the *Doll*; the new writing of the late sixties came from the 'springs of modernism rather than the billabongs of retrospectively manufactured nationalism'.[17] But it may be that the springs of modernism had trickled into Australia before Hibberd began to study Ionesco, Pinter, Brecht and Beckett, and Lawler's rejection of nationalism is apparent in the *Doll*.

Humphries also pursued modernism quite deliberately and Hibberd has shown an uneasy ambivalence towards Humphries. In 1981, Hibberd published a playscript called 'Breakfast at the Windsor' which depicted Humphries in the act of creating a new sketch. An intellectual and well-informed waitress, who is nevertheless working-class in status and sympathy, provides Humphries with his ideas. But he transforms her genuine understanding of art into a monologue of prejudice and ignorance: 'I do a spot of painting meself with some of the girls. We call ourselves the Lamington School.' Hibberd's anger that Humphries' art rests on ridicule and misrepresentation of the working class is apparent but, as well, his recreation of Humphries' sketch is brilliant. Hibberd knows and admires the skills which he believes to be misused.[18]

Hibberd is not alone among the new-wave dramatists demonstrating the heritage of revue. David Williamson's more naturalistic plays consist, in the main, of a series of short scenes each hinging on a clever joke. And Michael Boddy's and Bob Ellis' *The Legend of King O'Malley* (first produced in 1970) demonstrated the music-hall revue tradition better than even Hibberd or Williamson. The play is an extravaganza of song and dance, with interludes in the career of a mythologised version of the politician 'King' O'Malley. The loose plot allowed the writers to offer various satirical jibes at the current state of Australian politics.

These younger writers and actors were able to make fun of the vulgarities of Australian suburban life without being accused of attacking the working class partly because they *were* young and their attacks were directed at their elders. The RSL men who wanted to shoot moratorium protesters were no longer simple Sandy Stones but representatives of the stifling ideals which were preventing any kind of reform of Australian life.

Though the development of a lively national drama in Australia came after the period under review in this book, it is clear that several of its elements were being set down in the fifties. The growth of the universities and the expanding educational opportunities offered to the postwar generation were essential for the creation of writers, actors and audiences. The setting up of the National Institute of Dramatic Art on the campus of the University of New South Wales in 1958 eventually produced a body of professional actors and directors looking for interesting plays to perform. The Elizabethan Theatre Trust offered a degree of financial support to new dramatic enterprises. The production of Lawler's *Summer of the Seventeenth Doll* in the fifties showed that successful Australian plays were possible.

The other undeniable factor in the development of Australian drama was the commencement of television broadcasting in Australia in 1956. Though television did not reach beyond the major cities for several years and television ownership was not universal, its influence hangs over the late fifties and early sixties. Television did not destroy the novel, the drama or the poem in Australia but, by providing mass popular entertainment, it did appropriate some of the role of these forms and pushed them further towards high culture. It is difficult to argue that television has directly stimulated literary creativity but, in the case of Australian drama at least, it is possible to draw some conclusions about the relationship between television and the theatre.

Television gave employment to actors, directors and producers of drama and it also gave them a wider audience, and the audience who admires an actor or 'personality' on television is more likely to follow their performances in the theatre. But television also influenced, or reinforced, trends in the Australian theatre. Television's great strength in drama is the close approximation to the appearances of real life. Naturalism is its forte even when it is presenting the myths of the cowboy and the detective. There can be no large gestures on television, no effects which lift the audience from its seat. There can be no audience participation in events.

Drama, Old and New

Instead the television viewer is invited to act as voyeur on the small details of others' lives.

In Australia, playwrights have been aware that television is a very limited dramatic medium. For this reason, the Australian plays of the late sixties and early seventies have often challenged the passive spectator role of the audience by forcing it to take roles in the play (*Legend of King O'Malley, Dimboola*). These plays have abandoned 'naturalism' for the singing spectaculars of the music-hall, (*Toast to Melba, The Venetian Twins*), or they have offered unstructured plots, or the dramatic monologue of the stage comedian. All such devices remind the members of the audience that they are watching a play and that they must be wary of surrendering real life to the world of the play.

There is still room, of course, for the naturalistic play on the Australian stage, but these plays have the inevitable feel of a try-out for a film or television show. David Williamson's plays might be cited here, but most of these have proved disappointing on screen. Some of the verve of the playing is lost and, for all his brilliance at middle-class dialogue, Williamson remains resistant to structure and the carefully satisfying ending.

The most exciting developments in Australian drama came after 1965, but the foundations for this were being laid in the fifteen years before. Just as in the novel and poetry old traditions and attitudes were being challenged or worked through to their conclusion, so the amateur theatres and the few professional productions in the fifties were exploring and finally discarding simple naturalism. The popular image of Australian drama before 1965 as a long drought chooses to ignore the lively tradition of revue in Australia—especially university revue from the end of the thirties. It is this tradition of satirical sketches and musical pieces which has given the later playwrights a direction, other than naturalism, to follow.

At the same time, the emergence of the new drama must be related to the new generation which benefited from the greater educational opportunities after the war and which felt itself to be stifled by the prevailing conservative attitudes and to be threatened directly by the Vietnam War and conscription. The writers of the late sixties were excited by the prospect of creating not only a new drama but a more open and self-critical society in Australia; some could even hope for a new social and political order without the shadow of the old rigid communism. But Jack Hibberd is

207

one writer who insists that the important influences in the late sixties were intellectual rather than political. In his view, national theatre came from a rejection of nationalism and its naturalistic implications.

I have argued that the elements of modernism which Hibberd and other later playwrights claim to have brought to Australia already existed in the fifties, and that Lawler's play represented a rejection of the nationalism which the later playwrights were also anxious to reject. However, the successes of Lawler, Humphries, Beynon and others did not lead to the establishment of a continuing Australian drama and most of these writers left Australia to pursue careers in Britain. This disruption in the development of Australian drama came from a number of sources, including the lack of opportunity for production and work in the related areas of film-making and television.

Another factor was the perception of Australia as a backward and provincial society which could not accommodate the experimental art necessary to a developing art form. This was complicated by the political polarities of the early fifties where both the left nationalists and the politically conservative promoters of drama accepted traditional artistic doctrines. While the nationalists looked to stage realism as the dramatic equivalent of socialist realism— the work of Brecht was not influential—the internationalist entrepreneurs wanted an Australian drama modelled on the English naturalist play. Just as in poetry and the novel, conservative artistic attitudes dominated contemporary thinking.

In considering Australian drama with the novel, 1956 seems to mark the beginnings of emergence from this backward-looking atmosphere. In that year Patrick White's *The Tree of Man* re-examined the national tradition and offered criticisms which were deeper and more originally expressed than Lawler's but which had some elements of accord with them. In the years from 1956 to 1965, the elements of modernism which White had adopted in the novel became acceptable to Australian writers and readers, so that by the late sixties they were evident in all areas of Australian writing—in the novel, the drama and in poetry. The gradual loosening of the bonds between nationalism, radical politics and conservative art meant that writers could be both experimental and socially concerned, both 'international' in their interests and committed to the development of Australian art.

—

208

9

Australian Civilisation?

The most fascinating aspect of the period 1945 to 1965 for Australian writing is the way the rigidities of immediate postwar thinking about literature opened up to numerous and various ideas about the role of literature in the new society which Australia was becoming. By the end of the fifties, simple categorisations of writers into the political left and right, or the nationalists and internationalists, could no longer cope with the range of responses of Australian writers to their society.

At the same time, in politics, the splitting up of the Stalinist Communist Party of Australia, the formation of the Democratic Labor Party and the emergence of a left which resisted the simple moralities of good workers and evil capitalists created a much more complex range of political commitments. Socially, vast changes were taking place including the expansion of education and the increasing movement of Australian workers into white-collar employment.

By the end of the fifties a new generation of writers, innocent of those Cold War divisions between nationalist and Europeanist, communist and anti-communist, political and spiritual, had begun to publish. One of the features of this new generation was its willingness to look at contemporary Australian experience and to do this by means of the personalism so feared by older writers of all political persuasions in Australia. These younger writers were prepared to write personal poetry, autobiographical novels and even undisguised autobiography in order to examine the complexities of the Australian experience. Of the novelists emerging before the sixties Elizabeth Harrower, Christopher Koch, and Randolph Stow are particularly interesting. Each published first novels while still in their twenties, and curiously all three novelists produced little in the late sixties and seventies. Harrower has published no novel since *The Watchtower* in 1966.

Harrower's second novel, *The Long Prospect* (1958), was based on her own experiences growing up in industrial Newcastle. Koch's first novel, *The Boys in the Island* (1958), followed his own childhood and adolescence in Hobart and Melbourne. In 1965, Stow also published a novel based on his own childhood—*The Merry-Go-Round in the Sea*.[1]

Neither Harrower nor Koch were concerned with belonging to a national tradition. Their novels charted experiences they knew as Australian people, not some national legend. City life dominates their novels but it is not the city life of Ruth Park's romantic poor or Dorothy Hewett's workers. It was the emptiness, the boredom, the very lack of struggle in modern Australia which preoccupied these young writers.

All Elizabeth Harrower's novels make purposeless suburban life into a background for games of manipulation and threat. In her first novel, *Down in the City* (1957), Sydney is a city of sunshine, leisure, material well-being but without human comfort or sense of purpose. The new immigrants watch the Australians with envy and wisdom:

> Earnest and snubbed, the old-young New Australians went unsmiling through the streets, despising and fearing the lotus eaters among whom they now lived, despised and feared by them. 'They do not know life. They do not know what life is,' they told each other, and envy took its place beside contempt. They bent over their work with determination and ignored the heat and the happy laughter outside. But everyone else knew that summer had no end.[2]

But hope does not come from the bush—the bush representative, Stan Peterson, is brutal and dishonest. Australianness, country or city, is marked by vulgarity and cruelty.

The Long Prospect presents an even more stifling view of Australian postwar society. The sensitive little girl at its centre is confined and almost smothered by her grandmother's suburban hedonism. Her only comfort is the promise of intellect, understanding and love beyond suburban family life. In the final chapter of the novel, the girl's despair is mocked by the shining accessories and solid ugliness of her parents' new Sydney flat. Her parents bask complacently among their possessions while she faces life alone 'without kindness and communication, without a movement of the heart'.[3]

To attempt to draw Harrower's novels into the old Australian tradition is to face A.A. Phillips' problem with Barbara Baynton's stories. Baynton saw the bush as the setting for isolation and brutality, a place where the strong could oppress the weak. Phillips reconciled Baynton with the democratic tradition by arguing that she had a proper, nationalistic distaste for the 'peasant element' in Australian life. Harrower clearly finds such an element in postwar city life where her women and children are as isolated as Baynton's selectors' wives.

Furthermore, she identifies oppression as being connected with materialism and Australian vulgarity. Lilian, the grandmother of *The Long Prospect*, has a genuine enthusiasm for life, a vitality which makes her insensitivity dangerous to those around her. Lilian enjoys the Australian pleasures of drinking, horse-racing and idleness. Her likeness to Edna Everage suggests that this kind of matriarch was becoming an acknowledged stereotype of Australian life.

Christopher Koch, too, suggested in his first novel that the national characteristics might include cruelty and insensitivity. *The Boys in the Island*, like *The Long Prospect*, is an account of growing up in provincial Australia. The central character, Francis Cullen, like Harrower's sensitive young girls, finds the life around him unbearably routine: 'Staying in the same place, in the same cosy life, forever. That's my idea of Hell.' Francis' friend Shane Noonan announces the central fact about life on the island or in the city: '*I've realized that nothing happens.* I wonder whether you've ever admitted that to yourself?'[4]

Cruelty may give pleasure to the aimless city dwellers but Koch also sees it as an Australian heritage—the tradition of the bush as well as the town. V. B. Miles, the father of Francis' first girlfriend, is a man of the country and an Australian war hero. Koch observes him terrorising his wife and children and delighting in continual acts of cruelty. The scene where Miles chases and beats his wife in front of the young lovers recalls Patrick White's chase scene in *The Tree of Man*. Distaste for the 'peasant element' might be claimed as an Australian literary tradition. Certainly, in Koch's novel cruelty is a stronger residue of Australian country life than the independent, freedom-loving elements of the legend:

> Because it was a spiteful town, the boy thought. It had killed its unhappy convicts a century ago (little Heather's 'olden days' that she talked of solemnly), working them in chained gangs to build its bridge in the harsh, cruelly unsympathetic land, empty then even of the comfort of a forlorn house-roof, the hard red-coated masters whipping and driving them, until one (what grim horrors had his historic grey flesh endured?) had broken free of agony by a final agony, dashing himself clear from the tormenting bridge and his suffering mates forever, alone. Cruelty brooded through the grass here, and buzzed thinly with an insect's voice in the cold stone arches of the bridge. It still went on today. Miles was today's cruel master who kept it going.[5]

The heritage of Australian history is not the brotherhood of man but ignorance, insensitivity and the continuing practice of cruelty.

In the fifties novels of Harrower and Koch this cruelty and insensitivity are enshrined in the culture of the city with its garish materialism just as it may once have been in country life and poverty. There is no cultural support for those who seek a deeper and more honest attitude to life. Harrower leaves her young girl with parents whose 'world was Greenhills, their literature and philosophy Hollywood'.[6]

These novels adopted essentially realist techniques, though Koch stressed the unreal nature of Francis' attitudes by giving his experiences a dreamlike quality. The two novelists were not attempting to introduce experiment or modernism to Australia but they were criticising the Australian ethos promoted by Russel Ward, A.A. Phillips or Vance Palmer. In their novels the conformity of Australian life, its vulgarity and anti-intellectualism, did not promote universal well-being; on the contrary it left individuals to suffer in ugliness and cruelty. Where poets such as Hope or McAuley might pursue ways to escape Australian conformity and anti-intellectualism and Patrick White sought new techniques as a means of criticising these qualities of Australian life, Koch and Harrower could use traditional techniques without a corresponding need to defend or promote the Australian ethos.

They shared the attitudes which consistently surfaced among

social commentators on Australia in the fifties. A nationalism founded on materialism and mediocrity was not enough. Now that Australian society was settling down to a comfortable suburban life a degree of self-criticism seemed necessary; literature's role was no longer to draw attention to material deprivation through the novel or to seek a beauty beyond suburban life through poetry.

In Randolph Stow's novels a concern for technical experiment was more evident. After the melodramatic excesses of his two first novels, Stow, at the age of twenty-three, published the extraordinary *To the Islands*. Here was no socialist realist argument about material deprivation in Australia's cities or outback, nor a critical look at Australian cultural values. *To the Islands* dealt with the real world which Stow had experienced: the life of Aborigines and missionaries in outback Western Australia. But Stow examined the nature of human guilt and innocence in his story of a remorseful missionary.

In this and later novels, Stow was prepared to explore myths and religious ideas, and to consider the European loss of understanding and humanity accompanying the certainties of technology. Before *To the Islands* most novels about the Australian Aborigines had socialist realist sympathies; Herbert's *Capricornia* and Prichard's *Coonardoo*, with their notions of the 'spirit of the land', expressed outrage at the treatment of the Aborigines. Stow's novel was in many ways less patronising to the Aborigines but was also able to reflect on European moral and spiritual failures. His Aborigines are much less stage properties than White's Aborigines in *Voss*, and less romanticised than those in *Capricornia* or *Coonardoo*.

To the Islands was inevitably compared with *Voss* by contemporary reviewers. In 1959, David Martin wrote a piece for *Meanjin* called '"Among the bones"; what are our novelists looking for?' which considered the two novels together. Martin declared that symbolism had finally arrived in Australia but that it brought a corresponding loss in understanding of character and social reality. Martin, by this time, had left the Communist Party, but he retained his sympathy for the social novel about human problems as his later *The Young Wife* demonstrated. Martin commented: 'It serves us right, though. If we will insist that moral realities are not an integral part of social and historical realities we are bound to get moralities without basis in society and history.' Martin recognised the failure of socialist realism though he was loath to throw away the clarities of the social novel.[7]

Just as Stow knew more about the Aborigines and life in the deserts of Australia than Patrick White, his early fiction was more clearly based on social observation. In his children's novel, *Midnite* (1967), Stow even sent up White's ponderousness by introducing 'a rather miserable German man called Johann Ludwig Ulrich von Leichardt zu Voss', who has come to the desert to explore himself. Stow was intereseted in mixing his styles, in adapting realism and myth to his purpose. *Tourmaline* (1963) and *The Merry-Go-Round in the Sea* (1965) continued his interest in social reality and spiritual conflict. The two elements were not mutually exclusive.

In *The Merry-Go-Round in the Sea* Stow also revealed his impatience with Australian society in similar terms to those of White or Harrower. He allows Rick to voice a frustration shared by a growing number of Australians:

> 'I can't stand it', Rick said, 'this-ah, this arrogant mediocrity. The shoddiness and the wowserism and the smug wild-boyos in the bars. And the unspeakable bloody boredom of belonging to a country that keeps up a sort of chorus: Relax, mate, relax, don't make the pace too hot. Relax, you bastard, before you get clobbered.'[8]

In 1965 this was not taken as evidence of anti-nationalism or right-wing opinion; Rick was after all, a patriotic Australian who had suffered the agonies of the Burma railway.

In 1962 Jack Beasley could still attack Patrick White for his un-Australian interest in spiritual values, but the debate had clearly become more complex than it had been in the early fifties. There are clear signs that by the late fifties the old divisions which gave the social novel to the nationalist left and the 'metaphysical' to the right had broken down. Mona Brand, David Martin and other writers who had been relatively liberal in Communist Party literary discussion could see that Patrick White might be as socially and nationally concerned as any other nationalist writer.

When White asked himself what was wrong with Australia his answer was similar to that offered by a wide range of intellectuals; Robin Boyd, Barry Humphries, Ray Lawler, Elizabeth Harrower, A.D. Hope, Randolph Stow and many others would find much common ground with him. Australians lacked a sense of purpose, an understanding of the intangible values, an appreciation of beauty, a reverence for qualities which had no money-value. In allowing these concerns to be called 'spiritual' and 'aesthetic' and therefore the prerogative of the political right, the radical

—
214

nationalists had surrendered the most crucial cultural territory. The socialists and radical nationalists had handed over the most fundamentally humane activities, the very mysteries of human creativity, to their political opponents. All they had left was a hollow, old-fashioned nationalism.

Furthermore, the concern for nationalism weakened the left's ability to criticise Australian capitalism. In so far as the failures of Australian society were seen as part of British or American imperialism, Australian society itself was beyond reproach. Nationalism directed criticism away from the weakness of Australian attitudes towards the perceived evils of the old-world traditions of Britain and Europe and the new power of the USA.

On the other hand, writers such as Stow, White and Hope were being denied nationalism though they were preoccupied by the national as well as the universal plight. The Cold War polarities confused the nature of art and commitment, so that reconciliation between the nationalist and the 'universalist' was difficult. Politically, the changes since the fifties are graphically illustrated by Patrick White's emergence in the late sixties to march with trade unionists against encroachments on Centennial Park. After 1975, White stood on a public platform to declare himself a republican. In the eighties he has joined nuclear disarmament rallies. His position on these issues would make him a member of the left by the standards of the eighties. Yet White's concern for social values has not changed very much since the fifties. Then, however, republicanism and peace movements were the preserve of the socialist realist writers and even linked to communist fronts.

Elizabeth Harrower also identified herself with the new nationalism of the Whitlam years. In 1980, she was asked about her portrayal of 'the self-critical minority' in her fifties novels. She replied:

> They were different times. I'd say other things now.... A lot of people did discover each other in 1972. Many people who were very isolated in that uncongenial sort of Australia found themselves at home in their own country for the first time.... Society can legislate to open some gates, windows, so that lives aren't too much handicapped from the start...[9]

This movement of writers from an apparently 'elitist' attitude to Australian life in the fifties to an apparently left political position in the seventies, did not require much real movement at all. In the fifties socialism was identified with a complacent nationalism partly because of the rigidity of left attitudes. The right had been given the self-critical territory and aesthetic concerns. These were quite false divisions: Clem Christesen and his *Meanjin* colleagues were just as concerned about aesthetic values as McAuley and Hope; Patrick White worried about the state of the nation as much as Stephen Murray-Smith.

In the course of the sixties these divisions broke down so that issues such as preservation of the environment, town-planning, educational reform and support for the arts were claimed by the left. It was possible to be nationally self-critical, to be interested in 'spiritual' or metaphysical values and to vote Labor. Just as R.G. Menzies represented the kind of cultural and political values of the early fifties, Gough Whitlam represented them for the early seventies. Were they really so far apart?

In literature, the polarities were most clearly expressed in the novel form. David Martin's division of the two kinds of writing into the novel of social and historical realities and the novel of moralities might be expressed in John Docker's terms as 'social realist' (a broader term including both socialist realist writers and non-communists) and 'metaphysical'. In Australia, the social realist novel had become an extremely limited genre because of its allegiance to simple narrative structures and refusal to consider any reality beyond the external and obvious. The symbolic novel, in the hands of White and Stow, moved away from a concern with the social conditions of human life. Some reconciliation between the two extremes seemed necessary.

Communists, non-communists and anti-communists in the early fifties regarded personal writing as undisciplined self-indulgence and associated it with the irrational. Impersonality is one of the strongest common elements in Australian writing in this period, whether in the poetry of A.D. Hope or Judith Wright or the novels of Patrick White or Judah Waten. All of these writers kept a distance from their material or disguised personal experiences and emotions by various poses. Socialist realists, of course, had a duty to the working class to keep them from examining their own individual lives too closely. Others, such as A.D. Hope, used impersonality as a discipline for their own romantic tendencies.

However, the novels of Koch, Harrower and Stow had autobiographical elements, and the autobiography and the autobiographical novel offered ways for prose writing to deal with both

---

216

external reality and the less tangible elements of experience. In the sixties autobiographical writing emerged as a means by which writers could deal with Australian society without straying into dangerous modernist experiment nor adopting a left political stance. In *Quadrant* in the sixties the 'memoir' began to replace prose fiction, and autobiographical pieces tended to assert the authority of the writer to comment on politics and society. Autobiography placed an emphasis on the undeniable authority of experience and gave writers a firm base on which to comment on the wider social world.

Although Hal Porter belonged to the generation of White and Hope, he was the writer who demonstrated the possibilities of the autobiography for the postwar generation. Porter's novels *A Handful of Pennies* and *The Tilted Cross* have a quality of gothic extravagance about them. It is possible to argue that Porter has taken his cue from Patrick White and allowed narrative fiction to become merely a structure to be embellished by the novelist's wit. Porter's personality, his cynicism and scorn for human failing, is the strongest element in his prose. He has a reputaion as a stylist but his style is not an end in itself. It is the expression of a brilliant intelligence and a personality at odds with his society. Porter could never belong to the sentimental school of the common people. His eye seeks the grotesque, the odd, the absurd aspects of human behaviour.

Though his novels often seem overblown, Porter's autobiographies became the perfect vehicle for the strong personality which pervades all his writing. In *The Watcher on the Cast-Iron Balcony* (1963) and the later *The Paperchase* (1966) and *The Extra* (1975) Porter observed the actors in his own life with a sophisticated and jaded eye. Porter, the autobiographer, stands back from his own life and offers a number of perspectives on the nature of existence. Porter's life did have elements of the 'typical' Australian and he is always aware of a greater history moving beyond his immediate experience, but he reveals how extraordinarily individual a 'typical' life experience can be. Those ordinary people, his parents, become most extraordinary in his hands.

Porter was one of several innovators who emerged in the early sixties. Thomas Keneally and Thea Astley were others who demonstrated that Patrick White was not the only writer who scorned 'journalism'. But the innovations by these writers were not modernist explorations or even ventures into fantasy. The fantastic in

Porter's autobiographies is bound to his own experience as an Australian, while Keneally has sought his own preoccupations in moments of history. Thea Astley's wit pervades all her social observation but her novels are social, historical and moral in concern. Her work revived the notion that social writing could also be witty and stylish—without being unAustralian. In the early sixties, Australian writers were no longer limited to a choice between the earnest narrative or the mythic quest.

The pattern of rejection of the old, limited approach to nationalism was repeated in various forms in the late fifties and early sixties. Just as Ray Lawler in *Summer of the Seventeenth Doll* created his typical Australians in order to demonstrate the shallowness and sentimentality of the national myth, so George Johnston in his autobiographical novel *My Brother Jack* mapped the failings of the national hero. Both Lawler's and Johnston's works were ambivalent about the 'Australian' virtues; they seemed to celebrate the national virtues while revealing the essential childishness of the Australian hero.

My Brother Jack appears to be a continuation of the Australian nationalist tradition. It closely follows the experience of a generation of Australians born in the early years of this century. The Meredith family have inherited the Australian ideals of heroism and anti-authoritarianism through generations of Australian adventurers. Jack, not John, is the name for the first-born son of each generation; the name itself suggests an identification with the common man and a contempt for pomposity.

George Johnston used the Meredith family, closely if not accurately based on his own family, to examine the national inheritance. The First World War with its heroism and death is very real to the young Merediths through the presence in their house of maimed returned soldiers. To Davy, the critical son, the war means decay; to Jack it signifies heroism. The two brothers represent the two attitudes to nationalism evident in the fifties. Jack is the old-style nationalist—honest, generous, anti-authoritarian but simple; Davy is one of the new men in Australia—clever, critical, but always aware of the main chance. Johnston presents Davy as admiring Jack's openness and honesty but, as the novel progresses, it is clear that Davy is the brother with the skills to deal with the modern world.

Johnston recognises that the loyalty and heroism of the First World War had destroyed the nineties' ideal of the Australian.

Jack, the living embodiment of that ideal, is unable even to fight in the Second World War. Davy, the intellectual and sophisticate, becomes the Second World War hero.

Though Davy's qualities may be less inspiring or romantic than those of Jack, he is Johnston's true hero. Davy is able to earn money and support his family through the depression; Davy meets and marries the woman who is both warm and intellectual. David Meredith is a postwar success, and none of Johnston's protestations of admiration for Jack can save him from becoming a pathetic, outdated character by the end of the novel.

Yet Johnston also had comments to make on Australian suburban values. Although Davy sets up house in the suburbs with his first wife Helen before the Second World War begins, Johnston describes suburbia in terms common in the late fifties. The middle-class residents of Beverley Grove pursue conformity in their garden suburb with an enthusiasm for suburbia which was more widespread in the fifties. It is as if Johnston, writing his novel in the late fifties, wants to criticise contemporary Australia and so locates Australia of the fifties in Australia of the late thirties. When most Australians were still recovering from the depression, life in Beverley Grove cannot have been typical. It is, however, typical of the late fifties suburbia, and perhaps Johnston is showing us how much a man of the future David Meredith will be. For he not only owns a house in Beverley Grove with clipped lawns, he is advanced enough to protest at the ugliness of its red roofs and neat cement paths. David's separation from Helen is precipitated by his rejection of suburban conformity, specifically by planting a gumtree in the front lawn.

These are the acts of a man at one with Robin Boyd whose denunciaton of Australian suburbia, *The Australian Ugliness*, was not published until 1960, or with Barry Humphries whose Australian suburbanites did not appear until 1956. Boyd specifically criticised the suburban rejection of the gumtree and called the concern for cement drives and pipes unbroken by gumroots petty and ridiculous.

One of the fascinating aspects of *My Brother Jack* is the way Johnston justifies his own life through the character of Davy Meredith. The triumph of the intellectual man over the physical one is achieved rather too thoroughly. Yet the novel manages to make this intellectual man a new kind of Australian hero. Davy travels the world in the romantic tradition. Davy rejects the constrictions of woman-dominated suburban life. Davy is a new kind of bushranger or Anzac, free to move on to new experiences. Jack is left in the suburbs with wife and family.

When Davy climbs onto his suburban roof and scorns the life of Beverley Grove he identifies himself with his own working-class origins. His planting of the gumtree in the front lawn is an anti-authoritarian act, and so in sympathy with Jack and its values, but it is not a working-class act. In fact Davy is rejecting the bad taste of his neighbours. His real cultural identification is with Gavin Turley, whose upper-class breeding has given him aesthetic taste. Thus, *My Brother Jack* manages to claim the new cultural values—the concern for education, intellect, beauty, taste—for an Australian who is closely related to the old national hero (his brother).

Johnston's attitude to suburbia has striking similarities with that expressed by Patrick White in *Riders in the Chariot* published a few years earlier. Both novels attack Australian suburbia for its rejection of the artist and the intellectual. Both identify suburban values with women and treat their suburban women with some cruelty. White wrote his attack with the benefit of an 'upper-class' background while Johnston, like his narrator, was the 'second son of a tram driver'. Johnston's clear admiration for the values of the character Gavin Turley may explain the similarities between White's and Johnston's view. It is possible to see in *My Brother Jack* the newly arrived middle-class Australians looking to those of established wealth and education, such as Turley or White, for their values. Working-class values and loyalties may have been admirable and honest but the future seemed to demand more sophisticated attitudes.

White, of course, was interested in the spiritually sensitive character as well as the intellectual and the artist. Johnston does not pretend to such an interest and if there is something of the charlatan in his intellectual and artist then that, too, seems appropriate to the Australia of the sixties.

Most importantly, Johsnton's novel was a social novel about the experience of being an Australian in the twentieth century. Though Jack and Davy, Sheila, Helen and Cressida have representative roles to play they are not symbols. Johnston told his story in a clear, even journalistic, style. Yet his values were in accord with those of the 'symbolic' novelist, Patrick White. The two traditions—the clearly structured social novel and the experimental 'metaphysical' novel—were coming together. A writer in the mid-sixties could choose elements from the traditional social novel or follow White or Stow into the mythic without the consequence of a nationalist or elitist label. The Australian novel in the sixties was not marked by experiment so much as a relaxation of rules and a diversity of styles.

In poetry Hope, Wright, McAuley and Stewart remained prominent figures through the sixties. When A.D. Hope compiled his supplement to H.M. Green's *A History of Australian Literature* in 1963, he could state that no new developments had occurred in poetry since 1950. Of course, Hope was not likely to seek out evidence of new developments and he summarised the decade as follows:

> What [present-day Australian poets] have in common is a return to traditional verse and a retreat from experimental methods, free verse, surrealist logomania, fragmentary imagism, dislocated syntax and symbolist allusiveness. They use traditional metres and rhymes, aim at lucid and coherent exposition of themes, and at poems which are intellectually controlled and organized. [10]

When Hope looked for younger poets he found only Evan Jones, Chris Wallace-Crabbe and Alexander Craig worthy of comment. Though Hope's allegiance to form and tradition was clear, he saw the period 1950—62 as a time of consolidation of past achievements rather than a time of new discoveries. He could even express disappointment at the similarity of form and subject among Australian poets.

Commentators looking back over the period have come to different conclusions about the date when Australian poetry began to change direction. Some see the new decade as the turning point. But the change from the old traditionalism to the 'new poetry' of the late sixties and seventies was not dramatic. It began, as Rodney Hall and Thomas Shapcott put it, as 'new impulses' rather than revolutionary change. Francis Webb and Gwen Harwood had been publishing through the fifties and were as traditional in form and clarity as the other poets of their generation. But the imaginative and intellectual energy of these poets made them influential. Harry Heseltine has pointed to the publication of Bruce Beaver's *Under the Bridge*, Rodney Hall's *Penniless till Doomsday*, Thomas Shapcott's *Time on Fire* and Francis Webb's *Socrates and Other Poems* in 1961 as making that year crucial to change. Another milestone might be the publication of Bruce Dawe's first book of poems *No Fixed Address*, in 1962.[11]

John Tranter and others have argued that the new American poetry of the early sixties was the most significant influence for poetic change in Australia. In particular, Tranter cites two anthologies, Donald Allen's *The New American Poetry* (1960) and Donald Hall's *Contemporary American Poetry* (1962), as awakening mid-sixties Australians to new alternatives in poetry.[12] Nevertheless, the strength of the older generation through the sixties and even the seventies cannot be denied. The exaggerated way in which Tranter and other poets of the '68' generation have felt bound to attack Hope and Wright argues for a disproportionate influence on their part.

The very need to publish anthologies such as Alexander Craig's *Twelve Poets 1950–1970* (1971), Thomas Shapcott's *Australian Poetry Now* (1970) or the Shapcott and Hall *New Impulses in Australian Poetry* (1968) argues a determination to give attention to poets other than Hope, Wright, Stewart and Campbell. These poets remained so pre-eminent that they seemed in danger of swamping new voices.

At the same time, the new voices emerging in the early sixties were not remarkably experimental nor individual. The movement to less formal and more personal poetry was gradual. Evan Jones, Chris Wallace-Crabbe and Vincent Buckley were as concerned for craftsmanship as their predecessors. Geoffrey Lehmann and Les Murray, who published their first book of poetry *The Ilex Tree* jointly in 1965, fitted in their different ways Hope's criteria of lucidity, coherent exposition and intellectual control, even where they abandoned traditional metre and rhyme. Bruce Dawe's poetry brought a welcome shot against pomposity and a demonstration of the possibilites of the vernacular, but he was no less lucid than Hope himself.

It was not until the late sixties that a group of poets emerged who set out to attack the accepted orthodoxies of the fifties generation. The group of poets called the 'Generation of 68' were mainly born during and after the Second World War; 1968 marked an arrival to adulthood of a generation with little experience of Cold War politics and with no fear of the associations of modernism with fascism. In addition, Australia's involvement in the Vietnam War and the introduction of military conscription gave the poets a social and political cause. Radicalism in poetry, to this group

—

of poets, meant attack on the reigning traditionalists by every available means. A.D. Hope's belief that poetry was a long-term achievement, requiring years of practice and refinement, was cast aside for the immediate response and the momentary impression. Michael Dransfield's feat of composing twenty poems in two days might be compared with the years of craft in an A.D. Hope long poem.

A vast number of poems were written in the excitement of the late sixties, many by poets who were not heard of again. But the new radicalism did not become a new orthodoxy in Australia, partly because of the false demands of continual iconoclasm and, perhaps, because of the movement's links with the social and political moments of the poets' youth. With the change of government in 1972 and the consequent end of conscription part of the political battle was won. Certainly, in 1979 Tranter was prepared to declare that the new poetry movement was close to its end, having achieved the task of revitalising a 'moribund poetic culture'.[13]

Alongside the 'Generation of 68' poets, another kind of tradition, perhaps best represented by the poetry of Les Murray, has continued to flourish. This tradition has been content to maintain the older generation's concern for clarity and organisation while allowing itself some freedom with form. While poetic rivalries in contemporary Australia are as complex as the political arrangements of a Medici court, an observer can only offer the general comment that far from being a 'moribund culture' the poets of the fifties left a poetic achievement which it was difficult for younger poets to match. The concern to re-introduce modernism to Australia, with its resurrection of Ern Malley as hero, was a resort to extremes. The 'Generation of 68' found it necessary to protest too much.

The brief and belated flourishing of modernism in Australian poetry may have given poetry a new relevance to the Vietnam generation, but this generation was distinguished from that of their parents by clear educational advantages as well as little experience of national crisis. The universities were the focal point for the new poets, as they were for the dramatists of the late sixties. The audience for the new poetry, even more than for the new drama, were educationally privileged. Douglas Stewart's or David Martin's ideal of poetry for the people was even more remote by the end of the sixties than it had been in the early fifties. Les Murray alone has a significant popular following in the eighties, though a poet who scorns the status games completely such as Oodgeroo Noonuccal (Kath Walker) can surpass even Murray's sales of poetry. In the early fifties, however, for writers politically committed to the left, the appeal to a working-class audience was as essential as allegiance to working-class interests. David Martin's poetry of the fifties tried to express public sentiments, to be a public voice for the people who might not otherwise be heard. John Manifold's interest in folk ballads stemmed from his allegiance to the 'song of the people'.

The emerging criticism of Australian anti-intellectualism and poor taste grew to be a criticism of the 'average' Australian, the working man and woman. As poetry moved with little regret towards a remote and elitist audience, the drama and the novel directed their social criticism at 'ordinary' Australians—Barry Humphries' suburbanites, Patrick White's materialists. The old left ideal of the working-class struggling to understand its role through literature collided with the realisation that many working people were striving towards the middle class and unrepentantly enjoying the consumer pleasures of Menzies' 'peace and prosperity'. The socialist realists had romanticised the working class, though they often had to set their novels and short stories in the depression to do so. Humphries, White and others scorned the suburban working class for its failures of sensibility. John O'Grady's 'Nino Culotta' was more sympathetic to contemporary suburban Australia—his average Australian man and woman were materialistic and complacent, but why shouldn't they be in an age of war and chaos?

Ian Turner's 1959 'The Life and the Legend' article in *Overland* expresses the difficulties which the left had in reconciling itself to the aspirations of the Australian working people. Turner had been a member of the Communist Party until his expulsion in 1958 and had been secretary of the Australasian Book Society for a number of years. In 1959 he could review his commitment with a certain amount of disillusionment. He recalled that nationalism had given a new impetus to socialism after the war. Australian socialists had been excited to find that Australian history gave a heritage of democratic struggle to contemporary commitment. However, when Turner looked at the Australia of 1959 he saw entrenched inequalities and a working class content to accept such inequalities. In Turner's opinion, the Australian mateship ethos served to disguise the real inequalities in relationships between workers and their masters: 'So long as the worker is allowed to feel that he is as good as the next man, the boss, then unequal distribution of power in society goes unchallenged.'[14]

When Turner considered the cultural activities of the worker he found that the old hunger for 'self-improvement', literature and music had been satisfied by the mass culture of films, radio and sport. In such times, writers had to face massive difficulties. Turner wanted to hold onto the good things in the Australian tradition—its democratic and humane values—but he accepted that rigid doctrines could stifle creativity or lead writers back into antiquarian styles and interests.

David Carter has argued that Turner's 'The Life and the Legend' is symptomatic of a widespread distrust of ideology in the late fifties. Turner's personal experience at the hands of doctrinaire communism explained his need to rescue some elements from the nationalist tradition, but his rejection of the doctrinaire in favour of the individual was an attitude to be found among conservatives and liberals alike, among *Quadrant* writers as well as among *Meanjin* and *Overland* contributors. Carter identifies *Overland*'s use of nationalism and literature to de-politicise itself; he claims that by the sixties *Overland* was arguing that literature was above politics at the same time that literature should be humane and democratic.[15]

Clearly, Ian Turner and his friend, the editor of *Overland* Stephen Murray-Smith, now saw the socialist realist critical theories as narrowly prescriptive. But they did not want to abandon the search for a literature which cared for humane values and the fate of those at the bottom of the social heap. The difficulty was that the working class no longer appeared to care about literature; the Australasian Book Society, for example, was losing subscribers through the fifties and the sales of serious literature and poetry continued to be small. Perhaps the working class had never cared particularly for literature but in previous generations there had been strong worker education movements and promotion of the idea of the worker-writer. Towards the end of the fifties, writers clearly identified themselves as part of the intelligentsia rather than, as in the case of the socialist realists of the late forties and early fifties, worker-writers.

It is this feeling that the writer and the intellectual are distant from their society and that the pursuit of artistic achievement must be conducted apart from ordinary Australians which has created continuing problems for Australian writers. Patrick White's criticism of the mediocrity and materialism of Australians was only too easy to support by evidence of consumerism and devotion to the commercial culture. By the early sixties, a growing number of writers and critics with diverse political commitments shared this attitude. No matter how concerned a writer may have been about the inequalities in Australian society, he or she felt some of Turner's disappointment or despair that the people would not support the writer's challenge to the *status quo*.

In the Vietnam years some writers found support from audiences for their social and political views and then the audience consisted mainly of the privileged children of the postwar baby boom. It was the educated who attended Hibberd's and Williamson's plays at the Pram Factory, or who read Richard Tipping or Michael Dransfield. When political commitment became acceptable once again the writers made no pretence of supporting or addressing a working class. Indeed, many of them adopted the scornful attitude made popular by Barry Humphries and some identified the socially conservative worker as their enemy. Jack Hibberd, perhaps, saw the dilemma most clearly, and deliberately set out to celebrate the ordinary Australian as part of a political commitment. Yet even Hibberd's attempts to adapt popular entertainment to serious drama have had limited success and in 1986 he announced that he had stopped writing because of the 'lack of an intellectual context' for his work in Australia.[16]

The problems for writers in contemporary society have not been resolved by some magical Australian maturity dating from the late sixties. It is still difficult to find an audience for serious Australian fiction and poetry, and the serious drama of the sixties is now represented by David Williamson's slick and superficial entertainments. This is the nature of art: there is no simple progressive development which renders 1987's work greater or 'more mature' than the achievements of 1957.

Among the changes evident in the sixties was the loss of belief in literature's ability to transform Australian reality. The weakening of the Communist Party in the late fifties meant that socialist realism was no longer a significant literary force, and the prospect of literature preparing the way for a socialist revolution lost credibility. Less political versions of nationalism also lost the sense of urgency apparent in the forties; the impulse to assert Australian independence from Britain and the USA had been weakened by the influx of popular culture from the United States and by a growing criticism of the insularity and ignorance behind such nationalism.

Even Patrick White found that by the mid-sixties teaching ignorant Australians was less important than an examination of the artistic process itself. The didactic urges evident in the work of White, Clem Christesen, James McAuley or Judah Waten had lost their force, partly because the writers were not so certain that they had the answers and partly because writing no longer seemed an effective tool for social reform.

At the same time, an interest in social and political problems emerged in the sixties in the work of some writers, such as Judith Wright or David Campbell, who had appeared to be apolitical in the fifties. The difference lay in a rejection of programs which promised to transform the whole of Australian life. Once the simple answers of doctrinaire communism, nationalism, science and technology or even doctrinaire Catholicism had been discredited, writers were free to examine social, political and philosophical problems without offering cut-and-dried solutions to them. Instead of committing themselves to broad political causes or seeking to express their political commitment through particular literary styles Australian writers grew inclined to address specific issues, such as Wright's commitment to conservation, and to allow themselves some freedom from the bondage of political literary approaches, as in McAuley's personal lyrics of the late sixties.

This freedom from direct and obvious political alignment found expression in a poetry which combined the traditional with elements from a previously rejected modernism, in fiction which ranged from social narrative to prose poetry, in a drama which offered both the naturalist (Williamson) and non-naturalist (Hibberd) approaches. There were losses as well as gains in this new freedom. Since Patrick White's fifties novels, no Australian prose writer has been so eloquently passionate about the failings of Australian society. The admirable diversity in contemporary Australian poetry has not produced a younger poet with the sense of an urgent purpose which marks the work of Judith Wright or with the clear intellectual goals of A. D. Hope. The pleasures of Australian writing in the eighties are more various, more playful, more linguistically innovative than those of the fifties, but the writing is less certain of its role and less certain of its audience than it was thirty years ago.

While Australian writers now are able to experiment or choose traditional approaches without being accused of overt political commitment on the basis of this choice, the powerful incentives which led some Australians to write in order to transform society no longer exist. In the eighties it is difficult to imagine, for example, a group of workers teaching themselves and each other to write novels in order to assist changes in the social and political position of their class, but this did happen among the socialist realists of the late forties. While we accept that Catholicism is important to the writing of Les Murray, Christopher Koch and Bruce Dawe, none of these writers see their religion as the source of a political as well as supernatural order as James McAuley did in the fifties. Writers now have the freedom to express themselves in highly individual ways, but they are also more isolated from each other and from groups in the community with shared concerns.

This is not to argue that Australian writers in the eighties are not political. Literature always expresses ideology of some kind. However, the politics of contemporary writers usually may only be discerned by careful and informed reading of their work and often lies in an exploration of hidden injustices, as in the writing of Elizabeth Jolley or Olga Masters. Writers no longer feel the need to declare their politics by open commitment to particular forms.

In this book I have tried to examine the way in which the Second World War left Australian writers anxious to find new roles in a new society, and to explore the ways in which, for various writers, these roles changed with changing perceptions of the society. The influences on the writers have been complex and I cannot claim to have exposed every element in the network of forces which affected Australian writing in the years from 1945 to 1965. However, I hope that some understanding of the rationale behind writers' decisions in these years has emerged through this discussion and that readers will see some of the relationships between the work of writers during the period. A great deal can be gained by reading Patrick White's novels, for example, with reference to those of Judah Waten or the poetry of James McAuley, and by reading Judith Wright's poetry in the context of her contemporaries.

Equally importantly, I hope that the influences discussed in this book will enable readers to see poets such as A.D. Hope, Judith Wright and James McAuley not simply as 'metaphysical' in their interests and so apart from a social and political world but deeply involved in the intellectual, social and political arguments of their time. The difficulties which writers faced thirty years ago and the solutions which they sought cannot be dismissed as merely the unimaginative attitudes of an older generation dependent on the conventions of an even older civilisation, and they may prove instructive to writers today.

Endnotes

Introduction

1 For example, in John Tranter's introduction to his *The New Australian Poetry* St Lucia, 1979, and John Docker's *Australian Cultural Elites* Sydney, 1974.

2 John Docker *In a Critical Condition* Melbourne, 1984.

3 Marjorie Barnard, review of *The Harp in the South*, *Southerly* 9, 3, 1948, pp. 182–83.

4 Kathleen Barnes, review of *Australian Roundup*, *Southerly* 16, 1, 1955, p. 40; Cecil Hadgraft, review of *Twenty Australian Novelists*, *Southerly* 9, 2, 1948, pp. 116–18.

5 Max Dunn 'Some National Tendencies in Australian Poetry' *Southerly* 11, 3, 1950, pp. 122–26.

6 Lynne Strahan *Just City and the Mirrors: Meanjin Quarterly and the Intellectual Front 1940–1965* Melbourne, 1984.

7 'The Uneasy Chair: the wound as the bow' *Meanjin* 10, 1, 1951, p. 90.

8 Editor's note, *Meanjin* 2, 1, 1943, p. 2.

9 A.R. Chisholm, *Meanjin* 2, 1, 1943, p. 12.

10 *Meanjin* 2, 3, 1943, pp. 40–41; 'Tradition in Australian Literature' *Meanjin* 8, 1, 1949, pp. 19–22.

11 Vance Palmer *The Legend of the Nineties* Melbourne, 1954, p. 170.

12 A.A. Phillips *The Australian Tradition* Melbourne, 1958, p. 70.

13 Russel Ward *The Australian Legend* Melbourne, 1958; see, for example, P.K. Elkin's review of *The Australian Tradition*, *Southerly* 20, 1, 1959, p. 50.

Endnotes

14 George Johnston, in Ian Bevan (ed.) *The Sunburnt Country* London, 1953, pp. 148–53; F.W. Eggleston, in George Caiger (ed.) *The Australian Way of Life* Melbourne, 1953, pp. 1–22; P.H. Partridge in V.J. Aughterson *Taking Stock* Melbourne, 1953, p. 53; I am grateful to Richard White's article '"The Australian Way of Life"' *Historical Studies* 18, 1979, pp. 528–45, for drawing my attention to these books.
15 R.D. FitzGerald 'An Attitude to Modern Poetry' *Southerly* 9, 3, 1948, p. 153.
16 Richard Quinones *Mapping Literary Modernism* Princeton, 1985, p. 14.
17 Michael Dransfield 'Endsight: for Union Carbide, A.D. Hope & Sir P. Hasluck Askin Clutha etc' in *The Inspector of Tides* St Lucia 1972, p. 23.
18 Kenneth Slessor 'Australian Literature' *Southerly* 6, 1, 1945, p. 31.
19 Rubin Rabinovitz *The Reaction Against Experiment in the English Novel 1950–1960* New York, 1967.
20 John Docker *In A Critical Condition* chapter 4; S.L. Goldberg 'The Strong Contagion of the Gown' *The Critical Review* 9, 1966, p. 114.

1 Pursuing the National Tradition

1 A.A. Phillips 'The Cultural Cringe' *Meanjin* 9, 4, pp. 299–302.
2 Phillips, 'The Democratic Theme' in *The Australian Tradition* p. 70; Henry Lawson, 'The Uncultured Rhymer to His Cultured Critics' *A Camp-Fire Yarn: Henry Lawson Complete Works 1885–1900* Sydney, 1984, p. 513.
3 'A.A. Zhdanov at the First All Soviet Congress of Writers, August 17, 1934' in George J. Becker (ed.) *Documents of Modern Literary Realism* Princeton, 1963, pp. 486–88.
4 'Letter to Margaret Harkness April 1988' in Becker *Documents of Modern Literary Realism*, pp. 482–85.
5 'The Writer and the People' *The Realist Writer* (Melbourne) 1, 1952.
6 Frank Hardy 'My Problems of Writing' *The Realist Writer* (Melbourne) 6, 1953, p. 13.
7 Jack Beasley *Socialism and the Novel: a study of Australian literature* Sydney, 1957, p. 7.
8 ibid. p. 13.
9 Jack Beasley *Red Letter Days* Sydney, 1979.
10 Correspondence in the Frank Hardy papers, series 23, box 1, MS 4887, National Library of Australia (NLA).
11 David Martin 'How should we criticise?' *The Realist Writer* (Melbourne) 7, 1953, p. 3.
12 John Morrison 'Comment' *The Realist Writer* (Melbourne) 9, 1954, pp. 11–12.
13 Stephen Murray-Smith (ed.) *The Tracks We Travel* Melbourne, 1953, p. 10.
14 ibid. p. 10.
15 John Manifold *Collected Verse* St Lucia, 1978, p. 103.

16 David Martin *Poems of David Martin 1938–1958* Sydney, 1958, pp. 73–75.
17 Preface to *Poems of David Martin.*
18 Letter from Eric Lambert to Zöe O'Leary, 5 May, 1956, Mrs Zöe O'Leary papers, ML Document 1190, Mitchell Library (ML); Letter Dorothy Hewett to Frank Hardy, 1 April, 1961, Frank Hardy papers, Series 23, box 2, MS 4887, NLA.
19 Jack Lindsay 'Frank Hardy's Power Without Glory' in his *Decay and Renewal* Sydney, 1976, pp. 349–63.
20 Frank Hardy *Power Without Glory* St Albans, 1950, p. 25.
21 Judah Waten *The Unbending* Melbourne, 1954, p. 34.
22 Conversation with Judah Waten, May 1979; see also letters to Judah Waten from Vance Palmer, A.A. Phillips and Frank Dalby Davison in Judah Waten papers, series 2, MS 4536, NLA.
23 Dorothy Hewett *Bobbin Up* Melbourne, 1959, p. 141.
24 Dorothy Hewett '1954: Living dangerously' *Overland* 62, 1975, pp. 25–27; *Interview:* 'Dorothy Hewett' *Meanjin* 38, 3, 1979, pp. 350–67.

2 *Cultural Freedom and* Quadrant

1 Frank Hardy's speech to the Communist Party national congress, *Tribune* (Melbourne) 16 April 1958, p. 7.
2 Stephen Murray-Smith 'A General Demand for Art' *Overland* 14, 1959, p. 19.
3 Rex Chiplin '*Overland*—where's it being taken?' *Tribune* (Melbourne) 13 May 1959, p. 7.
4 'Author and readers write on review of *Overland*' *Tribune* (Melbourne) 27 May 1959; Ralph de Boissiere 'Author asks editor pertinent questions' *Tribune* (Melbourne) 3 June 1959; 'More letters on *Overland* criticism' *Tribune* (Melbourne) 10 June 1959.
5 *Commonwealth Parliamentary Debates* 1952, 28, pp. 717ff.
6 Letters from Richard Krygier to Francois Bondy and Michael Josselson, 1951–52, Australian Association for Cultural Freedom papers (AACF), NLA, MS 2031, box 15.
7 Letters to Sir John Latham, February-March 1954, Sir John Latham papers, NLA, MS 1009, series 71.
8 Letters, February-March 1954, Sir John Latham papers, series 71.
9 Clem Christesen to Sir John Latham, Sir John Latham papers, series 71.
10 Krygier to Josselson, 26 October 1954, AACF papers, box 15; Krygier's report, June 1955, AACF papers, box 6.
11 Krygier's report to Josselson, 14 March 1956, AACF papers, box 6.
12 Josselson to Krygier, 25 may 1957, AACF papers, box 6.
13 Krygier letters 9 February 1956, 25 October 1956, 30 October 1956, AACF papers, box 6; J.H. Wootten 'The Orr Dismissal and the Universities' *Quadrant* 1, 2, 1957, pp. 25–29.
14 Sol Stein, letter to Krygier, 1 February 1956, AACF papers, box 7.

Endnotes

15 Humphrey McQueen 'Quadrant and the CIA' in *Gallipoli to Petrov* Sydney, 1984, pp. 180−95; John Docker 'Cultural History and the Philosophy of History' *Arena* 52, 1979, p. 18.
16 Mentioned in letter, Krygier to Latham, 1 December 1955, Sir John Latham papers, series 71.
17 Proposals for literary journal, AACF papers, box 7.
18 James McAuley 'Comment: Right and Left' *Quadrant* 1, 2, 1957, p. 3.
19 James McAuley 'Comment: By way of prologue' *Quadrant* 1, 1, 1956−57, pp. 3−4.
20 James McAuley, review of *Meeting Soviet Man, Quadrant* 4, 3, 1960, pp. 91−92.
21 Peter Coleman (ed.) *Australian Civilization: a symposium* Sydney, 1962.
22 'The Legend and the Loneliness: a discussion of the Australian myth' *Overland* 23, 1962, pp. 33−38.

3 James McAuley's Quest

1 See James McAuley's curriculum vitae, May 1963, AACF papers, box 11.
2 James McAuley *The End of Modernity* Sydney, 1959; *The Grammar of the Real* Melbourne, 1975; biographical details also from Vivian Smith, *James McAuley*, Melbourne, 1970 and Peter Coleman *The Heart of James McAuley* Sydney, 1980.
3 For example, Livio Dobrez 'The Three McAuleys' *Southern Review* 9, 3, 1976, pp. 171−84; John Docker 'James McAuley: the poetry and the attitude' *Arena* 26, 1971, pp. 73−86; Despina Balzidis 'James McAuley's radical ingredients' *Meanjin* 39, 3, 1980, pp. 374−82.
4 'On being an intellectual' *Quadrant* 4, 1, 1959−60, reprinted in *The Grammar of the Real* p. 147.
5 Donald Horne *The Education of Young Donald* Harmondsworth, 1967, pp. 279−82.
6 Coleman *The Heart of James McAuley* p. 5.
7 James McAuley 'Comment: Right or Left' *Quadrant* 1, 2, 1957, p. 3.
8 Donald Horne referred me to 'Work in Protex' under the pseudonym 'Protex', *Hermes* 1939, p. 13.
9 Coleman *The Heart of James McAuley* p. 18.
10 See Michael McKernan *All In: Australia during the Second World War* Melbourne, 1983.
11 For an account of the Directorate see Richard Hall *The Real John Kerr: his brilliant career* Sydney, 1978, pp. 48−49.
12 James McAuley *Under Aldebaran* Melbourne, 1946.
13 Daniel Bell *The End of Ideology* New York, 1952.
14 Lionel Trilling *The Liberal Imagination* New York, 1951, pp. 97−98.
15 *The End of Modernity* pp. v−vi.
16 'The Magian Heresy', reprinted in *The End of Modernity* pp. 144−59.
17 *Australian Letters* 2, 3, 1959 has articles on *The End of Modernity* by Robert Hughes, Sister Mary Rosalie RSM and Geoffrey Dutton.

18 Quoted in Coleman *The Heart of James McAuley* p. 90.
19 See Richard Krygier 'Twenty years' *Quadrant* 21, 3, 1977, pp. 58−59.
20 Donald Horne 'In a Private Requiem', Peter Hastings 'A Kind of Tolerance' *Quadrant* 21, 3, pp. 31−32, 49.
21 *The End of Modernity* pp. vii−viii.
22 'Poetry in Australia: James McAuley' interviewed by John Thompson, *Southerly* 27, 2, 1967, p. 104.
23 James McAuley *A Vision of Ceremony*, Sydney, 1956; *Captain Quiros* Sydney, 1964.
24 'My New Guinea', reprinted in *The Grammar of the Real* p. 172.
25 Reprinted in *The End of Modernity* pp. 90−116.
26 Vincent Buckley *Essays in Poetry: mainly Australian* Melbourne, 1957, p. 194.
27 James McAuley 'The Gothic Splendours: Patrick White's Voss' *Southerly* 25, 1, 1965, pp. 34−44.
28 B.A. Santamaria confirms this reading of the stanza in 'So Clean a Spirit', *Quadrant* 21, 3, pp. 51−54.
29 According to Peter Coleman in *The Heart of James McAuley*, p. 91.
30 See, for example, Leonie Kramer 'James McAuley's *Captain Quiros*: the Rational Paradise' *Southerly* 25, 3, 1965, pp. 147−61; A.D. Hope 'The epic theme: James McAuley's *Captain Quiros*' in *Native Companions* Sydney, 1974, pp. 175−85.
31 See, for example, James McAuley 'Liturgy and Culture' in *Worship and Modern Man: papers delivered at the second Tasmanian liturgical conference* January, 1969.
32 *Surprises of the Sun* Sydney, 1969; James McAuley 'The Rhetoric of Australian Poetry' *Southerly* 36, 1, 1976, p. 22.
33 James McAuley and Patricia Giles *A World of its Own* Canberra, 1977.
34 James McAuley 'Commentary' *Quadrant* 20, 1, 1976, pp. 25−28.
35 Vivian Smith *James McAuley*; Chris Wallace-Crabbe ' "Beware of the Past": James McAuley's early poetry' *Meanjin* 30, 3, 1971, pp. 323−30; Dobrez 'The Three McAuley's': Docker 'James McAuley: the poetry and the attitude'.
36 Leonie Kramer 'James McAuley' *Quadrant* 20, 11, 1976, p. 6.
37 Smith *James McAuley*, p. 5.
38 See, for example, Les Murray's poem 'The New Moreton Bay (on the conversion to Catholicism of the poet Kevin Hart)' in *The People's Otherworld*, Sydney, 1983, p. 19.

4 Uncommitted Modern Man: A.D. Hope

1 Joy W. Hooton *A.D. Hope*, Melbourne, 1979, gives a full bibliography of Hope's writing to 1979. Poems discussed in this chapter appear in *Collected Poems: 1930−1970*, Sydney, 1977, *A Late Picking*, Sydney, 1975, *Antechinus*, Sydney, 1981.
2 In this chapter I have had the benefit of A.D. Hope's comments. The quote is from A.D. Hope's notes on a draft of this chapter.

Endnotes

3 'Australian Writers IV: A.D. Hope' interviewed by Desmond O'Grady, *The Observer*, 12 November, 1960, p. 10.
4 'Review of *From Life* by David Martin (1953)', reprinted in A.D. Hope *Native Companions*, Sydney, 1974, pp. 63–66.
5 'The Activists', first given as a talk to the Melbourne University literature club in 1960, reprinted in *The Cave and the Spring*, Adelaide, 1965, pp. 29–37.
6 *The Cave and the Spring*, pp. 29–37.
7 '15 years later', *Quadrant*, 15, 5, pp. 17–18.
8 Hope's notes and comments.
9 Conversation with Manning Clark, 1985.
10 Lynne Strahan *Just City and the Mirrors* Melbourne, 1984, p. 200.
11 John Docker 'The image of woman in A.D. Hope's poetry', in his *Australian Cultural Elites* pp. 42–58; Andrew Taylor 'A.D. Hope: the Double Tongue of Harmony' *Southern Review* 17, 1, 1984, pp. 81–95; Rodney Hall *Collins Book of Australian Poetry* Sydney, 1981; Geoffrey Dutton *Snow on the Saltbush* Ringwood, 1984, pp. 148–49.
12 Leonie Kramer *A.D. Hope* Melbourne, 1979.
13 'The Practical Critic' in *The Cave and the Spring* pp. 76–90.
14 'Christopher Brennan: an interpretation' in *Native Companions* pp. 140–60.
15 ibid. p. 152.
16 *Australian Cultural Elites* p. 58.
17 'Rough riders in the chariot' *Quadrant* June 1981, p. 70; this satire revived Hope's old rift with Patrick White.

5 *Douglas Stewart and the* Bulletin

1 Douglas Stewart *Writers of the Bulletin: 1977 Boyer lectures*, Sydney, 1977.
2 'The Changes in the Bulletin', *Bulletin*, 18 January, 1961, p. 4.
3 Graeme Kinross Smith, 'David Campbell—a profile', *Westerly*, 3, 1973, p. 34.
4 Douglas Stewart 'First Views of David Campbell' in *The Broad Stream* Sydney, 1975, p. 223.
5 'Poetry in Australia: Douglas Stewart' interviewed by John Thompson in Brian Kiernan (ed.) *Considerations*, Sydney, 1977, p. 118.
6 'Norman Lindsay's Novels' in *The Broad Stream* p. 125.
7 Norman Lindsay, *Creative Effort*, Sydney, 1920.
8 Douglas Stewart *The Flesh and the Spirit*, Sydney, 1948, p. 275.
9 ibid. p. 279. Italics original.
10 Humphrey McQueen 'The thinker from the push: Norman Lindsay' in *Gallipoli to Petrov* Sydney, 1984, p. 83.
11 Vincent Buckley 'Utopianism and Vitalism', *Quadrant*, 3, 2, 1959.
12 A.A. Phillips 'The Poetry of Douglas Stewart' in *Considerations*, pp. 181–90.

13 Humphrey McQueen discusses Lindsay's attitude to Hope in *Gallipoli to Petrov*, pp. 84–85, and in his *The Black Swan of Trespass* Sydney, 1979, p. 85.
14 Jack Lindsay *Life Rarely Tells* London, 1958, p. 129.
15 *The Flesh and the Spirit* pp. 78–102.
16 ibid. p. 99.
17 Poems discussed in this chapter are from *Elegy for an Airman* Sydney, 1940; *Sonnets to the Unknown Soldier* Sydney, 1941; *Glencöe* Sydney, 1947; *Sun Orchids* Sydney, 1952; *The Birdsville Track* Sydney, 1955; *Rutherford* Sydney, 1962.
18 See Nancy Keesing *Douglas Stewart* Melbourne, 1969, p. 27.
19 *Australian Bush Ballads* Sydney, 1955; *Old Bush Songs* Sydney, 1957; *Who Wrote the Ballads?* Sydney, 1964; *The Penguin Australian Song Book* Ringwood, 1964.
20 Rodney Hall *J.S. Manifold: an introduction to the man and his work* St Lucia, 1978, pp. 172–74.
21 'The Big Boss Voss' *Bulletin* 5 March 1958, p. 2.
22 See Keesing *Douglas Stewart* p. 30.
23 Douglas Stewart *Selected Poems* Sydney, 1973, p. 122.
24 Vincent Buckley *Essays in Poetry, mainly Australian* Melbourne, 1957; Paul Kavanagh 'Preternatural mimickry: the lyric poetry of Douglas Stewart' *Southerly* September 1983, pp. 265–81; Dennis Robinson 'Douglas Stewart's Nature Lyrics' *Southerly* 47, 1, 1987, pp. 52–69.
25 See Australasian Book Society papers, ML MSS 2297.
26 Geoffrey Dutton *Snow on the Saltbush* Ringwood, 1984 pp. 150–51.

6 *The Writer and the Crisis: Judith Wright and David Campbell*

1 Judith Wright 'The Writer and the Crisis' in *Because I Was Invited* Melbourne, 1975, pp. 165–79; Poems discussed in this chapter are from Judith Wright's *The Moving Image* Melbourne, 1946; *Woman to Man* Sydney, 1949; *The Gateway* Sydney, 1953; *The Two Fires* Sydney, 1955; *Birds: Poems* Sydney, 1962; *Five Senses* Sydney, 1963; *The Other Half* Sydney, 1966; *Collected Poems 1942–1970* Sydney, 1971; *Alive* Sydney, 1973; *Fourth Quarter* Sydney, 1976; *Phantom Dwelling* Sydney, 1985.
2 *Because I Was Invited*, pp. vii–xii.
3 'Some problems of being an Australian poet' in *Because I Was Invited* pp. 56–58.
4 *Because I Was Invited* pp. 129–37.
5 ibid. p. 135.
6 Marian Theobald, 'Classroom Lament, by Judith Wright' *Sydney Morning Herald* 19 October, 1985, p. 1.
7 Judith Wright *Preoccupations in Australian Poetry* Melbourne, 1965, pp. xi–xii.
8 Shirley Walker *The Poetry of Judith Wright: a search for unity* Sydney, 1980.

Endnotes

9 Douglas Stewart *The Flesh and the Spirit* Sydney, p. 273.
10 H.P. Heseltine 'Wrestling with the Angel: Judith Wright's poetry in the 1950s' *Southerly* 38, 2, 1978, pp. 163–71; Rodney Hall 'Themes in Judith Wright's poetry' in *The Literature of Australia* edited by Geoffrey Dutton, Ringwood, 1976, pp. 388–405.
11 *The Generations of Men* Melbourne, 1959; *The Cry for the Dead* Melbourne, 1981.
12 *Charles Harpur* Melbourne, 1963; *Shaw Neilson* Sydney, 1963.
13 Wright *Preoccupations in Australian Poetry*, pp. xiv–xix.
14 'Our Vanishing Chances' in *Because I Was Invited* p. 238.
15 Reprinted in *Sideways from the Page*, edited by Jim Davidson, Melbourne, 1983, pp. 391–415.
16 Walker *The Poetry of Judith Wright* p. 155.
17 'Brevity' in *Phantom Dwelling* p. 27.
18 Vincent Buckley 'A new Bulletin School?' in his *Essays in Poetry* Melbourne, 1957, p. 72.
19 Thomas Shapcott 'Australian Poetry since 1920' in Geoffrey Dutton (ed.) *The Literature of Australia* 1976, p. 123.
20 Kevin Hart 'New Directions: an interview with David Campbell' *Makar* 11, 1, 1975, p. 4; Poems discussed are from *Selected Poems 1942–1968* Sydney, 1968; *Selected Poems* Sydney, 1978.
21 Nancy Gordon 'The Opinion interview: David Campbell' *Opinion* 5, 3, 1976, pp. 11–12.
22 Robin Gollan 'David Campbell at War' in Harry Heseltine (ed.) *A Tribute to David Campbell: a collection of essays* Kensington, 1987, pp. 28–38.
23 David Campbell 'Autobiographical Sketch' *Poetry Australia* 80, 1981, p. 5.
24 ibid. p. 5.
25 Roderick Shaw 'A conversation with David Campbell' *Poetry Australia* 80, 1981, pp. 26–32.
26 Leonie Kramer 'The Surreal Landscape of David Campbell' *Southerly* 41, 1, 1981, pp. 3–15; R.F. Brissenden 'The Poetry of David Campbell' *Quadrant* October 1983, pp. 66–71.

7 A new kind of novel: the work of Patrick White

1 Patrick White *The Vivisector* Ringwood, 1973, p. 110.
2 Novels discussed in this chapter are *The Aunt's Story* London, 1948; *The Tree of Man* New York, 1955; *Voss* London, 1957; *Riders in the Chariot* London, 1961.
3 Patrick White 'The Prodigal Son' *Australian Letters* 1958, reprinted in *The Oxford Anthology of Australian Literature* Melbourne, 1985, p. 337.
4 Patrick White *Flaws in the Glass* London, 1981, p. 106.
5 'The Prodigal Son' p. 337.
6 See Mona Brand 'Another Look at Patrick White' *The Realist Writer* (Sydney) 12, 1963, p. 21; see earlier debates in *Tribune* (Melbourne) July 1959 and *The Realist Writer* (Sydney) 9, 1962.

7 Alan Lawson 'Unmerciful dingoes? The critical reception of Patrick White' *Meanjin* 32, 4, 1973, pp. 379–91.
8 *Flaws in the Glass* p. 104.
9 Martin Boyd *Day of My Delight* Melbourne, 1965, pp. 233–34.
10 *Voss* Harmondsworth, 1960, pp. 89–90.
11 ibid. p. 387.
12 Ann McCulloch *A Tragic Vision: the novels of Patrick White* St Lucia, 1983.
13 *Voss* p. 443.
14 ibid. pp. 446–47.
15 *Flaws in the Glass* p. 104.
16 *Riders in the Chariot* Harmondsworth, 1964, p. 70.
17 *The Tree of Man* Harmondsworth, 1961, p. 14.
18 *Riders in the Chariot* p. 75.

8 Drama, old and new

1 Leslie Rees *The Making of Australian Drama* Sydney, 1973 and *A History of Australian Drama volume 2: Australian Drama in the 1970s* Sydney, 1978.
2 Ruth Cracknell 'The First Ten Years' *Meanjin* 43, 1, 1984, pp. 6–11.
3 'The First Ten Years' p. 11.
4 David Walker *Dream and Disillusion* Canberra, 1976.
5 For a fuller account see Ken Harper, 'The Useful Theatre: The New Theatre Movement in Sydney and Melbourne 1935–1983', *Meanjin*, 43, 1, 1984, pp. 57–71.
6 Jack Hibberd, 'After Many a Summer: the Doll trilogy' *Meanjin*, 36, 1, 1977, p. 109.
7 This discussion refers to Ray Lawler *Summer of the Seventeenth Doll* Sydney, 1957 and Barry Humphries *The Humour of Barry Humphries* selected by John Allen, Sydney, 1984.
8 Joy Hooton, 'Lawler's demythologizing of the Doll: Kid Stakes and Other Times', *Australian Literary Studies*, 12, 3, 1986, pp. 335–46.
9 *The Humour of Barry Humphries* p. 82.
10 Interview, *The Advertiser* (Adelaide) 29 November 1983, p. 23.
11 Elizabeth Harrower *The Long Prospect* London, 1958.
12 Stephen Murray-Smith 'A New Satirist' *Overland* 14, 1959, p. 39.
13 See, for example, Craig McGregor 'What's wrong with Barry Humphries' *National Times* October 3–9, 1982, p. 12–13.
14 Letter to author from Barry Humphries, 9 August 1984.
15 Vivian Smith 'Poetry' in Leonie Kramer (ed.) *The Oxford History of Australian Literature* Melbourne, 1981, p. 371.
16 Jack Hibberd *White With Wire Wheels* in *Four Australian Plays* Ringwood, 1970; *A Stretch of the Imagination* Woollahra, 1977; *Dimboola* Ringwood, 1974.

Endnotes

17 'After Many a Summer'; Jack Hibberd 'National Drama as Melodrama' *Westerly* 4, 1978, p. 57.
18 Jack Hibberd 'Breakfast at the Windsor' *Meanjin* 40, 3, 1981, pp. 395–99.

9 *Australian Civilisation?*

1 Elizabeth Harrower *The Long Prospect* London, 1958; Christopher Koch *The Boys in the Island* London, 1958, reprinted Sydney, 1974; Randolph Stow *To the Islands* London, 1958; *The Merry-Go-Round in the Sea* Harmondsworth, 1968 (f.p. 1965).
2 Elizabeth Harrower *Down in the City* London, 1957, p. 117.
3 *The Long Prospect* Melbourne, 1966, p. 189.
4 *The Boys in the Island* pp. 165, 210.
5 ibid. pp. 126–67.
6 *The Long Prospect* p. 14.
7 David Martin '"Among the bones": what are our novelists looking for?' *Meanjin* 18, 1, 1959, pp. 52–58.
8 *The Merry-Go-Round in the Sea* p. 273.
9 'Interview: Elizabeth Harrower' reprinted in *Sideways from the Page* pp. 252–53.
10 A.D. Hope *Australian Literature 1950–1962* Melbourne, 1963, p. 4.
11 H.P. Heseltine, introduction to *The Penguin Book of Modern Australian Verse* Ringwood, 1981.
12 John Tranter, introduction to *The New Australian Poetry* p. xvii.
13 ibid. p. xxvi.
14 Ian Turner 'The Life and the Legend' *Overland* 16, 1959–60.
15 David Carter 'Coming Home after the Party: *Overland's* first decade' *Meanjin* 44, 4, 1985, pp. 462–76.
16 Candida Baker 'An ailing playwright takes the cure' *Age* 22 March 1986, pp. 3, 12.

Index

Index

Bevan, Ian, *The Sunburnt Country*, 12, in endnotes, 231
Beynon, Richard, 191–2, 208
Blake, William, 71, 75, 79, 110, 125
Blamey, General Thomas, 73
Blight, John, 122
Boddy, Michael, 192; *The Legend of King O'Malley*, 192–3, 205, 207
Bollinger, Max, 33
Bondy, Francois, in endnotes, 232
Boyd, Martin, 47–8, 152, 158, 177–8; in endnotes, *Day of My Delight*, 238
Boyd, Robin, 63, 172, 186, 199, 203, 214; *The Australian Ugliness*, 172, 219
Brand, Mona, 26, 30, 174, 195, 214; in endnotes, 237
Brecht, Bertolt, 23, 25, 193, 205
Brennan, Christopher, 7, 63, 71–2, 75, 112, 152; in endnotes, 235
Brissenden, R.F., 162; in endnotes, 237
Buckley, Vincent, 63–5, 68, 81, 85, 94, 124, 126, 136, 156, 222; *Essays in Poetry*, 156, in endnotes, 234–7
The Bulletin, 67, 120–5, 130–1, 137, 156; in endnotes, 235
Burke, Joseph, 60–1
Burstall, Tim, 65

Caiger, George, *The Australian Way of Life*, 12, in endnotes, 231
Calvinism, 98, 106, 124
Calwell, Arthur, 185
Cambridge University, 18, 130, 169
Campbell, D.A.S., 55
Campbell, David, 2–3, 35, 117, 122–3, 130, 133, 139, 147, 156–66, 169, 172, 176, 188, 222, 227, in endnotes, 235, 237; 'Bellbirds', 163; *The Branch of Dodona*, 160; 'Cocky's Calendar', 159; 'Come Live With Me', 158; 'Conroy's Gap', 157, 160; 'Droving', 157; 'Harry Pearce', 157, 160–1; 'Hawk and Hill', 159; 'Hotel Marine', 160; 'Jack Spring', 157; 'Kelly and the Crow', 157; 'Men in Green', 160; *The Miracle of Mullion Hill*, 157; 'My Lai', 160; 'Operation Moonprobe', 160; *Poems*, 157; 'Portents over Coffee', 163; 'Red Bridge', 163; in endnotes, *Selected Poems*, 237, 'Soldier Settlers', 158; 'Soldier's Song', 157, 160; 'Song for a Wren', 159; 'Song for the Cattle', 161, 163; *Speak with the Sun*, 122, 157,

160; 'Wether Country', 163; 'Who Points the Swallow', 159; 'Windy Gap', 158; 'Words and Lovers', 159
Campbell, Roy, 131
Canberra University College, *see* Australian National University
Carter, David, 224, in endnotes, 239
Casey, Gavin, 31, 33, 43, 122
Casey, R.G., 55
Catholic Action, 79, *see also* The Movement
catholicism, 39, 52–3, 56–7, 76, 79–80, 83, 86, 88, 93–4, 98–9, 103, 227–8
Caudwell, Christopher, *Illusion and Reality*, 24
censorship, 66
Central Intelligence Agency (CIA), 55, 58–9, 67
Cheever, John, 17
Chiplin, Rex, 50, in endnotes, 232
Chisholm, A.R., 8–9, 15, 63, 230
Christesen, Clem, 6–10, 20, 55–6, 61, 97, 101–2, 118, 143, 216, 227; in endnotes, 232
Christesen, Nina, 10, 101
Clark, Manning, 9, 60–1, 63–5, 101, 116; in endnotes, 235
Cleary, Jon, 22, 47, 167; *The Sundowners*, 22
Clift, Charmian, 186
cold war, 4–5, 9, 11, 19, 61, 92, 160, 185, 188, 203, 209, 215–16, 222
Coleman, Peter, 64, 66–7, 73, 92; *Australian Civilization*, 64–5, in endnotes, *The Heart of James McAuley*, 233–4
Collinson, Laurence, 26, 33–5, 50
Commonwealth Literary Fund, 51–2, 97
Commonwealth Parliamentary Debates, 232
communism, 21, 23–49 *passim*, 77–9, 93, 139
Communist Party, 11, 19, 23–51, 53–4, 58, 63, 67, 185, 195, 209, 214, 224, 226
Conlon, Alfred, 60, 73, 90
Covell, Roger, 59–60
Cracknell, Ruth, 193–4; in endnotes, 238
Craig, Alexander, 221; *Twelve Poets*, 222
The Critical Review, in endnotes, 231
Culotta, Nino, *see* John O'Grady
cultural cringe, 20, 152
Cultural Freedom, 3, 19, 49–70, 90, 100–1, 191, 202; Australian

---

241

Index

Index

'Confession', 90; 'Convalescence', 92; *The End of Modernity*, in endnotes, 233–4; 'Envoi', 75, 82, 87; 'Father, Mother, Son', 90; 'Gnostic Prelude', 75; *The Grammar of the Real*, in endnotes, 233–4; 'Henry the Navigator', 86; 'The Incarnation of Sirius', 75; 'In the Huon Valley', 92; 'Jesus', 81; 'Jindyworobaksheesh', 75; 'Landscape of Lust', 75; 'A Letter to John Dryden', 85–6; 'Mating Swans', 74; 'My New Guinea', 82–3, 87; 'New Guinea', 82–3; 'Numbers and Makes', 136; 'A Note on Maritain's View', 84; 'One Tuesday in Summer', 91; 'Pieta', 91; 'Released on Parole', 91; 'Revenant', 75; 'Sacred Art in the Modern World', 84; 'Sequence', 81, 84; *Surprises of the Sun*, 90–2, 136, in endnotes, 234; 'Tabletalk', 90; 'Terra Australis', 75, 87; 'To the Holy Spirit', 81, 84; 'The True Discovery of Australia', 75, 85; 'A Tune for Swans', 74; *Under Aldebaran*, 70, 73, 74–5, 78, 86, in endnotes, 233; 'Vespers', 83; *A Vision of Ceremony*, 74, 81–6, in endnotes, 234; 'When Shall the Fair', 74–5; 'Work in Protex', 72; *A World of Its Own*, 92, 136, in endnotes, 234; in endnotes, *Worship and Modern Man*, 234

McCallum, Douglas, 64
McCulloch, Ann, 179; in endnotes, *A Tragic Vision*, 238
McCarthy, Mary, 17
McCrae, Hugh, 124, 127
McCuaig, Ronald, 122
McGregor, Craig, in endnotes, 238
Mackenzie, Kenneth, 122, 127, 137; *The Refuge*, 127
McKernan, Michael, in endnotes, *All In*, 233
McKinney, Meredith, 153
McQueen, Humphrey, 58, 126; in endnotes, *The Black Swan of Trespass*, 236; in endnotes, *Gallipoli to Petrov*, 233, 235–6;
Malenkov, 27
Malouf, David, 1
Mallarmé, 112
Malley, Ern, 16, 62, 70, 74–5, 86, 202, 223; 'Durer: Innsbruck, 1495', 74

Maloney, J.J., 55
Malraux, André, 53
Manifold, John, 2, 26, 30, 33–7, 46, 50, 70, 102, 130–1, 142, 169, 224; 'The Bunyip and the Whistling Kettle', 33; *The Death of Ned Kelly and other Ballads*, 130; 'L'embarquement pour Cythère', 34; *The Penguin Australian Song Book*, 130, in endnotes, 236; 'Red Rosary Sonnets', 33–4; 'The Tomb of Lt John Learmonth, AIF', 33–4, 130–1; *Who Wrote the Ballads?*, 130, in endnotes, 236; in endnotes, *Collected Verse*, 231
Mannix, Archbishop Daniel, 39
Marshall, Alan, 21, 31, 138; *How Beautiful are Thy Feet*, 21; *I Can Jump Puddles*, 21
Martin, David, 2, 25, 29–31, 33–5, 46, 50, 56, 58, 63, 65, 99, 142, 213, 216, 223–4, in endnotes, 239; *From Life*, 99, in endnotes, 235; 'A Letter to President Eisenhower', 34; *Poems of David Martin*, 34–5, in endnotes, 231; *The Young Wife*, 213; in endnotes, 231
Marxism, 23–49, 99; *see also* communism, socialist realism
Mayer, Henry, 64
Mead, Philip, 156
Meanjin, 6–11, 55, 59, 61–2, 64, 66, 97, 101, 142, 154, 213, 216, 225, in endnotes, 230
Melbourne, University of, 8, 18, 55, 97, 196, 204
Melbourne University Magazine, 97
Melbourne Realist Writers Group, 26
Melville, Leslie, 55
Menzies, R.G., 52, 59, 79, 185, 203, 216, 224
Meredith, Gwen, *The Lawsons*, 195
Metropolitan Theatre, 193
Milgate, Wesley, 56, 60–1
modernism, 13–17, 26, 48, 74–5, 77–8, 80, 91, 95–6, 100, 102–3, 127, 139, 164, 171, 185, 193, 208
der Monat, 53
Molnar, George, 62
Moore, Tom Inglis, 64
Moorhouse, Frank, 1
Morrison, John, 26, 29–31, 36–7, 46, in endnotes, 231; *Port of Call*, 37–8; *The Creeping City*, 38

Index

Rattigan, Terence, 191; *The Sleeping Prince*, 191
The Realist Writer (Melbourne), 26–7; in endnotes, 231
Rees, Leslie, 192; in endnotes, *A History of Australian Drama*, 238; in endnotes, *The Making of Australian Drama*, 238
Rene, Roy, 195
Returned Services League (RSL), 66, 120–1, 200, 206
Richardson, Henry Handel, 152, 167–8; *The Fortunes of Richard Mahony*, 40, 167–8
Robinson, Denis, 136–7; in endnotes, 236
Robinson, Roland, 143
Roderick, Colin, *Australian Roundup*, 7
Ronan, Tom, *Moleskin Midas*, 22
Rosalie, Sister Mary, in endnotes, 233
Ross, Lloyd, 66
Russell, Bertrand, 64

Salinger, J.D., 17
Santamaria, B.A., 60, 79, 101, in endnotes, 234
Sartre, Jean Paul, 26
Seymour, Alan, 191–2
Schlunke, E.O., 68
Shapcott, Thomas, 156, 161, 221, in endnotes, 237; *Australian Poetry Now*, 222; *New Impulses in Australian Poetry*, 222; *Time on Fire*, 221
Sharman, Jim, 194
Shaw, Roderick, 162; in endnotes, 237
Shute, Nevil, *A Town Like Alice*, 22
Sinclair, Upton, 53
Slessor, Kenneth, 16, 56, 59, 124; in endnotes, 231
Smith, Graeme Kinross, in endnotes, 235
Smith, Joshua, 16
Smith, Vivian, 94, 202, in endnotes, 238; in endnotes, *James McAuley*, 233–4
Snow, C.P., 17, 113
socialist realism, 2, 17, 19, 23–49, 51, 65, 78, 85, 93, 99–100, 118, 120, 126, 138, 140, 147, 167, 173, 189–90, 192, 216
Somerville, Oliver, 72
Southerly, 6–11, 87, 97, 174, in endnotes, 230
Spender, Stephen, 56, 77
Spence, Catherine Helen, 98

Stalin, Josef, 23–4, 33, 36, 38, 46, 58, 77
Stead, Christina, 152
Stein, Sol, in endnotes, 232
Steinbeck, John, 53
Stewart, Douglas, 2–3, 34–5, 63, 80, 122–41, 146, 149, 155, 156–9, 161, 169, 174–5, 188, 198, 222–3; in endnotes, 235–7; *Australian Bush Ballads*, 130, in endnotes, 236; 'Bird's eye', 135; *The Birdsville Track*, 133, 135–6, 156–7, in endnotes, 236; 'Brindabella', 135; in endnotes, *The Broad Stream*, 235; *Elegy for an Airman*, 128, 131, in endnotes, 236; 'Escapes from Art', 127; 'Everlasting', 135; *The Fire on the Snow*, 128, 131, 190, 195; in endnotes, *The Flesh and the Spirit*, 234–7; *Glencöe*, 128, 132, in endnotes, 236, *The Golden Lover*, 129; 'The Goldfish Pool', 133–4; 'The Green Centipede', 133–4; 'The Gully', 133–4; 'Kindred', 133–4; 'The Man from Adaminaby', 137; 'Mosquito Orchid', 135; *Ned Kelly*, 128–9; 'Nodding Greenhood', 133; *Old Bush Songs*, 130, in endnotes, 236; 'A Robin', 133–4; in endnotes, *Rutherford*, 236; 'Rutherford', 148; in endnotes, *Selected Poems*, 236; *Shipwreck*, 128–30; 'The Silkworms', 137; 'The Snow-gum', 135; *Sonnets to the Unknown Soldier*, 128, in endnotes, 236; *Sun Orchids*, 133–5, 157, in endnotes, 236; 'To Lie on the Grass', 133–4; in endnotes, *Writers of the Bulletin*, 235
Stewart, Harold, 74, 203
Stivens, Dal, 138; *Jimmy Brockett*, 22
Stow, Randolph, 65, 210, 214–16, 221; *The Merry-Go-Round in the Sea*, 210, in endnotes, 239; *Midnite*, 214; *To the Islands*, 213–14, in endnotes, 239; *Tourmaline*, 214
Strahan, Lynne, 7, 102; in endnotes, *Just City and the Mirrors*, 230, 235
Swift, Jonathan, 103, 106–7, 110; *Gulliver's Travels*, 107
Sydney, University of, 60, 70, 72, 98
Sydney Morning Herald, 97, 174
Sydney Teachers' College, 97

Tasmania, University of, 57–8, 90

247

Index

Moving Image, 144–6, 148, 149, 151, in endnotes, 236; 'Nigger's Leap, New England', 144; 'Old House', 149; *The Other Half*, 154, in endnotes, 236; *Phantom Dwelling*, 156, in endnotes, 236–7; *Preoccupations in Australian Poetry*, 148, 151–2, in endnotes, 236–7; 'Remittance Man', 145; 'Request to a Year', 150, 154; 'South of My Days', 145, 149; 'Spring After War', 146; 'To Another Housewife', 154; 'The Train Journey', 149; 'Transformations', 149; 'The Traveller and the Angel', 149–50; 'The Twins', 146; *The Two Fires*, 149–50, 154, in endnotes, 236; 'The Typists in the Phoenix Building', 154; 'The Wattle Tree', 150; *Woman to Man*, 146, 148–51, in endnotes, 236; 'Woman to Man', 146; 'The Writer and the Crisis', 141

Yeats, William Butler, 71, 74–5, 111, 147, 157–8; 'Running to Paradise', 158
Young, Bishop Guildford, 90

Zhdanov, A.A., 24; in endnotes, 231

For Product Safety Concerns and Information please contact our EU
representative GPSR@taylorandfrancis.com
Taylor & Francis Verlag GmbH, Kaufingerstraße 24, 80331 München, Germany